Joseph Parker

**A homiletic analysis of the Gospel by Matthew**

Joseph Parker

**A homiletic analysis of the Gospel by Matthew**

ISBN/EAN: 9783337714369

Printed in Europe, USA, Canada, Australia, Japan

Cover: Foto ©ninafisch / pixelio.de

More available books at **www.hansebooks.com**

# A HOMILETIC ANALYSIS

OF

## THE GOSPEL BY MATTHEW.

By JOSEPH PARKER, D.D.,

AUTHOR OF "ECCE DEUS," ETC.

WITH AN INTRODUCTORY ESSAY ON

THE LIFE OF JESUS CHRIST,

*Considered as an Appeal to the Imagination.*

London:
HODDER AND STOUGHTON,
27, PATERNOSTER ROW.

1870.

# INTRODUCTORY ESSAY

ON

THE LIFE OF JESUS CHRIST CONSIDERED AS AN APPEAL
TO THE IMAGINATION.

THE fact that Christian doctrines have on the one hand been considered too sacred for purely intellectual analysis, and on the other have been confined to the excited sphere of polemical divinity, has almost entirely concealed the argument which is involved in the ideal completeness of Christianity when strictly regarded as an appeal to the imagination. If in this attempt partially to develop that argument, the foregone conclusions of the dogmatic theologian are overlooked, it is through no defect of reverence for settled Christian conviction; and if we assume the attitude of students of what (for want of a better term) may be described as the artistic side of Christianity, it is through no desire to determine the scope of Divine inspiration by the uncertain and debateable canons of human criticism. To dismiss from recollection every remembrance of theological doctrine and every trace of theological bias is almost essential to a just appreciation of the artistic argument. We put no inquiry as to the historic credibility of the New Testament writers; we do not discuss any questions in grammar or exegesis; we know nothing of commentators or schools of interpretation; we hardly care, in fact, in the first instance, to make any inquiry into the *moral* import of New Testament teaching: our business is simply to ascertain how far the reported life of Jesus Christ is consistent with itself; is there any law of harmony between the parts; is the progress of the narrative merely a high monotony, or is there in it an ascending motion carrying each point to higher significance, and covering the whole with accumulating glory? As a work of fiction, is the written life of Jesus Christ ideally complete? Is there anything so peculiar in its ideal completeness as to destroy the theory that it is a work of fiction? This is the one line along which it is proposed to carry an inquiry, and if again and again the reader be reminded of this fact it will be to save him from wandering into collateral questions which would distract attention from the main issue.

The miraculous conception of Jesus Christ at once addresses the boldest challenge to the imagination, and determines the unique and perilous line of artistic judgment. How can *such* a beginning have a corresponding progress and an appropriate culmination? Under the ancient economy God had elected his ministers in a manner which was directly inverted in the birth of Jesus Christ; in the ministers of the Old Testament God had sought to call up the human to the Divine, but in the Minister of the New Testament God brought down the Divine to the human. Viewing the Old Testament dispensation as an elaborate attempt to train a Man who should so far overcome all natural and incidental difficulties as to exert upon society the influence of a life absolutely perfect in its purity and aspirations, we are driven to the conclusion that the attempt, though conducted by the mysterious power of the Holy Ghost, was partially unsuccessful; in Abraham, Jacob, Moses, and David, it is not difficult to find the blemish which proves this, and in proving it suggests the impossibility of training an ideally perfect ministry. In reading the Old Testament we cannot escape a sense of gloomy and humiliating disappointment with the defective quality of its foremost men. They have great excellencies, and they have also great blemishes; they have excellencies, and yet are not excellent; their character can be spoken of in sides and aspects, not in its unity and indivisible massiveness; only momentarily do they get away from the common herd of men, and afterwards they are the weaker for their transient elevation. The prophet and the minstrel often descend from their ecstacy, and resume the ordinary associations of life; the warrior never quite advances to victory; and the sufferer always falls a little short of the perfection of patience. Under these circumstances the promise of a *New* Testament does not altogether allay the anxiety of hope so long deferred, and so vexed and mortified. Through forty centuries God has failed to train "a man;" He "looked and there was no man;" He bade His messengers run to and fro through the streets of Jerusalem and seek in the broad places thereof if they could find "a man;" He sought for a man that should make up the hedge and stand in the gap before Him, but He found none; He saw that there was no man, and wondered that there was no intercessor; how, then, will He proceed? Let imagination pause awhile at the last of the prophets, and attempt the task of outlining a Testament that shall be *New*; New and yet related to the Old; that shall be faithful to the great purpose of the former dispensation, yet bring to bear upon it an order of instrumentality that shall neither make a machine of man, nor convict God of capricious changeableness in His methods of working. A great task will thus fall to the lot of imagination; let us see what it is: imagination has before it, in the Old Testament, a written account of the creation of man, the giving of law, the establishment of family life, the appointment of ritual, worship, and service, and the history of mankind for thousands of years; on the other hand, the world is disquieted and tormented exceedingly, every method of alleviation seems to have been exhausted, and every new proposition is treated with angry or sorrowful distrust. It is now required of Imagination to propose a Testament that shall be *New*. Abandoning the task as intellectually hopeless, Imagination may justly be allowed to encounter with the severest criticism any suggestion that may be offered as a solution of the difficulty. Now, it must be admitted that the writers of the New Testament do instantly address themselves to the one point which the Old Testament failed to reach; with most startling abruptness they invert the ancient method, so that instead of man being made by God, God Himself becomes man—a virgin is found with child of the Holy Ghost, and for "thus *saith* the Lord" we have thus *is* the Lord! True or not true, is not the immediate question; here is progress; the first page of the New Testament presents a more wonderful revelation than all the pages of the Old, and that is at least an encouragement to inquire whether God has not thus answered the inarticulate, yet not the less urgent and painful, desire of the world. The whole Christian argument must stand or fall with the Incarnation, and so must the collateral argument which is now being attempted. If the account of Jesus Christ's birth is fabulous, Jesus Christ's life must, in all its higher bearings, be fabulous too; if Jesus Christ could have been what He was *without* miraculous conception, then the Old Testament method of training men was an elaborate mockery, because their life might have been made as pure as His: if, on the other hand, the account of Jesus Christ's birth is true, there can be no lack of illustrative and confirmatory evidence in the life and doctrine detailed in the New Testament. A miraculous birth cannot be followed by a common-place life, yet there must be in that life, if its mission be to recover and sanctify the world, such simplicity and approachableness as shall secure for it a position in ordinary society; it must proceed to its loftiest acts with the stoop of condescension, and do its lowliest work with original and inimitable dignity. With a test so unique the least flaw in homogeneousness must be instantly detected.

Beginning with Jesus Christ's outward course, the artistic student will press the inquiry: does the manner of life correspond in tone and quality with the assumed Fatherhood of the agent? There is sufficient material in the Gospels to justify the formation of an opinion; reports of wonderful works, methods of meeting difficulties ordinary and extraordinary; intercourse with most different classes of persons; how, then, did One professedly of Divine generation conduct Himself in the discharge of duty? Starting upon the basis of the Incarnation, the artistic student will put in two conditions, the fulfilment of which he must regard as essential to the ideal completeness of Jesus Christ's claim. In the first place, he will demand in an agent of professedly Divine descent, such redundance of power as shall carry him through all his engagements with the most perfect ease, he must never go up to his work as if it lay above him, but continually *descend* upon it as if his most marvellous achievement were rather a relaxation than an effort of his strength. If in any case there be a *strain* upon the power, the laboriousness of the attempt must tell against his claim; if in any case there be the slightest possible *failure* of power, the aspirant must be convicted of the most shameful wickedness. We must never meet with *almost* a miracle; we must not be satisfied with comparative superiority of power; we must have omnipotence, anything short of the Almightiness of God will be unpardonable sin. In what direction, then, does the evidence point? There are four witnesses, in what proportion do they approach unanimity? There are blind, deaf, lame, leprous and lunatic sufferers claiming Jesus Christ's attention; He is brought to the sick, the dying, and the dead; He is asked to appease hunger, to expel devils, to silence storms; and the artistic critic demands that He do all these things with infinite ease, with inexhaustible wealth and exuberance of power. The New Testament says that Jesus Christ did so. Can a single instance be pointed out in which Jesus Christ's power to work miracles ever showed the faintest sign of exhaustion? The disciples failed, and they confessed the failure; when did the Master fail? The artistic student must insist that the ease which marks the first chapter of Genesis mark also the whole course of Jesus Christ; there must be creativeness in His fiat if He be Emmanuel,—God with us. The attribute of power must be swallowed up in His essential Almightiness; He must be more than powerful, He must be *power*. The universe in all its compass and wonderfulness must lie in the hollow of His hand, and be as perfectly under His control as it is dependent on His sufficiency; He must not avail Himself of any calculus of probability; the law of distance, weight, force, adaption, must be in Him as an element of His sovereignty; His word must carry with it creation and destruction; He must *fill all things*. An occasional exercise of power, however startling and however beneficent, would rather excite suspicion than work conviction; great efforts are often unintended signs of weakness, securing momentary applause for the discipline which they imply, but also eliciting pity for the exhaustion which they leave behind; a life of great efforts is a life of great failures.

The difficulty of the most honest and patient discipline is to keep a steady hold of its highest points, and so to become permanently equal to its tasks and aspirations. The most resolute disciplinarian can instantly point out the line of his ability; within that line he is mighty, beyond it he is powerless. In Jesus Christ, the artistic student must insist on finding something higher than discipline; there must not, in fact, be any sign of training or preparation in His work; His power must be native, instant, immeasurable. He must, too, stand clearly out, having, so to speak, nothing with Him but His *life*, and with that He must rule the universe as with the Almightiness of God. The source of His power must not only be secret, it must necessarily confound every attempt to discover it, and its effects must be so thorough and so numerous as to force astonishment to the point of distraction, and to drive men to intellectual despair where they are not won to spiritual homage. Clearly so, because where the intelligence of the observer is equal to the execution of the worker, the disparity may be accounted for on those natural principles which are everywhere illustrated in the distribution of human gifts. In the case of Jesus Christ there must not be any measurable relation between the intelligence of His critics and the capacity of His own power; His critics must confess their inability to discover the secret of His might; and His power must come before them so often and so gloriously as to extort from them either exclamations of bewilderment or expressions of reverent and thankful joy. What of the life of Jesus Christ, in the light of these principles ? The people "were astonished and said, Whence hath this man this wisdom and these mighty works?" "Whence then hath this man all these things?" "No man can do those miracles that thou doest, except God be with him." "They were beyond measure astonished, saying, He hath done all things well: he maketh both the deaf to hear and the dumb to speak." "They were sore amazed in themselves beyond measure, and wondered." "The multitudes marvelled, saying, It was never so seen in Israel." Now, the artistic student has nothing to do with the theologic import of these passages; his one business is to determine how far they are such expressions as harmonise with the supposed descent of the worker who elicited them: are they the common expressions of vulgar amazement, or do they carry with them the wonder and pathos of the heart? From the public opinion which was formed upon Jesus Christ's work, as well as from his own estimate of it, we may infer whether it was worked by the opulence and quietness of power which may be supposed to distinguish the processes of omnipotence. What can have been the richness of the power, which led one poor suffering woman to utter the greatest saying about it that probably was ever uttered: If I may but touch the hem of his garment I should be made whole! The artistic student will put peculiar value upon this testimony, because it condenses into one pathetic sentence a great body of public opinion; if it be merely a stroke of inventive genius, it is a stroke of consummate power; if it be historically true it is conclusive evidence that Jesus Christ had produced in the public mind of His day an impression that His power was at once beneficent and boundless. There is, too, in connection with this incident a feature which the artist will appreciate as showing that the power was not lawlessly expended; instantly that the woman was healed Jesus Christ exclaimed that virtue had gone out of Him, and demanded to know who had touched Him,—though thronged by the press, one hand had touched the fountain of His life, and His communication of power gave Him the right of inquiry and judgment. There is nothing, then, in the written life of Jesus Christ to shew that in any instance His power was unequal to the occasion; on the contrary, the whole evidence maintains, alike by direct statement and incidental illustration, perfect consistency between the supposed birth of the agent and the Divine ease with which He met every claim upon His power.

In the second place, the artistic student will demand that in no case shall the exercise of Jesus Christ's ability, how useful or splendid soever the result, be accompanied with any sign of astonishment on the part of the worker. Whilst astonishing the world, He alone must be free from astonishment. All unexpected successes, like all great efforts, betray the weakness of the workers as well as show their strength, and on this account every discovery in civilisation is quite as certainly a lamp hung over human ignorance as it is a contribution to the brilliance of human wisdom. The artistic student will proceed upon the principle that as omnipotence can never put itself into doubtful competition with a difficulty, so God can never be surprised at the results of His own work. Surprise comes of ignorance, and elation of weakness. Yet, looking at the written life of Jesus Christ, the absence of astonishment is most marked, and not a trace of vain self-satisfaction has been left on the whole of the narrative. Amazement is not forbidden to common workers; it may, indeed, be advantageous to them, as well as to those in whose interest they work, for wonder should stimulate to progress, and every opening door be regarded as an invitation to profounder study. There is no monotony in the highest intellectual life, for even where youthful passion subsides it is only to be succeeded if by a more placid yet by a more exquisite enjoyment; the young worker may be unable to suppress his Eureka, but the silence of the maturer thinker is not to be mistaken for insensibility. Can men receive Divine revelations of the depth and beauty of truth without emotion? Or can they put into common words the Divine addresses which they have received, in the secrecy of their own souls, without being startled by every tone that successfully reproduces the mystic music which divides the realm of speech from the realm of silence? Articulation is the difficulty of the highest thought. What, if successful articulation should occasionally betray surprise and joy on the part of the speaker? Nothing will be more natural or more rationally explicable. We account him the strong man who can suppress his emotions while prosecuting his work, and so highly is this suppression valued, that not seldom is the dignity of noble self-control counterfeited by the unhealthy and demoralising conceit of indifference in the presence of the most exciting events. Let it be assumed, however, that strength brings quietness, and that conscious power holds surprise in check, we have to account for the fact that an unlettered man healed the lame, the blind, the deaf, the leprous, and all manner of diseased people, that He quelled the tempests, expelled devils, and raised the dead, and never discovered any symptoms of surprise, was never startled by unexpected results, or by successes which filled society with the most bewildering amazement. This self-control is not found along one special line of discipline, but is common to the whole course of Jesus Christ's ministry; the worker is never excited; the worker is always greater than His work; He works as though power were the least of His characteristics, and were only put forward as an introduction to a higher blessing. The artistic student will find that his demand for the entire absence of surprise is thoroughly satisfied by the written life of Jesus Christ, and in noting the completeness of the evidence he will not overlook an incidental but most vivid illustration of Christ's estimate of surprise in others; on one occasion the disciples told Him with wondering joy that even the devils were subject to them through His name, and He answered that they were not to rejoice in such events, but rather to rejoice because their names were written in heaven,—personal rightness being better than functional success. Another aspect of the same teaching is shown in an instance of surprise at their failure : they had tried to expel a devil, and their word was powerless; Jesus Christ expelled the tormentor, and told the disciples privately the spiritual conditions by which alone success was possible in such cases. So that he had to deal with the operation of surprise, and to save His disciples from the effects of elation and disappointment by drawing them into deeper appreciation of purely spiritual privilege and discipline.

But how to humanise such a life, how to make it approachable, how to adapt it to ordinary society? Up to this point, the artistic student has been working on the supposed Divine side of Jesus Christ's life; but Jesus Christ was the Son of Mary as well as the Son of God, and therefore, for His course to be artistically complete, He must supply conditions in many respects almost irreconcileable with the claim of divinity. If He has entered into the flesh that He may be visibly nearer men, and more sensibly accessible to them, he must so conceal His divinity as not to alarm them by unearthliness, and so display it as to secure their confidence and homage, He must answer the question, can God in very deed dwell with men upon the earth? To be God and man, so distinctly that each can be felt, so unitedly that no division line can be seen, is the intricate part which He has to play. This is surely a great problem in art, and there is scope enough for failure; one slip will dispossess Him of His crown, one false accent will prove Him the most daring of empirics. He must be *with* and yet not *of* them; on the earth and yet in heaven; familiar with men, yet separate from sinners; He must enlighten the world, and yet be as a sun that is far off: how to simplify the infinite—how to stoop from heaven!

The artistic student will notice that Jesus Christ lived much in public, and so gave opportunity enough for general criticism. There is no evidence in the narrative that He was ever indisposed on the ground of fear to meet any section of society; He conversed with equal freedom with the well-taught and the ignorant, and His social life was even too liberal for the narrow notions of conventional purists. His was not a monastic life; He went to be guest with men that were sinners; He sat at the tables of men whose hospitality was intended as a temptation; He went to the marriage-feast, and to the house of mourning; He loved Martha and her sister and Lazarus; He took little children in His arms and blessed them; and spoke hopefully to women who had lost the standing of sisterhood. And in what manner did He do all this? Was there in his manner any originality of movement, any savour of heavenliness, any omnipotence of simplicity? The artistic student will look everywhere for the Divine signature; the minutest things must bear the Divine initials, and the greatest the incommunicable name. When God descended into the bush, He filled it with undestroying fire,—when He walks along the common highways of life will it be with insufferable brightness? In ordinary life there is seldom any difficulty in distinguishing the quality of the actor, even in the simplest actions; a tone will tell the education of the speaker, a courtesy will discover his status. Are there not two ways of accosting a poor man? There is a way which tells him he is a man, there is also a way which only tells him that he is poor. Are there not two ways of giving an alms? There is a way that doubles the gift, there is also a way that makes it a burden. Nor can the quality of the actor be altogether concealed by external accidents; under the richest surface it is not difficult to see the native meanness of some souls, whilst through the poorest raiments there may shine transfiguring light. Little natures reserve themselves for great occasions, majestic natures make all occasions great. There are codified lives that can move only as the book permits, there are controlling lives that hold prescription in contempt. The artistic student will carry the remembrance of this fact into his examination of Jesus Christ's life, and give to Jesus Christ the advantage which would be justly conceded even to an unknown name. When Jesus Christ sat down to meat with the leading men of the times, did He ever fail to turn the conversation towards heaven? When an ardent admirer exclaimed, "Blessed is the womb that bare thee, and the paps which thou hast sucked," did He not instantly answer, "Yea, rather, blessed are they that hear the Word of God, and keep it"? When called upon to define neighbourliness, did He fear to exalt the despised Samaritan above the priest and the Levite? When the disciples would have turned away the aspiring mothers who brought their children to be blessed, did He not receive the little ones with condescending grace, and say, "Of such is the kingdom of heaven"? Did He fear to put a higher value on the mites of the widow than on the gold of the rich? The artistic student will carefully weigh the answers which may be given to these questions, and will be as critical as to the method in which the work of Jesus Christ was done, as to the quality of the work itself. And this, too, he must not fail to notice, viz., that whilst Jesus Christ was much in public, He was also much in secret, He withdrew to solitary places, and was accustomed to be alone in prayer. These withdrawments must have some meaning, they throw an air of solemnity over the narrative, and almost constrain criticism into worship. What if in some instances they imply weakness, and even exhaustion, on the part of the worker? This is precisely what the artistic student wanted to complete the argument upon the all-sufficiency and redundance of Jesus

Christ's power, for nowhere along the line of that power did he come to any assurance of Jesus Christ's *manhood*, it steadily ascended, rather, towards the terribleness of omnipotence! What was wanted was a pause, a break of weakness, perhaps a cry of exhaustion. An unwearying flesh could hardly have prepared us for a compassionate divinity; it required the imperfection of infirmity to complete the perfection of strength :—" Great is the mystery of godliness." Yet the artistic inquirer will watch tremblingly lest there be any decay of power on the supposed Divine side: he will read that Jesus was weary with His journey, and yet at the same time that Jesus offered to give the water which springeth up into everlasting life; he will find that Jesus felt the desire of hunger, and yet that His word withered the fruitless fig-tree; he will see Jesus Christ asleep in the ship, tired with long service, and quickly hear Him silencing the winds and the waves; he will find that Jesus wept, and while the tears were yet in His eyes, He commanded Lazarus to come forth. The artist must say whether in this dual manifestation, there is any such consistency as is required to support the theory that Jesus Christ was begotten of the Holy Ghost, and he must assign some value to the fact that in no instance did Jesus Christ employ what may be termed the purely Divine side of His power to save Himself from the infirmities incident to ordinary human life; He wrought no private miracle for merely selfish protection, but was in all points tempted as other men; in short, He never made any deceptive use of His omnipotence, He was not a man by mere pretence, professedly weak and suffering, yet secretly availing Himself of sources inaccessible to His deluded disciples. And the consideration of this circumstance is the more important because all the signs of destitution which marked the life of Jesus Christ were precisely such as common reason would pronounce incompatible with the claim of a Divine ministry;

they provoked contempt, they enfeebled and actually contradicted the very aims which Jesus Christ was so desirous to subserve. Then, how to find consistency in such manifest inconsistency? The artistic student will pause to ask whether it is not through apparent contradictions that the verity of truth is most strongly established? Falsehood descends from verity to contradiction; truth ascends from contradiction to verity: the child smiles at the idea, that motion that can be so rapid as to become rest,—the man knows that but for this fact the universe would stagger and perish. What if Jesus Christ has shown that to be most a man it was necessary to be hardly a man at all,—that is, to go down to the lowest possible point and to be without form or comeliness or reputation?

Passing from the works of Jesus Christ, the artist has next to consider whether the scope and tone of His teaching (regarded as a spiritual revelation and an ethical testimony) are in keeping with the theory of His miraculous conception. The student must insist that Jesus Christ's teaching has properties which contradistinguish it even from the inspired teaching of Moses, the psalmists, and the prophets; and here arises the exciting question: How can inspiration exceed itself? This inquiry is met by the bold answer that in the development of Divine truth, we have been conducted from inspiration to the Inspirer, a teacher whose words are rather a living Presence than a written testimony. The artistic student must bear in mind that this supposed Son of God cannot be allowed to contradict Moses, the psalmists, and the prophets; he must work strictly in their line, and undertake to carry their work forward to the point of culmination; he cannot be permitted to begin by ignoring the moral history of the world; he must accept it, and prove his authority not by disputation but by fulfilment. To deny, or under-rate, the claim of Moses and the prophets, would be to bring Divine inspiration into discredit; on the other hand, to give them a higher signification, and actually to displace them as the fruit displaces the blossom, is the most difficult, as it is the most ambitious, work which any man can propose to accomplish. Now, candour requires instant recognition of the fact, that in the narrative Jesus Christ addresses Himself to this apparently impossible task, and this dauntless courage must not be overlooked in considering the validity of His title to the Messiahship. In the meantime it is not necessary to do more than to bear it in mind, because mere intrepidity, considered strictly *in se*, may amount to nothing,—yet the *absence* of intrepidity would properly destroy any claim to divinity : necessarily so, for God cannot hesitate, omnipotence cannot falter. That Jesus Christ accepts the history of the Divine government of men, as expounded or administered by inspired agents, is clear from His own words: "Think not that I am come to destroy the law or the prophets, I am not come to destroy but to fulfil." At this point, the intrepidity of Jesus Christ assumes peculiar value because He defines its function, and that function is sublime alike in its difficulty and purpose. He admits nothing of failure in preceding dispensations; He does not depreciate the work of others that He may magnify His own; He undertakes to deal with the necessary incompleteness of introductory economies, and to complete the circumference of Divine revelation to men. The artistic student cannot fail to observe that Jesus Christ proceeds on the theory that God's government is *one*, always consistent with itself, constantly evolving homogeneous and progressive truths. If it be held that teachers are reliable in proportion to the compass and grasp of their minds, it cannot be denied that Jesus Christ is represented in the narrative of His ministry as dealing with doctrines which relate with equal boldness and precision to the growth and destiny of human nature. Instead of denying the beginning He founded a distinct claim upon it,—" Had ye believed Moses ye would have believed me, for he wrote of me; but if ye believe not his writings, how shall ye believe my words?" A great plea for the oneness and simplicity of God's government.

As in the case of the works, so in the case of the words; there are two conditions which the artistic student must require to be fulfilled: (1.) An unequivocal claim on the part of Jesus Christ to be the Inspirer, and (2.) A corresponding excitement on the part of those to whom the claim was addressed. Let us attend to each of these conditions. With regard to the first, we cannot but be struck with the persistent identification of His own personality with the doctrine which He taught: He said not I *teach* the truth, but I *am* the truth; not I *show* the life, but I *am* the life— I am not inspired, I *am* the Inspirer Himself! The inspired man is the exceptional man; of the inspired man it may be said not so much he *knows* as he *is*, for inspiration increases and sanctifies the volume of being. Most men stop at education, they cannot attain the higher point; they have property, but not life; they are an accumulation of details; they *know* much, but *are* nothing. In the case of Jesus Christ we find Him constantly working from His personality, thus: "The words that I speak unto you, they are spirit and they are life; I am the bread of life, he that cometh to me shall never hunger, and he that believeth on me shall never thirst; he that believeth on me hath everlasting life; I am the bread of life; I am the living bread which came down from heaven; I am the vine, ye are the branches; without me ye can do nothing; I am the way, the truth, and the life; no man cometh unto the Father but by me; I am the good shepherd; I am the door; I give unto my sheep eternal life; he that seeth me, seeth him that sent me; he that hath seen me hath seen the Father; I and my Father are one." Here is distinctively a new type of man; to have conceived the notion that truth was capable of embodiment, and that life was the consummation of law, was a great advance upon all former thinking, while to set Himself forth as that embodiment and that law was an assumption not to be justified but by the highest evidence. Yet the accord between such an assumption and such a birth is at once appreciable; if never man *spake* like this man, it was because never man was *born* like this man. The deliberate exposition of His personality was sustained in the completest manner by His instantaneous answers to all kinds of questions suddenly and carefully put; attempts were made to take Him unawares, to entangle Him in His speech, and to draw Him on to dangerous ground, yet He confounded the wise and took the crafty in their own craftiness; He never asked for time; He never complained of inequality; He was never betrayed into unguarded expressions—all this is on the record, and with that fact our immediate business begins and ends. And is not this instantaneousness what might have been expected from one who professed that in Him dwelt all the fulness of the Godhead bodily? Is there not a complementary accord between the statement that there was virtue even in the hem of His garment, and the fact that His most unpremeditated speech put to silence the most astute cavillers? Unquestionably we are met, in the terms of the first proposed condition, with the most unequivocal demand on the part of Jesus Christ to be considered the Inspirer; what, then, of the second condition, viz., a corresponding excitement on the part of those to whom the demand was addressed? In answering this question, it should be borne in mind, that the people who heard Jesus Christ had enjoyed the advantage of long training, ancestral and personal, in

Divine things, and were by so much qualified to form an opinion upon ordinary religious teaching: "Unto them were committed the oracles of God . . . to them pertained the adoption, and the glory, and the covenants, and the giving of the law, and the service of God, and the promises;" to them had been addressed the question: "What nation is there so great that hath statutes and judgments, so righteous as all this law?" Upon such a people it will be difficult, with commonplace sentiment and utterance, to make a deep impression; yet, according to the narrative, Jesus Christ roused their deepest emotions: "The people were astonished at his doctrine, for he taught them as one having authority, and they were all amazed, insomuch that they questioned among themselves, saying, what thing is this? what new doctrine is this?—and all bare him witness, and wondered at the gracious words which proceeded out of his mouth; they were astonished, and said, whence hath this man this wisdom and these mighty works?—they were astonished at his doctrine, for his word was with power." On the other hand, He provoked contemptuous criticism; He came from a proscribed place; He adopted the most lowly surroundings; He drew upon Himself the murderous hatred of so-called righteous men; in His case the law of analogy and sequence was upset; the ascertainable elements of His personality did not account for the sum total of His being; so there He stood, at once a plague and a blessing,—a stranger, a friend, a mystery,—a monster or a God! The artistic student has to consider whether such results are ideally complete; whether the Inspirer could have hesitated to make a positive standing ground for Himself; whether the Inspirer could have taken any but the foremost position; and whether the rejection of the Inspirer does not bring to a crisis the sin and madness of the world.

A difficulty may present itself to the artistic mind at this point. A man who claims to have been begotten by the Holy Ghost may be expected to be so transcendental in his teaching as to disqualify himself for being a factor in practical morals; his stand-point will be so distant and so unappreciable that even the strongest reasoners will be unable to follow him; his teaching will be so apocalyptic and celestial as quite to miss the earthward and disciplinary side of human life. In reference to this difficulty the student may probably remember how nearly impossible it has been for some of the highest mortal minds to simplify themselves so as to be understood even by average thinkers; those minds have almost originated planes of their own, and the universal language has been minted into new values by the unique uses to which it has been turned. This, however, will but remotely touch the difficulty in hand, because Jesus Christ's pretensions exclude Him from the class of so-called original thinkers; such is the professedly *benevolent* purpose of His mission that we must insist that out of the heavens of divinity must be shed the light which may keep men from stumbling. In a word, there must be the approachableness on the side of His wisdom which was happily discovered on the side of His power. Of the existence of such approachableness there are two sources of proof; there is, first of all, the direct ethical teaching of Jesus Christ,—notably the sermon on the mount, abounding in laws and maxims which the most ordinary perception can comprehend; and secondly, there is a most considerate reticence on the part of Jesus Christ, shown in such passages as: "He spake the word unto them as they were able to hear it,—I have many things to say unto you, but ye cannot bear them now." Was it the least of His mercies that He carried *the burden of truth* for His Church? His followers were eventually to bear it for themselves, yet it was to be so gradually and effectually wrought into their very being by the Holy Ghost that instead of being a burden it was to be their peace and joy. So we come upon a power, boundless and terrible, yet controlled and repressed; a power, in fact, that becomes the very perfection of gentleness; and we come upon a doctrine that reaches beyond the ken of all human sagacity and genius, and yet descends into common daily life, calling all men to a morality lustrous as the purity of God. In doing and teaching all this, there is on the part of Jesus Christ a most sweet harmony of power and wisdom and love: what He *could* have done, what He *could* have said, and yet as God, Almighty and All-good, so adapted the light to the eye and the eye to the light as to bless men with the golden gifts of day and summer, so this worker of miracles and setter forth of strange doctrines tempered His majesty by an unspeakable condescension.

As the narrative of Jesus Christ's life moves towards its more tragic scenes, the artistic student feels at a loss to anticipate an exit which will be in keeping with the advent. For a time the line of consistency, if not broken, is most darkly obscured. The mighty man is bound as a prisoner; the Inspirer is dumb; He who saved others does not save Himself; He who never paused for an answer allows His life to be sworn away by false witnesses. Here (unless there be a purpose to serve which men never conceived) the line of consistency is at an end, and Christianity perishes in an ignominious anti-climax. To the artistic student who has taken a deep interest in his work, this is a moment of almost intolerable excitement. In his distress he may forget the saying, " Thou fool, that which thou sowest is not quickened except it die,"—a law which should give all men the true view of life and all its labour. With a most courageous determination the Christian narrative proceeds to illustrate this law, by carrying forward the story to the highest point of triumph—bringing back Jesus Christ from the dead, holding "all power in heaven and on earth." Still there remains the question, how is He to leave the world into which he came so mysteriously? And to this question there is returned the quiet but most exciting answer, *He ascended!* Not in a chariot of fire as if He had been sent for, He went of His own will and by His own power, and the consenting heavens received Him out of sight. This, then, concludes the appeal which is made to the imagination, and the artistic student has to pronounce upon its consistency and completeness:—Has the high tone of the beginning been sustained? Is the Ascension worthy of the Conception? Are the works and words of the same quality as the extreme points of the history? Are the small particles of the story gold or dross? These are questions which the artist will have no wish to escape.

To all this there is, of course, an obvious objection; it may be contended that as all writers of fiction endeavour to secure artistic unity, so the writers of the Gospels may have succeeded in inventing a coherent romance. The objection is quite as pointless as it is obvious.

First: No dramatist, in fact no mythologist, ever attempted to work with such extraordinary conditions as are found in the life of Jesus Christ.

Second: The Christian narrative is singularly defective in the very kind of unity which mere artists regard as essential to completeness—so defective that many critics have not hesitated to say that they have discovered in it several discrepancies. In the construction of the Gospels there is no sign of artistic effort, the unity is spiritual and latent, not literal and demonstrative.

Third: The most conclusive answer is, that the moral purpose proposed to be accomplished by the Gospels makes it impossible that they can be mere inventions of dramatic genius. That moral purpose is to save men, to bring them to God, and to give them peace; the inconsistency of such a purpose with the representation of a dramatic personage as a living Saviour is so gross as to be not only an offence in letters but a crime in morality.

# A HOMILETIC ANALYSIS

OF

# THE GOSPEL BY MATTHEW.

*CHAPTER I.*

1. The book of the generation of Jesus Christ, the Son of David, the son of Abraham.
2. Abraham begat Isaac; and Isaac begat Jacob; and Jacob begat Judas and his brethren;
3. And Judas begat Phares and Zara of Thamar;* and Phares begat Esrom; and Esrom begat Aram;
4. And Aram begat Aminadab; and Aminadab begat Naasson; and Naasson begat Salmon;
5. And Salmon begat Booz of Rachab; and Booz begat Obed of Ruth;†  and Obed begat Jesse;
6. And Jesse begat David the king; and David the king begat Solomon of her that had been the wife of Urias;
7. And Solomon begat Roboam; and Roboam begat Abia; and Abia begat Asa;
8. And Asa begat Josaphat; and Josaphat begat Joram; and Joram begat Ozias;
9. And Ozias begat Joatham; and Joatham begat Achaz; and Achaz begat Ezekias;

---

\* "It is to be noted that no holy woman is reckoned in the genealogy of Christ, but such as undergo some reproach in the Scripture, that He which came for sinners, being born of sinners, might do away the sins of all, without respect to the greatness thereof."—*Jerome.*

† "While Orpah wants bread in her own country, Ruth is grown a great lady in Bethlehem, and advanced to be great-grandmother to the kings of kings."—*Trapp.*

10. And Ezekias begat Manasses ; and Manasses begat Amon ; and Amon begat Josias ;

11. And Josias begat Jechonias and his brethren, about the time they were carried away to Babylon ;

12. And after they were brought to Babylon, Jechonias begat Salathiel ; and Salathiel begat Zorobabel ;

13. And Zorobabel begat Abiud ; and Abiud begat Eliakim ; and Eliakim begat Azor ;

14. And Azor begat Sadoc ; and Sadoc begat Achim ; and Achim begat Eliud ;

15. And Eliud begat Eleazar ; and Eleazar begat Matthan ; and Matthan begat Jacob ;

16. And Jacob begat Joseph the husband of Mary, of whom was born Jesus, who is called Christ.

17. So all the generations from Abraham to David are fourteen generations ; and from David until the carrying away into Babylon are fourteen generations ; and from the carrying away into Babylon unto Christ are fourteen generations.

1. Every human name more or less historic. 2. Some persons exercise a *direct* historic influence; others are but *incidentally* associated with the great facts of time. 3. To be even incidentally connected with CHRIST involves a great honour and a corresponding responsibility—all these persons were connected with the Promised One. 4. All generations travail in birth with one greater than all preceding, Christ alone excepted. 5. Those were illustrious lines along which the Man of Prophecy came ; kings were in it and men of mighty arm, yet these lines converge upon a point which appears to lie far below their majestic range ; "below," however, is but a relative term,—"below" is really of more importance than "above ;" the *root*, the *foundation* are both below, yet without them forests and temples are impossible. 6. Grace is not hereditary; bad people have been the sons and daughters of prophets and righteous kings. 7. The *accident* is mutable, the *purpose* changes not. Along the line, whether the links be gold or lead, the great Saving Man comes. 8. Christ's having come through all sorts of characters may be typical of His all-inclusive mission. " This

Man receiveth sinners." 9. Christ did not come through the *eldest* sons in all cases; the Son of man came from various grades, that He might be the Son and Saviour of all. 10. Why did not Christ come *earlier?* Why was not His name first on the list? God moves *gradually.* Take the analogy of the universe so far as we know it. Christ came the first moment He could have been comprehended. From "the foundation of the world" He was *ready,* He *waited;* was it with the impatience of yearning love? We know not His feelings *prior* to His incarnation; what a period was *that!* What visions, struggles, forereachings!

[Subject for discourse: CHRIST'S PRE-INCARNATE LIFE READ IN THE LIGHT OF HISTORY. In developing this theme take the New Testament over the birth-line, and under the shadow of the grief which Jesus Christ endured throughout His early ministry, read what *could* have been the life which, from all the ages of eternity, had *such sorrow perpetually in anticipation.*]

Taking the entire seventeen verses, a discourse might be constructed on THE CHRISTOLOGY OF HUMAN DEVELOPMENT: I. Up to the time of Mary the race was preparing for Christ: (*a*) through good men, (*b*) through bad men, (*c*) through captivity. II. The race is *still preparing* for Christ, not now through the narrow line of a family, but throughout the whole range of its being. *This Christ-element is the secret of all history.* Even now it passes through bad men, bad churches, corrupt institutions, and captivities in Babylon; but it lives on, and shall live, until the full time.

Taking the seventeenth verse separately, it might be regarded as setting forth the DIVINE REGULATION OF TIME. (*a*) God has set times for the accomplishment of His purposes; (*b*) these times are beyond human control; (*c*) the duty of impatient man is to *wait:* (*d*) every generation shortens the duration of the Satanic empire; (*e*) every peal of the great time-bell of the universe announces the advancing step of Christ; (*f*) good ideas have everything to hope from time, but bad ideas everything to fear.

Appeal on the ground *that, though not one of us can be in the family line of Christ, yet all may be spiritually related to Him.* We cannot have our names put down on *this* list, but they may be "written in heaven." Appeal also on the ground *that the tumultuous "generations" bring the peaceful Christ.*

18. Now the birth of Jesus Christ was on this wise: When as his mother Mary was espoused to Joseph, before they came together, she was found with child of the Holy Ghost.
19. Then Joseph her husband, being a just man, and not willing to make her a public example, was minded to put her away privily.
20. But while he thought on these things, behold, the angel of the Lord appeared unto him in a dream, saying, Joseph, thou son of David, fear not to take unto thee Mary thy wife; for that which is conceived in her is of the Holy Ghost.
21. And she shall bring forth a son, and thou shalt call his name JESUS; for he shall save his people from their sins.
22. Now all this was done, that it might be fulfilled which was spoken of the Lord by the prophet, saying:
23. Behold a virgin [ἡ παρθενος=*the* virgin, or even a virgin] shall be with child, and shall bring forth a son, and they shall call his name Emmanuel, which being interpreted is, God with us.
24. Then Joseph being raised from sleep, did as the angel of the Lord had bidden him, and took unto him his wife:
25. And knew her not till she had brought forth her firstborn son: and he called his name JESUS.

1. Here the great exceptional birth transpires. Up to this point we have run on in an easy line; everything has been ordinary and accountable. 2. The whole life of Christ, indeed, was the great Exception of Being. 3. Here is the direct contact of the human with the Divine; heretofore in all birth we have simply had the human and the human, but in the 18th verse we have the human and the Divine. This birth comes from the heavens and the earth; the child is at once Son of GOD and Son of MAN. 4. God has never

ceased to take an interest in the human race, but only once has He inserted into it a New Man—a personal, redeeming, transforming life. 5. The race had no power in itself to give birth to a Saviour; it might continue a progeny of sinners, but no Saviour would ever appear apart from direct Divine interposition. 6. Joseph affords a marked illustration of the fact that *men often misinterpret their circumstances*. Joy has often been threading its way to us through the entangled lines of our perplexity. 7. The marriage of Joseph and Mary was useful in showing that Mary was not superhuman; that she was an ordinary member of the human family, and that so far Jesus Christ was bone of our bone, and flesh of our flesh. 8. Christ was the only man born with a special mission in relation to "sins" (verse 21). Every other man since Adam was born *in sin*, but this Man descended as it were upon it to destroy its power. In addressing Himself, however, to this aspect of humanity He in reality addressed Himself to all aspects. Man is never found *out* of sin, hence the inclusiveness of the Redeemer's mission. He came to the *heart*. Christ's was not a mission to accidents and details, but to *manhood*,—not manhood in any time or place, or transient condition, but manhood in its reality and permanence. 9. This was all in fulfilment of prophecy. (*a*) Time, a great realising power. (*b*) The announcements of one age are the men of another. (*c*) All prophecy, good or bad, may safely be left to the determining power of *time*. (*d*) Great events may require preparation. God puts a word of hope into the world's heart, and for ages that word sings or burns, keeping man in joy, or lighting him through the gloom. (*e*) Wonderful connection between the Prophets and the Facts; one man is permitted merely to speak a word, another is honoured with seeing that word become a life! "Herein is that saying true, One soweth and another reapeth." Isaiah and Jeremiah sowed, and *we* stand amid landscapes clothed with golden harvests! 10. Joseph's being asleep when the announcement was made to him is a suggestive circumstance. (*a*) Man's life is not all comprised in the little bustle of his wakeful hours. (*b*) Some communications can be effectually made only when men are most dissociated from the external and material. (*c*) In sleep, man is as thoroughly *alone* as he possibly can be in this world, and (in a certain sense) is *more entirely in the power of God* than in any other condition. There is a theology of sleep; there is also a theology of dreams. All things, in fact, and specially all life and thought, are theological. Atheism itself is but theology in shadow!

GENERAL NOTE ON THE FIRST CHAPTER.

The opening chapter of the Old Testament and the opening chapter of the New Testament afford, when taken together, some striking points of analogy and contrast:

I. The former is mainly occupied with the building of a universe; the other with the birth of a Man.

II. The former concludes with the making of the first Adam; the latter with the birth of a second.

III. The former shows how out of chaos came the orderly creation; the latter how out of a fiercer tumult came the calm Redeemer.

IV. The former shows the progress through the inferior creation up to man; the latter reveals the progress of the Divine idea through sinful generations up to man's Saviour.

V. The former shows how man, as a creature, is dependent on the Creator; the latter how man, as a sinner, is dependent on the Redeemer.

VI. The former says, Let us *make* man; the latter, Let us *save* man.

## CHAPTER II.

1. Now when Jesus was born in Bethlehem of Judæa, in the days of Herod the King, behold, there came wise men from the east to Jerusalem,
2. Saying: Where is he that is born King of the Jews? for we have seen his star in the east, and are come to worship him.
3. When Herod the king had heard these things, he was troubled, and all Jerusalem with him.
4. And when he had gathered all the Chief Priests and Scribes of the people together, he demanded of them where Christ should be born.
5. And they said unto him, in Bethlehem of Judæa; for thus it is written by the prophet,
6. And thou Bethlehem, in the land of Juda, art not the least among the princes of Juda; for out of thee shall come a Governor, that shall rule my people Israel.
7. Then Herod, when he had privily called the wise men, enquired of them diligently what time the star appeared.
8. And he sent them to Bethlehem, and said, Go and search diligently for the young child; and when ye have found him, bring me word again, that I may come and worship him also.
9. When they had heard the king, they departed; and, lo, the star which they saw in the east, went before them, till it came and stood over where the young child was.
10. When they saw the star, they rejoiced with exceeding great joy.

ENQUIRY RESPECTING CHRIST.—I. The world's interest is in *life*, not in mere age; enquiry is made respecting "the young child." Men should be interested in *facts*, not in accidents: "Born," sets forth the fact; "young," merely indicates a passing circumstance. II. All classes concerned in this birth—"Wise men, kings, chief priests and scribes of the people." The power of one life to rouse a world. III. The different purposes of enquiry respecting Christ; to worship, to destroy (verse 13), to speculate upon. Every man enquires according to his own moral condition;—hope, fear, reverence, love, are expressions of moral life. Christ's incarnation was a perpetual appeal to moral consciousness: his life was a daily judgment upon the race. IV. The different results of enquiry respecting Christ: Herod was "troubled;" the wise men "rejoiced with exceeding great joy." (*a*) No man has "troubled" the human heart so much as Christ. His whole course was a rebuke of all evil. A babe "troubling" a king! See here the punitive force of goodness. The good have ever "troubled" the bad. The nefarious book-keeper is "troubled" by the eye of his honest companion; he fears that eye more than the lightning. The world's bitterest trouble has ever arisen from *moral* causes. (*b*) No man has ever given such "joy" to the human heart as Christ. The highest joy, too, comes from moral causes. A right relation to Christ ever inspires gladness. V. Behind holy words there may be wicked designs,—Herod *said* "worship," but *meant* "destroy."

1. All men *must*, in one relation or another, come into contact with Christ. 2. Some have seen "His star," but have not cared to see Himself. Go from the flame to the hand that kindled it. 3. It was well that a star should herald Him who was the light of the world. All light should lead to the Saviour.—Taking the 6th verse alone, it shows: 1. That the world has been taught to hope for Rulership. 2. That Rulership is right only in proportion as it is derived from Christ. 3. That all false Rulership trembles before the government of the Redeemer. 4. That Rulership is often connected with improbable circumstances—(*a*) improbable place—Bethlehem; (*b*) improbable person—"young child." The Ruler does not come from the Metropolis—does not appear as an imposing personage. 5. True Rulership is moral. Gain a *moral* mastery if you seek a permanent triumph. (Collate the passages which announce the subjugation of all Rulerships to Christ.)

11. And when they were come into the house, they saw the young child with Mary his mother, and fell down, and worshipped him: and when they had opened their treasures, they presented unto him gifts; gold, and frankincense, and myrrh.

12. And being warned of God in a dream that they should not return to Herod, they departed into their own country another way.

13. And when they were departed, behold, the angel of the Lord appeareth to Joseph in a dream, saying, Arise, and take the young child and his mother, and flee into Egypt, and be thou there until I bring thee word: for Herod will seek the young child to destroy him.

14. When he arose, he took the young child and his mother by night, and departed into Egypt:

15. And was there until the death of Herod: that it might be fulfilled which was spoken of the Lord by the prophet, saying, Out of Egypt have I called my son.

1. Worship is the true attitude of man towards Christ. 2. Worship associated with oblation indicates the proper spirit of the Christ-seeker. 3. The right position of wisdom is at the feet of Christ. Verses 12—15. 1. God is in constant communication with the right-minded. 2. Distinguish between the dream of the spirit and the dream of the stomach; there are foolish fantasies arising from indigestion, as well as communications from Heaven vouchsafed to the restful spirit. Never mistake delusion for inspiration. 3. The angel of the Lord is watching the affairs of men; he warns Joseph, he watches Herod, he points out a safe retreat. How much we owe to the *Invisible!* How near is heaven to earth! A dream may connect the worlds—a vision of the night may reveal the unity of creation! 4. Man's simple business in perplexity is to obey; sometimes obedience requires *activity*—"flee into Egypt;" sometimes it requires simple *quiescence, patient waiting*—"be thou there until I bring thee word." 5. The true interpretation of human purposes is from God,—"Herod will seek the young child to destroy Him." Herod had said "worship," but God read the heart. 6. Egypt, the asylum of weakness, will become the starting-point of imperial and all-conquering power. A retreat need not be a tomb.

16. Then Herod, when he saw that he was mocked of the wise men, was exceeding wroth, and sent forth, and slew all the children that were

34    HOMILETIC ANALYSIS.

in Bethlehem, and in all the coasts thereof, from two years old and under, according to the time which he had diligently enquired of the wise men.

17. Then was fulfilled that which was spoken by Jeremy the prophet, saying,

18. In Rama was there a voice heard, lamentation, and weeping, and great mourning, Rachel weeping for her children, and would not be comforted, because they are not.

19. But when Herod was dead, behold an angel of the Lord appeareth in a dream to Joseph in Egypt,

20. Saying, Arise, and take the young child and his mother, and go into the land of Israel: for they are dead which sought the young child's life.

21. And he arose, and took the young child and his mother, and came into the land of Israel.

22. But when he heard that Archelaus did reign in Judæa in the room of his father Herod, he was afraid to go thither; notwithstanding, being warned of God in a dream, he turned aside into the parts of Galilee:

23. And he came and dwelt in a city called Nazareth: that it might be fulfilled which was spoken by the prophets, He shall be called a Nazarene.

Verses 16—18. 1. The power of goodness is moral; the power of selfishness is physical. 2. The spirit of goodness is preservative; the spirit of selfishness is destructive. 3. The result of goodness is "Good-will towards men;" the result of selfishness is "lamentation, and mourning, and great weeping." 4. See what the world would come to under a selfish Rulership! Passion flees to the sword; disappointment thirsts for blood! Say, who shall be king— Christ or Herod? The apparent blessings connected with the reign of Herod are connected with danger. It is always dangerous to be seeking flowers on the slopes of a volcano.

Verses 19—23. 1. The angel of the Lord is ever mindful of the good. 2. The good have everything to hope from time. 3. The good have everything to fear from the family of sinners, forasmuch as sons may be sworn to their father's purposes. 4. The bad perish, but the good live; "they are dead which sought the young child's life." This is the summing up of all attempts to arrest the Messianic progress. Again and again, from age to age, until every rival be subdued, shall men say—" They are dead which sought the young child's life." The "young child" cannot die! His enemies go down to the dust, and are buried in shame and confusion, but the "young child" lives on without a wrinkle on His brow; He shall hear of many deaths, but no arrow shall strike His own heart,—the grave shall cover His foes, but He shall be the light and joy of the universe for ever.

GENERAL NOTE ON THE SECOND CHAPTER.

This chapter presents the difficulties which always attend the setting up of the Kingdom of Heaven among men. Here, for example, are :—1. Trials of the *individual*: Joseph and Mary. 2. Trials of the regnant power: Herod. 3. Trials of families: the massacre of infants. 4. Trials of the Coming Sovereign : withdrawal of Christ into Egypt. Concerning these trials three things are to be critically noted :—

I. THE KINGDOM OF HEAVEN IS NOT RESPONSIBLE FOR THEM. Is the surgeon responsible for the pain inflicted by the excision of a limb ? Truly not ; the limb was diseased ; the limb was so diseased as to be endangering the life of the sufferer; therefore, pain was associated with a beneficent application of scientific skill. The Kingdom of Heaven came to operate upon morally putrid humanity ; and the putridity must be blamed for the agony, not the Kingdom of Heaven.

II. THEY ARE THE NECESSARY ATTENDANTS OF ALL WIDENING CIVILISATION. Education always involves pain. Whenever the age receives a wider or deeper truth into its heart, there is a massacre somewhere in the social sphere. It is so even in material civilisation; when civilisation so liberalised itself as to receive the locomotive engine, what unsettlement, what temporary loss, what re-arrangement of parties, took place! So it is everywhere; the greater the change, the greater the pain. Hence, when the Kingdom of

Heaven came to be established in the person and work of Christ, it was through much rending and shaking of the old condition of things. The innocent suffered through the guilty, yet who can tell what place in Heaven the Bethlehem infants fill who were slain instead of Christ? For the passing hour the parents wailed in great agony, but what is their feeling *now?*

III. THEY ARE BUT HINTS OF THE GREATER SUFFERING OF GOD. When Christ was thus received, did God suffer nothing? And, if suffering be in proportion to the capacity of the sufferer, to what insignificance are all human sufferings reduced? We forget that the sensibilities of God are wounded by every rejection of His mercy, and that the establishment of His kingdom costs Him greater pain than any of His creatures can endure or comprehend.

(*a*). The Kingdom of Heaven does not fight with hand against hand.

(*b*). The Kingdom of Heaven is introduced into every soul, much as Christ was introduced into the world, through struggle, trial, difficulty, &c.

(*c*). The Kingdom of Heaven, though withdrawn for a time, is not defeated. (Refluent wave.)

### CHAPTER III.

1. In those days came John the Baptist, preaching in the wilderness of Judæa,
2. And saying, Repent ye : for the kingdom of heaven is at hand.
3. For this is he that was spoken of by the prophet Esaias, saying, The voice of one crying in the wilderness, Prepare ye the way of the Lord, make his paths straight.
4. And the same John had his raiment of camel's hair, and a leathern girdle about his loins; and his meat was locusts and wild honey.
5. Then went out to him Jerusalem, and all Judæa, and all the region round about Jordan,
6. And were baptized of him in Jordan, confessing their sins.

1. Convergent historic lines,—Christ in Nazareth, John in the wilderness. 2. One worker necessary to another. 3. Solitude a preparation for service;—every day at Nazareth means strength, wisdom, patience. 4. The cry of all civilisation has been "Repent,"—change your purposes,—turn round! How much more, in what fuller and profounder sense, is this so with *Religion!* This cry, "Repent," shows (*a*) that men were in a false position; (*b*) that they had power to alter it; and (*c*) that such power was immediately associated with a great opportunity; "the kingdom of heaven is at hand." 5. All servants of the highest interests of humanity have had to engage in a *negative* work; this is expressed in the cry, "Repent." This negative work (*a*) brings them into collision with violent antagonisms; (*b*) absorbs strength which might have been employed in direct edification; and (*c*) prevents for a long period the full exhibition of what is superficially termed *Success*. The idea of success in spiritual work is much perverted and misunderstood. (Foreign missions,—look at initial difficulties, tradition, habit, prejudice, distrust of foreign race, &c.) 6. Every preacher of Repentance is a fulfilment of prophecy, inasmuch as he expresses and interprets the Divine purpose respecting apostate humanity. Such preachers are united with an illustrious line; yet the glory of their position is tarnished by the reflection that so many "voices" have cried in vain. 7. This call to "Repent" must be deepened and prolonged, though under the most depressing circumstances, for it is a Divine testimony in a corrupt age. 8. The moral majesty of an earnest man. John shakes Jerusalem and all Judæa, and all the region round about Jordan. He is only an individual, yet his march is like that of an army intent on victory. What is his work? Twofold—(*a*) Preaching; (*b*) Baptizing. This twofold work permanent during man's apostacy; preaching calls to the truth; baptizing symbolises its acceptance, or preparation

for its acceptance. The moral signification of John's baptism was that all cleansing must come from beyond man; it must be done by another, and water was but as an emblem of that mightier Power.

7. But when he saw many of the Pharisees and Sadducees come to his baptism, he said unto them, O generation of vipers, who hath warned you to flee from the wrath to come?
8. Bring forth therefore fruits meet for repentance:
9. And think not to say within yourselves, We have Abraham to our father: for I say unto you, that God is able of these stones to raise up children unto Abraham.
10. And now also the ax is laid unto the root of the trees: therefore every tree which bringeth not forth good fruit is hewn down and cast into the fire.
11. I indeed baptize you with water unto repentance: but he that cometh after me is mightier than I, whose shoes I am not worthy to bear: he shall baptize you with the Holy Ghost, and with fire:
12. Whose fan is in his hand, and he will throughly purge his floor, and gather his wheat into the garner; but he will burn up the chaff with unquenchable fire.

1. Men may come to religious ordinances from a wrong motive. 2. Men may come to such ordinances through misapprehension of their import. 3. Men may avail themselves of such ordinances for selfish purposes. 4. All men who come to religious ordinances should be faithfully warned of their spirit and duty; this faithful warning will (*a*) call things by their proper names; (*b*) will demand not ceremonialism, but heavenly fruitfulness of life; (*c*) will destroy all false grounds of moral descent, by throwing every man on his own personal character; (*d*) will keep up the grand judicial idea in all its awfulness and sublimity; (*e*) will broadly distinguish between outward observances and spiritual processes.

This is not such an inauguration of the Messianic era as we should have expected. The ages have been waiting for the Son of Peace, but there comes before Him a man whose voice is thunder, whose glance is lightning. No gentle word escapes the lips of this fierce man; the stormy whirlwind has caught him and borne him on through the wilderness of Judæa, and as if a great fire were behind him he urgently makes his way. Strangely terrible are his words, "Repent," —"Prepare,"—"Ax,"—"Purge his floor,"—"Burn up the chaff with unquenchable fire." In all this there is not one tone of conciliation, one smile of amiability, one overture of cordiality. Yet this man comes before the Prince of Peace! Nor does he allude to the gentler aspects of the Coming One. He is taken up with the idea of *power;* hence he says, "He that cometh after me is MIGHTIER than I." This preacher in the wilderness dwelt on the idea of strength,—strength as a terror to evil,—strength as an irresistible judicial power. The soft, melodious hymn, such as Peace would sing in a garden of flowers, might have been expected; trembling, quivering with hopeful joy; but instead there is a roar as of a sudden storm, a cry as of unexpected terror. This circumstance is, however, quite coincident with the course of history. God is always setting aside human expectations, and building His temples in unlikely places or with unlikely materials. God uses the storm. The ages are not all made up of long, radiant, summer days. Night, and storm, and battle, as well as day, and calm, and peace, are God's servants. This age requires "voices" that can be heard. The world's vast wilderness is open—pray God to send into it men crying "Repent." The Church is now in danger of over-feeding the few, and forgetting the hungering many. There is a work to be done in the wilderness. The manner appropriate to the wilderness may not be appropriate to the Church: what is wanted, therefore, is adaptation: the loud cry or the subdued tone,—both are required to meet the world's great want.

A ministry of Repentance ought always to precede a ministry of salvation. In our day the former has been much overlooked. The ministry of Repentance should be modelled upon the ministry of John :—1. John dealt with the corruptions of the age; 2. John uttered the preparative, not the final word; 3. John demanded "fruits" in proof of sincerity; 4. John preached of judgment; 5. John grounded his ministry on first principles. He called to *duty*, "Repent;" he announced a *fact*, "The kingdom of heaven is at hand." It is the business of some men simply to *initiate*. They blow a trumpet-blast, and having roused attention, they retire before the teacher sent from God. Let ministers be judged by this rule; there is a ministry of *initiation*, and there is a ministry of *education*. Some men, Christ for example, combine these ministries.

13. Then cometh Jesus from Galilee to Jordan unto John, to be baptized of him.
14. But John forbad him, saying, I have need to be baptized of thee, and comest thou to me?
15. And Jesus answering said unto him, Suffer it to be so now : for thus it becometh us to fulfil all righteousness. Then he suffered him.
16. And Jesus, when he was baptized, went up straightway out of the water : and, lo, the heavens were opened unto him, and he saw the Spirit of God descending like a dove, and lighting upon him :
17. And lo a voice from heaven, saying, This is my beloved Son, in whom I am well pleased.

Christ's baptism could not imply that he was called to "repentance." It showed :—1. *That Christ identified Himself with the current of the Divine purposes as shown in human history.* He did not stand apart in an unapproachable loneliness; He worked *with* man as well as *for* man. This identification begets sympathy, and sympathy is one of the prime conditions of moral sovereignty. 2. *That the right use of present dispensations is compatible with the highest ideal of destiny.* The ages have been conducted to a great crisis; the prophets of an olden time had passed away; and now prophecy in its sublimest power was incarnated in one man; the past and the future converged, so to speak, upon this "voice crying in the wilderness." Christ, then, identified Himself with the contemporary dispensation, and through *that* passed on to His mediation. Men should study the divinity of each age, and become co-workers with God. God has some method of working in every generation, and our business should be to ally ourselves with Him, according to the speciality of the revelation. 3. *That obedience to the spirit of the time ever brings fuller disclosures and attestations of the Divine blessing.* In a peculiar sense this was so with Christ, yet each of His followers is honoured, proportionally, in the same way. The heavens are opened to every obedient man, and the Spirit of God descends on the last as on the first. Christ's was, of course, a special inauguration; so far He stands entirely and for ever *alone*, yet all who come within His mediation, penitently and believingly, receive according to their degree the same tokens of Divine complacency. 4. *That the less is auxiliary to the greater.* John shrunk from the service, saying, "I have need to be baptized of thee, and comest thou to me." Men must "come to" one another, sometimes even in an inverted order, so that Divine plans may be carried out.

GENERAL NOTE ON THE CHAPTER.

This chapter contains the history of a whole dispensation. "In those days came John . . . . This is my beloved Son." Sometimes a dispensation stretched through centuries; in this case it was comparatively but an hour. God makes history with varying degrees of rapidity. Hardly have we finished the awful words of Malachi, "Smite the earth with a curse," until we read, "Blessed are the poor in spirit, for their's is the kingdom of heaven."

History has thus culminated in a new name. We have

come from Man, Servant, Prophet, Messenger, up to SON! There is a profoundly significant moral element even in this nomenclature : we pass from "make" to "begotten ;" from "upright" to "beloved;" from the "us" of the creating Trinity to the "my" of the benignant Father. There has been a Divine ideal in the race, towards which all revolution, all war, all discovery, all worship, has been a struggle. Visions of prophecy, songs of hope, agonies of prayer, have had this mystery before them—a mystery which has been inspiration, a mystery which has been a great "burden."

Christ has been in *all* the dispensations, why should He be excluded from John's ? " Beginning with Moses and all the prophets, he expounded unto them in all the scriptures, the things concerning himself." Should there, then, be one dispensation without Him ? Truly not. He had been the inspiration of all epochs, and as they moved on to the immediate fulfilment of God's purpose He came nearer to the vision, until at last, baptized with water, standing on the earth, under the opened heavens, He was pronounced " my Son," and the "very good " of the first Adam was exchanged for the " well pleased " of the second.

## CHAPTER IV.

1. Then was Jesus led up of the spirit into the wilderness to be tempted of the devil.
2. And when he had fasted forty days and forty nights, he was afterward an hungred.
3. And when the tempter came to him, he said, If thou be the Son of God, command that these stones be made bread.
4. But he answered and said, It is written, Man shall not live by bread alone, but by every word that proceedeth out of the mouth of God.
5. Then the devil taketh him up into the holy city, and setteth him on a pinnacle of the temple.
6. And saith unto him, If thou be the Son of God, cast thyself down : for it is written, He shall give his angels charge concerning thee : and in their hands they shall bear thee up, lest at any time thou dash thy foot against a stone.

7. Jesus said unto him, It is written again, Thou shalt not tempt the Lord thy God.

8. Again, the devil taketh him up into an exceeding high mountain, and sheweth him all the kingdoms of the world, and the glory of them;

9. And saith unto him, All these things will I give thee, if thou wilt fall down and worship me.

10. Then saith Jesus unto him, Get thee hence, Satan: for it is written, Thou shalt worship the Lord thy God, and him only shalt thou serve.

11. Then the devil leaveth him, and, behold, angels came and ministered unto him.

1. THE TIME,—"Then;" (*a*) immediately after a great blessing; (*b*) in fulfilment of God's earliest promise. 2. THE MANNER,—"led up of the Spirit;" (*a*) every man must be tempted; (*b*) no man knows his strength until he has known the discipline of temptation; (*c*) great destinies are often approached through great afflictions. 3. THE PROCESS: I. (*a*) An appeal to immediate necessity,—"he was an hungered;" (*b*) a temptation breathing the spirit of benevolence,—make bread; (*c*) a temptation which was apparently harmless,—there could be no harm in making bread, but there was infinite harm in making it at the devil's suggestion. II. (*a*) A temptation to presumption,—"cast thyself down;" (*b*) a temptation breathing the spirit of faith,—"he shall give his angels charge concerning thee;" (*c*) a temptation surrounded by the most religious circumstances,—"holy city;" "pinnacle of the temple:" temptations may be adapted to places. III. (*a*) A temptation to ambition,—"the kingdoms of the world and the glory of them;" (*b*) a temptation breathing the spirit of generosity,—"all these things will I give thee;" (*c*) a temptation to the most ruinous of all attitudes,—"if thou wilt fall down and worship me." 4. THE ANSWERS: (*a*) a profound view of life,—"man shall not live by bread alone;" (*b*) a profound view of moral limitations,—"thou shall not tempt the Lord thy God;" (*c*) a profound view of the duty of the creature to the Creator,—"thou shalt worship the Lord thy God, and

him only shalt thou serve." In all these answers, Christ asserts *the ultimate authority of written Revelation*. Christ, not Satan, began the quotation of scripture. We now see how He employed His solitude: He did not come to the wilderness unprepared. Instantly He interposed the written word between Himself and the temptation. Revelation was thus shown not to be a speculative statement, but a final and practical support to tried humanity. 5. THE ISSUE,— "the devil leaveth him, and, behold, angels came and ministered unto him." (*a*) The true method of resisting the enemy; (*b*) an encouragement in the terrible contest,—angels watch the tempted!

There are certain peculiar characteristics of the Temptation; (*a*) it was adapted to the subject by its refinement; (*b*) it proceeded upon a recognition of the deepest instincts of human nature; (*c*) it revealed a perfect knowledge of the various approaches to the human heart; (*d*) it began by professedly aiming at Christ's benefit, and ended by an avowed design for extended dominion. What harm could there be in proving His divine Sonship by an instant transformation of the stones into bread? Might not the act have ended the temptation, and sent Satan back confounded and dismayed? Were it possible for the devil to suggest a good action, *men should never do even a good deed at the devil's bidding.*

1. It is to be noted that Sonship does not exempt men from temptation:—"this is my beloved *Son* . . . . . *tempted* of the devil." Temptation, in fact, implies a measure of goodness on the part of the tempted. 2. Temptation is not sin; the Saviour was tempted, but He did not commit sin. The spiritual history of the good is often overshadowed by confounding temptation with transgression.

In this temptation, Christ teaches three things respecting God:—1. That true life is derived from Him; 2. That faith, not presumption, is acceptable to Him; 3. That He is the only proper object of adoration.

The temptation of Christ has a twofold bearing:—1. ON THE BELIEVER; (*a*) the best are most tempted; (*b*) the strength comes from revelation, not from human nature; (*c*) there is now added to the doctrine of revelation the personal sympathy of the tempted Redeemer. "There are but three particular temptations mentioned in all the forty days of our Saviour's temptation, and two of them run so, '*If thou be the Son of God;*' wherein Satan labours to draw a cloud upon Christ's assurance, and to write an IF upon his childship."—(*Bridge.*)

2. ON THE UNBELIEVER; (*a*) Your master aspires to Godhead; (*b*) your master offers what he can never bestow; (*c*) your master prostitutes Divine promises into encouragements to presumption. "When Satan tempted Christ in the wilderness, he alleged but one sentence of Scripture for himself, and that Psalm out of which he borrowed it (Psalm xci. 11), made so plain against him that he was fain to pick here a word, and there a word, and leave out that which went before, and skip in the midst, and omit that which came after."—(*Henry Smith*, 1560-1591.)

12. Now when Jesus had heard that John was cast into prison, he departed into Galilee;
13. And leaving Nazareth, he came and dwelt in Capernaum, which is upon the sea coast, in the borders of Zabulon and Nephthalim:
14. That it might be fulfilled which was spoken by Esaias the prophet, saying,
15. The land of Zabulon, and the land of Nephthalim, by the way of the sea, beyond Jordan, Galilee of the Gentiles;
16. The people which sat in darkness saw great light: and to them which sat in the region of the shadow of death light is sprung up.
17. From that time Jesus began to preach, and to say, Repent: for the kingdom of heaven is at hand.

1. The fall of one man may mark the inauguration of another. 2. The worker may be imprisoned, but the work

goes on. 3. The tetrarch "shut up John in prison," but he could not imprison the "great light" which shone on the land of Zabulon and the land of Nephthalim. 4. Every movement of Christ was (verse 14th) a fulfilment of prophecy; and could we see God's purposes concerning ourselves, we should see that He fixes the bounds of our habitation. Wherever in the sacred record we find a statement of details, we discover that they are set forth as part of a plan, and so it is through all human life. Could we but see the book that is on high, we should find that we move hither and thither "that it might be fulfilled." 5. Local beginnings are compatible with universal endings; Zabulon and Nephthalim see the early gleam, but the broad noontide bathes the world in heavenly glory. 6. Danger should develop courage: Jesus went forth when John was in prison.

Verse 17th brings Christ before us as a preacher. 1. He passed a long period of silence and preparation. 2. His preaching was negative and positive. Mark gives a fuller account of the ministry: "Jesus came into Galilee preaching the Gospel of the kingdom of God and saying, The time is fulfilled, and the kingdom of God is at hand: repent ye, and believe the Gospel." (*a*) Negative, "repent;" (*b*) positive, "believe."

Christ is compared to a "great light:" (*a*) Light is a revealer; (*b*) Light is a deliverer: (*c*) Light is a condition of progress.

GENERAL NOTE ON CHRIST'S PREACHING.

Preaching ceases to be a great moral power as it becomes merely scholastic, critical, and artistic. The work of the preacher is to call men to repentance and faith. The preacher is "a *voice* crying in the wilderness." There is a moral condition which he must reprove; there is a spiritual exercise to which he must call. Ungodly men are not able to enter into the spiritual meaning of the written word; in the first instance, there must be an alarm,—"repent," and then a rest,—"believe." When a heart is awakened, the first inquiry does not relate to the canonicity of a given number of manuscripts, or to a settlement of conflicting readings. The matter lies deeper, goes nearer the life, penetrates the moral core. The first act of a man who heeds the call to repentance is an act of introversion of self-analysis, and self-estimation. This act is conducted under the illumination of the Holy Spirit. The heart becomes conscious of its corruption, and conscious of a want which it cannot supply. Then it utters the prevailing prayer of earnestness, and having done the "will," God gives it to know the "doctrine." The honoured servant who is charged with the double gift, —the gift of preaching and the gift of teaching—will proceed to feed the heart with the word of truth, so that it may grow in the knowledge of our Lord Jesus Christ;" but the simple work of the preacher, as such, is to say (with all variety, force and argumentativeness), "Repent, and believe the Gospel." Afterwards, when the moral faculty is quickened, there is a supremely important work to be done with the written word. The moral faculty alone, however, can properly deal with moral questions; while that is dormant, the written word is sealed; but after it is quickened, it sees light above the word, and light in the word, and its sublime apprehensions of the spiritual meaning reduce all verbal difficulties to their proper magnitude. A marked distinction then, should be made between preaching and teaching; but according to the conventionalities of British ecclesiasticism, the minister must do the double work of preacher and teacher, and the pulpit is persistently turned into the prelector's desk. Any appeal to the purely intellectual faculty of the ungodly hearer is a deferential tribute to his pride, such as Christ and His apostles never paid. They cried, Repent; they called to the immediate discharge of a moral duty. The physician does not call the sick man to the study of treatises on physiology and therapeutics, but gives the medicine adapted to the urgency of the crisis. The moral physician calls first to repentance,—to a right moral condition, and then the penitent and trusting soul may betake itself to theological pursuits. This process is often reversed; we first teach theology, and then preach repentance; and no wonder that we are deprived of "times of refreshing from the presence of the Lord." The oral discourse should be as different as possible from the printed treatise: it is as impossible to print what may be called the electricity of an oration, as to print a thunderstorm, or a summer shower. Preachers generally, cannot compete with authors; most have not the time, many have not the culture. The sermon, then, should not be merely a vocal-book, or an articulated manuscript; it should be marked by a life which cannot be printed, an urgency which awakens emotion rather than provokes criticism. The preacher who merely vocalises a manuscript courts comparison with the author; but the orator who utters well-ordered thought in the language of the moment, develops the strongest *contrast* by occupying a plane peculiarly his own. When the preacher is called to address a select audience, capable of following an intricate argument, or appreciating the delicate refinements of genius, the case is unique, and must be judged accordingly. But the preacher who addresses promiscuous assemblies, should, in the degree of his power, reproduce the examples of New Testament preaching.

18. And Jesus, walking by the sea of Galilee, saw two brethren, Simon called Peter, and Andrew his brother, casting a net into the sea : for they were fishers.

MATTHEW IV.

19. And he saith unto them, Follow me, and I will make you fishers of men.
20. And they straightway left their nets, and followed him.
21. And going on from thence, he saw other two brethren, James the son of Zebedee, and John his brother, in a ship with Zebedee their father, mending their nets ; and he called them.
22. And they immediately left the ship and their father, and followed him.
23. And Jesus went about all Galilee, teaching in their synagogues, and preaching the gospel of the kingdom, and healing all manner of sickness and all manner of disease among the people.
24. And his fame went throughout all Syria ; and they brought unto him all sick people that were taken with divers diseases and torments, and those which were possessed with devils, and those which were lunatic, and those that had the palsy ; and he healed them.
25. And there followed him great multitudes of people from Galilee, and from Decapolis, and from Jerusalem, and from Judæa, and from beyond Jordan.

1. Every true minister is immediately *called* of Christ ; the call may be determined by (*a*) personal conviction, (*b*) favourable circumstances, and (*c*) the concurrent opinion of good men.  2. He who calls to the work gives the power—"I will make ; " "without me ye can do nothing." (*a*) The true minister can ever bind Christ to His promise ; (*b*) power over men is a Divine gift ; (*c*) the ingathering of men to Christ the highest triumph of spiritual power.  3. Jesus, even when accompanied by two disciples, exercised the incommunicable right of *vocation ;* He who called the first called also the last.  4. The Divine call makes men superior to all earthly claims,—"they immediately left the ship and their father."

*All* calls to higher life must proceed from the Perfect One.  He calls to repentance, to faith, to service.  This shows (*a*) God's interest in man ; (*b*) man's capability of progress ; (*c*) that there is an element in man kindred to the nature of God.

Verses 23—25. 1. The twofold ministry of Christ,—to the soul, to the body ; (*a*) His compound nature encompassed

E

the entire nature of man; (*b*) the sweep of His sympathy indicated the range of His mission. 2. The unity and indivisibility of Christ's theme,—"the Gospel of the kingdom;" (*a*) indicative of earnestness; (*b*) prophetic of success. 3. The moral uses of Fame,—"His fame went throughout all Syria." (*a*) Fame never despised but by the unfamed; (*b*) Fame gives opportunities of usefulness; (*c*) Fame is properly employed when it draws men to the true Teacher and the unfailing Healer; (*d*) Fame must not be sought, but when found, should enlarge the sphere of gracious service.

The last verses might be regarded as showing :—1. The lamentable condition of man; 2. The all-sufficiency of Christ; 3. The wisdom of taking human nature at its most accessible points,—the wants of the *body*.

The body has been neglected by the ministers of Christ. Why so? He who made the mind made the body; and without the body, how is the mind accessible? How far are the ministers of Christ justified in the plea that to feed the body may be to corrupt the soul? Is no distinction to be drawn between bribery and benevolence? It is a remarkable, and should be an instructive, fact that Christ and His apostles paid most careful attention to the physical condition of men. As with them, so with us,—physical benefits were abused; but were they therefore withdrawn? Did Christ cease to feed the hungry because some followed Him only for the loaves and fishes? Did Christ avoid all lepers because nine of their number returned not to bless their healer? It is well, indeed, to be guarded, but better to err on the side of generosity than on the side of penuriousness; better do good to one side of man's nature than not do him any good at all: if we cannot feed men into a good spiritual mood, it is extremely improbable that we can starve them into salvation. I would that the Church should become a generous almoner of earthly things; it should deal out its bread to the hungry, and offer a guiding hand to the blind, and lead the thirsty to fountains of water. Men can appreciate kindness better than dogmas; religion better than theology; light better than astronomic science. To this method of Christian service the objections are not so good as the answers: (*a*) It might encourage indolence,—that would be the fault of the almoners; (*b*) it might be a temptation to hypocrisy,—that, too, would be largely the fault of the almoners; (*c*) it might discourage the spirit of self-help,—again the almoners would be chiefly to blame. Because a man is charitable, is he therefore a fool? Can he not use his eyes and ears? Will not charity itself sharpen his sagacity? Let him blight the hypocrite like an east wind; but let him remember that men are won sooner by trust than by suspicion; "men may overget delusion, not despair." Churches would sooner be filled if Christians took a deeper interest in the well-being of the body; and who shall say that through the body the soul may not be captured for Christ? The preacher is powerless if he have no hearers; first, therefore, get the hearers,—"compel them to come in," fill the house,—and then tell the all-subduing story. While the Gospel is a Gospel for all, it is peculiarly a Gospel for the poor; the poor man Christ went to the poor men of His time, fed them, healed them, comforted them, and then told them of a love of which all feeding and healing were but poor manifestations.

## CHAPTER V.

1. And seeing the multitudes, he went up into a mountain : and when he was set, his disciples came unto him :
2. And he opened his mouth, and taught them, saying,
3. Blessed are the poor in spirit : for their's is the kingdom of heaven.

52   HOMILETIC ANALYSIS.

4. Blessed are they that mourn : for they shall be comforted.
5. Blessed are the meek : for they shall inherit the earth.
6. Blessed are they which do hunger and thirst after righteousness : for they shall be filled.
7. Blessed are the merciful : for they shall obtain mercy.*
8. Blessed are the pure in heart : for they shall see God.
9. Blessed are the peacemakers : for they shall be called the children of God.
10. Blessed are they which are persecuted for righteousness' sake ; for their's is the kingdom of heaven.
11. Blessed are ye when men shall revile you and persecute you, and shall say all manner of evil against you falsely, for my sake.
12. Rejoice, and be exceeding glad ; for great is your reward in heaven: for so persecuted they the prophets which were before you.

Verse 1. 1. Christ's relation to the multitude always depend upon the *spirit* of the multitude ; that spirit might be (*a*) fanatical; (*b*) worldly; (*c*) earnest. 2. Christ spake to His disciples as a special body : thereby showing (*a*) that a certain degree of moral preparation is requisite to understand the words of Christ; (*b*) that the few may be the teachers of the many ; (*c*) that the propagation of truth may begin at the lowest possible point, either in numbers or influence.

Christ brings truth to the Church, the Church must bring receptivity of heart to Christ.

Verse 2. The opening of Christ's mouth was :—1. A signal of His personal authority ; 2. A fulfilment of long-cherished hope ; 3. A completion of Divine revelation. When Christ speaks the Church should be silent.

Verses 3—12. Instead of going into the lessons of each beatitude, the beatitudes may be looked at as a group. So looked at, we see :—1. That some of them look towards God, and others towards man ; theology and morality

* The texts we least need are the ones we like best, and remember longest. A kind-hearted, *lazy* man will remember "Blessed are the merciful" long after he has forgotten the injunction to be "diligent in business."—*(Beecher.)*

should be united. 2. That some persons are included beyond our expectations, and others are excluded contrary to our expectations; the poor in spirit, the mourners, and the weak are here; but where are the rich, the famous, and the mighty? 3. That right moral relations to Christ are always associated with the richest personal rewards; the good enjoy not only a blessed *condition*, but shall enjoy an ample *compensation*. 4. That men have always mistaken the direction in which "blessedness" lay. 5. That the enemy himself shall be a contributor to the saint's joy.

Christ's ministry summed up in two words—"Repent," "Blessed."

Three things noticeable about the beatitudes:—1. Their intense spirituality; 2. The possibility of exemplifying their practical conditions in daily life; 3. The present and personal blessedness which they affirm.

13. Ye are the salt of the earth: but if the salt have lost his savour, wherewith shall it be salted? It is thenceforth good for nothing, but to be cast out, and to be trodden under foot of men.
14. Ye are the light of the world. A city that is set on an hill cannot be hid.
15. Neither do men light a candle, and put it under a bushel, but on a candlestick; and it giveth light unto all that are in the house.
16. Let your light so shine before men, that they may see your good works, and glorify your Father which is in heaven.

1. *Christ summons man to a high standard.* — There is Divine wisdom in this. Christ does not degrade humanity, but elevates it by hopeful words. "Men may overget delusion, not despair." In proportion as responsibility is thrown upon man, does man rise to the dignity of the occasion. Educate common men into gentlemen by treating them as gentlemen; the same principle holds good in the higher life. Show men that great things are expected of them, and the latent power will be developed. 2. *Christ recognises the true*

*influence of good men.*—Salt, light, elevation. 3. *Christ recognises the active and passive aspects of influence;*—salt and light (active); city set on a hill (passive); both conjoined in true Christian character. Some persons are more pungent than lustrous, others more conspicuous than penetrating; others more dazzling than cheering.

In this display of influence three things are obvious—(*a*) secrecy, "salt;" (*b*) supremacy, "light of the world;" (*c*) publicity, "city set on an hill." In all this there is perfect *silence;* silent as the salt, silent as the light, silent as the city on an hill. Wonderful that so much life should be associated with so much silence: it is so in the body: the *heart* is silent, the hand demonstrative; the *brain* makes no sign, the tongue "no man can tame."

1. Every man has a light peculiar to himself; 2. There is a right way of shedding light, "*so* shine;" 3. Men are to see the works, not the worker; 4. Works are to have a heavenly tendency.

"The Christian is called a light, not lightning. In order to act with effect on others, he must walk in the Spirit, and thus become the image of goodness: he must be so akin to God, and so filled with His dispositions, that he shall seem to surround himself with a hallowed atmosphere. It is folly to endeavour to make ourselves shine before we are luminous. If the sun without his beams should talk to the planets, and argue with them to the final day, it would not make them shine; there must be light in the sun itself, and then they will shine of course."—*(Bushnell.)*

Men are affected by what they "see."

17. Think not that I am come to destroy the law or the prophets: I am not come to destroy, but to fulfil.

18. For verily I say unto you, Till heaven and earth pass, one jot or one tittle shall in no wise pass from the law, till all be fulfilled.

19. Whosoever therefore shall break one of these least commandments, and shall teach men so, he shall be called the least in the kingdom of

heaven : but whosoever shall do and teach them, the same shall be called great in the kingdom of heaven.

20. For I say unto you, That except your righteousness shall exceed the righteousness of the Scribes and Pharisees, ye shall in no case enter into the kingdom of heaven.

1. The possibility of mistaken conceptions regarding Christ. 2. The final worker should never disparage the preparatory worker. 3. The law is one. 4. Christ fulfilled it. Summer fulfils spring; noon fulfils morning; the fruit fulfils the blossom; manhood fulfils infancy. 5. All trifling with law involves at least the degradation of the trifler. (6) All honour of the law secures exaltation in the kingdom of heaven. Whether "the kingdom of heaven" be taken in a limited or in the widest sense, this principle holds good. 7. Man is to regulate his conduct by Divine law, and not by human standards. He who walks at noonday by the light of a taper will be held guilty for stumbling, delay, and ignorance. 8. Mutual comparison of "righteousness" is forbidden; man is not to compare with man, but to judge himself by the law. Failure in this duty will lead to exclusion from the kingdom of heaven. "We dare not make ourselves of the number, or compare ourselves with some that commend themselves: but they measuring themselves by themselves, and comparing themselves among themselves, are not wise." (2 Cor. x. 12.) The *Absolute* is the only standard by which man should determine his moral relations and his moral courses.

21. Ye have heard that it was said by them of old time, Thou shalt not kill; and whosoever shall kill, shall be in danger of the judgment:

22. But I say unto you, that whosoever is angry with his brother without a cause shall be in danger of the judgment; and whosoever shall say to his brother, Raca! shall be in danger of the council; but whosoever shall say, Thou fool! shall be in danger of hell fire.

23. Therefore, if thou bring thy gift to the altar, and there rememberest that thy brother hath ought against thee;

24. Leave there thy gift before the altar, and go thy way; first be reconciled to thy brother, and then come and offer thy gift.
25. Agree with thine adversary quickly, whiles thou art in the way with him; lest at any time the adversary deliver thee to the judge, and the judge deliver thee to the officer, and thou be cast into prison.
26. Verily I say unto thee, Thou shalt by no means come out thence, till thou hast paid the uttermost farthing.

1. God has been educating the race up to the highest *spirituality;* from "killing" to evil speaking; from evil speaking to confession, contrition, restitution, the course of religious education has proceeded. It is so in the human family circle. The child is cautioned against violent deeds, before it can understand the wrongfulness of unkind words; education, therefore, keeps pace with the unfolding capabilities of the pupil. Much education (including much pulpit teaching) fails through beginning at the wrong point, or through incorrect perception on the part of the educator. 2. The *principle* of evil is the same, though its manifestations vary; in "kill," "angry without a cause," "Raca," "fool," we find precisely the same *principle*, though the modifications are various. Differences of *degree* are not to be confounded with differences of *nature*. 3. Reconciliation to man is an essential part of true religion.—" First be reconciled to thy brother." Man cannot be right with God while wrong with his fellow-man. Philanthropy and religion are hemispheres; put them together, else unity and revolution are impossible. 4. Human antagonisms are strengthened by delay,—"agree quickly" (ταχύ); come to him in the right mental mood ("Ἴσθι εὐνοῶν, be well-minded); the wrong mood leads to the wrong action, the wrong action provokes retribution, and thus the sinner becomes his own tormenter; stifle wrong while yet it is in the *mind*,—bruise the serpent's head.\*

\* A recent publication, entitled "ECCE HOMO," contains this statement:—"The primitive man had no obligations, no duties, to any except his parents, his brothers, and his parent's brothers, and their families.

27. Ye have heard that it was said by them of old time, Thou shalt not commit adultery:

28. But I say unto you, that whosoever looketh on a woman to lust after her hath committed adultery with her already in his heart.

29. And if thy right eye offend thee, pluck it out, and cast it from thee; for it is profitable for thee that one of thy members should perish, and not that thy whole body should be cast into hell.

30. And if thy right hand offend thee, cut it off, and cast it from thee: for it is profitable for thee that one of thy members should perish, and not that thy whole body should be cast into hell.

31. It hath been said, Whosoever shall put away his wife, let him give her a writing of divorcement;

32. But I say unto you, that whosoever shall put away his wife, saving for the cause of fornication, causeth her to commit adultery; and whosoever shall marry her that is divorced committeth adultery.

The same idea of bringing the race forward to spiritual conceptions, and founding education upon a spiritual base, characterises this passage. The two voices are again heard; the first "by them of old time" (τοῖς ἀρχαίοις to the ancients); the second that (apart from divinity) of a dogmatist—solemn, impressive, in his individuality—('Ἐγω λέγω ὑμῖν). There is no division of responsibility—all rests upon that 'Ἐγω! 1. All human impulses are to be held in perfect mastery. 2. There is a judgment upon the *heart* as well as upon the outer life. 3. When the bodily appetites and the spiritual nature come into collision, let the body suffer, not the soul. A whole body (a body wholly gratified) or a maimed soul, which? 4. There are bodily temptations as well as mental temptations. (Trace the reciprocal action of body and soul.)

When he met with a man unrelated to him he would without hesitation take his life and his property. But the life and property of a relation were sacred, and the Greeks held that there were certain supernatural powers called Erinyes, who vindicated the rights of relatives." This statement must not be accepted without duly considering instances which Homer himself supplies, proving the direct contrary. Medon killed a man, not improbably a brother (γνωτός); Tlepolemus killed the maternal uncle of his father, and when settled in Rhodes was blessed by the peculiar favour of Jupiter; and Epeigeus killed his cousin. Even the family circle was not guarded by insurmountable walls.

The mind has advantages in the probationary state which the body has not;—*death* has yet to pass upon the body; the body is not to be wholly purified or transformed until the resurrection; the mind, on the contrary (except so far as modified by the body), may be "set on things above." 5. Christ, in this paragraph, shows the bearing of His specific truths on the body, and bodily relations; (*a*) personal mastery; (*b*) personal mastery may require the severest measures; (*c*) personal mastery required in the maintenance of the conjugal bond.

"Saving for the cause of fornication." This is a clause which we do not find in the conjugal laws of the heroic age. Whilst it is true that the Greeks detested the crime of adultery, it is also true that they did not allow it to break the marriage bond. Helen lived for many years in *de facto* adultery with Paris; but when the war ended, she resumed her place in the house of Menelaus, and though she never quenched the tormenting fire of her shame, yet the nuptial tie continued in full force and virtue. In this point, the Homeric and Christian code are at variance.

33. Again, ye have heard that it hath been said by them of old time, Thou shalt not forswear thyself, but shalt perform unto the Lord thine oaths :
34. But I say unto you, Swear not at all : neither by heaven ; for it is God's throne :
35. Nor by the earth ; for it is his footstool : neither by Jerusalem ; for it is the city of the great King.
36. Neither shalt thou swear by thy head, because thou canst not make one hair white or black.
37. But let your communication be, Yea, yea ; Nay, nay ; for whatsoever is more than these cometh of evil.

1. Language should be the simple expression of the heart. 2. Social intercourse can never be right until the heart is right. 3. The heart can never be right until Christ's word is its supreme law. 4. All violent expression is suggestive of con-

scious weakness, exasperated temper, or want of social faith.

5. Christianity seeks to simplify human communications.

Morality demands *exactness* in speech; exactness of speech is much promoted by exactness of observation, a clear, unprejudiced, comprehensive perception of facts; to fall back upon "heaven," "earth," "Jerusalem," or the "head," as illustrative realities, is rather to pander to human disbelief than to trust to the simple dignity of the truth.

38. Ye have heard that it hath been said, An eye for an eye, a tooth for a tooth:

39. But I say unto you, That ye resist not evil; but whosoever shall smite thee on thy right cheek, turn to him the other also.

40. And if any man will sue thee at the law, and take away thy coat, let him have thy cloak also.

41. And whosoever shall compel thee to go a mile, go with him twain.

42. Give to him that asketh thee, and from him that would borrow of thee turn not thou away.

43. Ye have heard that it hath been said, Thou shalt love thy neighbour, and hate thine enemy;

44. But I say unto you, Love your enemies, bless them that curse you, do good to them that hate you, and pray for them which despitefully use you, and persecute you:

45. That ye may be the children of your Father which is in heaven: for he maketh his sun to rise on the evil and on the good, and sendeth rain on the just and on the unjust.

46. For if ye love them which love you, what reward have ye? Do not even the publicans the same?

47. And if ye salute your brethren only, what do ye more than others? Do not even the publicans so?

48. Be ye therefore perfect, even as your Father which is in heaven is perfect.


1. The superiority of the moral over the passional in human nature. 2. Material compensation not equal to moral satisfaction. 3. Only the lowest part of the human constitution can be appeased by revenge on the physical nature of an enemy. 4. The patient endurance of wrong may be a most useful illustration of the grandeur of personal rectitude. 5. Where compulsion ends, generosity

may begin. 6. A right relation to Christ places men in a right relation to one another—friends, enemies, suppliants, borrowers. 7. Men who thus occupy a right relation to one another attest their filial relation to God,—"that ye may be the children of your Father which is in heaven." It is common to say respecting a son who reproduces the characteristics of his father, "He is his father's son." Christ, in putting the case so, does not disturb the relation of cause and effect. 8. God's universal goodness, as displayed in material benefits, is not to be regarded as indifference to moral distinctions. God supplies the conditions, which, properly accepted and worked out, are designed to lead to repentance; but which, neglected or abused, aggravate the sinner's impenitence. 9. Man is even in his moral aspirations to advance towards the Absolute.

GENERAL NOTE ON THE FIFTH CHAPTER.

The enthusiasm of perfect love seems to be the spirit in which all duties can alone be fulfilled. Christ shows men how to find "blessedness" in all states of life, some of them apparently much opposed to blessedness — "sorrowing," "persecution," being examples. Where there is enthusiasm of love, there will be a reverent regard for the "*least* commandments" as well as the greater; our "righteousness will *exceed;*" our brotherly affection will overcome our personal antipathies; our fleshly passions will be lost in holy ecstasy of delight in God; our right eye, right hand, or right foot will be as nothing to us when we are borne away by a sublime fervour of love; our sincerity will be so great that the heart need not be inflamed, chafed, and irritated by "swearing;" our magnanimity will transcend the murky region of revenge; he who takes the coat may have the cloak also; and two miles shall be walked, where only one was "compelled;" and even more, our very "enemies" shall feel the benignity of our love, and our whole life shall be an upward struggling towards the perfectness of "our Father which is in heaven." All this regarded as mere *law* is impracticable; but descended upon from the heavenly altitude of God-like love, it becomes easy, sweet, and most profitable. This is the *ideal* towards which we are tending, while as yet our faith is but a grain of mustard-seed. Men are not commanded to *begin* here, but we shall truly end here if we "abide" in Christ; these "sayings" become plain to us just as we increase in heart-depth and intensity of moral emotion. Love carries us upward from the pined and dwarfed "righteousness of the Scribes and Pharisees" into the infinite sublimity and unquenchable fervour of the perfectness of God. Our religion, then, is to be the passion of our nature, fire fusing and refining everything—this fire is love, for "love is the fulfilling of the law." The grammar and the lexicon help us little in understanding these maxims, but love reads them as one would read his native language, and executes them as one would fulfil the behest of life's dearest friend. The height is high; only love's unwearying wing can reach it.

## CHAPTER VI.

1. Take heed that ye do not your alms before men, to be seen of them; otherwise ye have no reward of your Father which is in heaven.
2. Therefore, when thou doest thine alms, do not sound a trumpet before thee, as the hypocrites do in the synagogues and in the streets, that they may have glory of men. Verily I say unto you, They have their reward.
3. But when thou doest alms, let not thy left hand know what thy right hand doeth;
4. That thine alms may be in secret: and thy Father which seeth in secret himself shall reward thee openly.

The word translated "alms" may be more literally rendered "righteousness." The word is thus translated in chap. v. 20. 1. THERE IS AN ELEMENT OF RIGHTEOUSNESS IN ALMSGIVING. This is not generally understood. Charity is usually dissociated from ideas of righteousness, justice, and the like. It is *righteous* on the part of the strong to help the weak—not merely charitable or good-natured, but deeper than this, *righteous*. Being righteous, its chief side lies towards heaven and not towards earth ; this being the case, then, 2. RIGHTEOUS ACTIONS SHOULD BE CONFINED TO THE UTMOST POSSIBLE EXTENT TO THE DIVINE COGNISANCE. Philanthropy is the practical side of theology. A philanthropic course may be started from one of two points,— either natural kindliness of heart, or a profound sense of the DIVINE IDEAL IN MAN, serving which is serving God Himself. (Matt. xxv. 35—40.) Philanthropic service is deep and permanent in proportion as it works from the latter centre. Even the lower considerations are better promoted by working from a high spiritual plane, than by working immediately for them; hence, 3. THE SECRECY OF RIGHTEOUS ACTIONS DOES NOT DEPRIVE THEM OF PUBLIC RECOGNITION AND REWARD. " Thy Father which seeth in secret himself shall reward thee openly." It may be considered singular that "righteousness" should be succeeded by "reward." It must be borne in mind, however, that it is "righteousness" which was realised in the face of the most terrible allurements in the direction of self-glorying. One of man's greatest trials is to overcome the weakness and the downward tendency of his own flesh. Righteousness is, indeed, in a deep sense, its own reward ; it brings a calm rest and a holy joy into the heart,—not only so, it enlarges, refines, and ennobles the whole nature; yet, in addition to this interior reward, there is an open, public recognition which God works out on the righteous man's behalf. The necessary tendency of "hypocrisy" is towards decay; hypocrisy strains nature, and brings the "reward" of ruin. The tendency of "righteousness," on the contrary, is towards expansion, strength, and immortality: it is of the nature of God, and brings with it the joy of the ever-blessed Father. Poor are the prospects of the hypocrite! There is a terrible irony in the Saviour's words, "Verily I say unto you they have their reward." Peter uses the same word when he speaks of "the *reward* of unrighteousness," and again of "the *wages* of unrighteousness," and Jude employs it in the expression, "Woe unto them! for they .... ran greedily after the error of Balaam for *reward*." The "hypocrite" loses the very object for which he toils; he toils for "reward," he obtains it, and lo! it wastes in his hand, and mocks his expectations.*

The word δίκαιος is Homeric as well as Christian, and in Homer it is employed to describe not only the duty of man to man, but of man to the gods. This circumstance certainly elevates our idea of Greek ethics; to have the same

---

\* Christ does not undervalue public opinion as a moral check, but here, as everywhere, throws men upon interior considerations and motives rather than upon outward circumstances. The spring of all true service in Christ's kingdom is love; whatever is less than this, though collateral and subsidiary, will be burnt up by the final fire. Public opinion (δήμου φάτις) was highly prized by the Greeks as a moral restraint. Numerous instances are given in Homer. When Nausicaa desired Ulysses not to enter Scheira in her company, she found her apology in the φῆλις ἀδευκής, "the bitter gossip" of the people. Public opinion may still be turned to good account; it is the great unwritten *law* which surrounds a man like an atmosphere; at the same time he who acts only that he "may be seen of men" has no reward of his Father in heaven. A most distinguished Homeric critic suggests that the uses of the single word αἰδώς (which occurs only twice in the New Testament—1 Tim. ii. 9, and Heb. xii. 28, where it is rendered "shamefacedness" and "reverence") with the cognate verb and adjective, which occur in Homer, would to a large extent establish the fact that the Greeks of his age "were in a condition of high civilisation, in that which constitutes its most essential part, namely, that which relates to the affections and passions of man; the expansion of moral forces by the one and the compression of the other." Hesiod gave it as one of the characteristics of the iron age that αἰδώς had fled from the earth; most men are, however, still capable of feeling "shame," and upon such, public opinion may operate very usefully.

word employed in complimenting Telemachus for handing the cup first to seniority, as is employed in referring to the character of men who had omitted the usual sacrifices, clearly shows the idea which the Homeric age held as to the connection between morality and religion. We should do well to consider that almsgiving and prayer are equally included by Christ under this term. Christian morality is surely not less inclusive than Homeric righteousness.

5. And when thou prayest, thou shalt not be as the hypocrites are: for they love to pray standing in the synagogues and in the corners of the streets, that they may be seen of men. Verily I say unto you, They have their reward.

6. But thou, when thou prayest, enter into thy closet, and when thou hast shut thy door, pray to thy Father which is in secret; and thy Father which seeth in secret shall reward thee openly.

7. But when ye pray, use not vain repetitions, as the heathen do: for they think that they shall be heard for their much speaking.

8. Be not ye therefore like unto them: for your Father knoweth what things ye have need of before ye ask him.

9. After this manner therefore pray ye: Our Father which art in heaven, Hallowed be thy name.

10. Thy kingdom come. Thy will be done in earth, as it is in heaven.

11. Give us this day our daily bread.

12. And forgive us our debts, as we forgive our debtors.

13. And lead us not into temptation, but deliver us from evil: For thine is the kingdom, and the power, and the glory, for ever. Amen.

14. For if ye forgive men their trespasses, your heavenly Father will also forgive you:

15. But if ye forgive not men their trespasses, neither will your Father forgive your trespasses.

The most needless passage in all Holy Writ, we are sometimes tempted to exclaim! Earnest men, we argue, will surely know *where* to pray and *how* to pray. We know not whereof we affirm. The Teacher is still proceeding on a distinct recognition of the weakness of the flesh, and man's innate self-idolatry. There are three directions respecting prayer:—1. Secrecy; 2. Brevity; 3. Comprehensiveness. Brevity is quite compatible with fulness. No man can be long in prayer until after he has exhausted his heart;

so long as the heart speaks, pray on, though it be from morning until night, and through the night till the daybreak. It is when the lips alone talk, that prayer is long, and then, even a sentence is tedious. The Saviour then tells His disciples how to pray; He shows that they are to remember:—

1. That they are adoring children. 2. That they are subjects. 3. That the Father's will is of universal application. 4. That daily mercies should be daily sought. 5. That good men need daily forgiveness. 6. That temptation is to be prayed against. 7. That all ascription of majesty and praise is due to the Father alone. Much practical truth may be evolved by considering this as a *daily* prayer: be adored *this* day; thy kingdom come *this* day; thy will be done *this* day, &c. This gives us concentration of idea, and ought to give extraordinary vividness and steadfastness to our hope. Think of all these petitions being answered "*this* day"!

The Lord's *Prayer* may be looked at as a summary of the Lord's *Life*.

The 14th and 15th verses show that men are to prove the reality of their prayers by the magnanimity of their conduct. *They are not to expect from God what they are not prepared to render to man.* Men are thus made *co-workers* with God. As men ask forgiveness from God, so men should ask forgiveness from one another. As God will not grant forgiveness except it be asked for sincerely, so men ought not to grant forgiveness except on the same condition; but as God always forgives the sincere penitent, so ought men to forgive their contrite enemies. *Forgiveness without penitence is immorality.*

16. Moreover, when ye fast, be not as the hypocrites, of a sad countenance: for they disfigure their faces, that they may appear unto men to fast. Verily I say unto you, They have their reward.

17. But thou, when thou fastest, anoint thine head, and wash thy face;
18. That thou appear not unto men to fast, but unto thy Father, which is in secret: and thy Father, which seeth in secret, shall reward thee openly.

It is a mistaken view of civilisation which affirms that the greater the number of man's wants the further is he removed from barbarism. There is a higher civilisation, which enables a man to say, "I know the value of comforts and luxurious enjoyments, yet I shall so master myself as to be superior to their temptations." Education rather than self-indulgence, is the main element in pure civilisation. The barbarian does not know the relative value, or the manifold uses of things; to know these, and yet to hold the appetite in restraint, is to be truly civilised. Fasting may serve—1. To keep the body in proper subordination; 2. To purify and strengthen the operations of the mind; 3. To excite sympathy with those who fast without their own consent; 4. To bring into prominence the fact that there is a higher life than bread can satisfy. These uses can be served effectually only in connection with the *secret* observance of fasting. The true purpose of fasting is *the moral education of our nature*. Our Lord's direction as to *appearances* is remarkable; He does not teach duplicity, but secrecy; He wishes to check all glorying before men.

In the three points of Giving, Praying, and Fasting, our Lord confines the action (to the utmost possible extent) to the individual and God himself. Too narrow a view of this circumstance would give false impressions of the religious life. There is a side of spiritual life which is secret; there is also a side which is public. In proportion as the secret side is cultivated, will the public side be luminous, persuasive, influential. There are men whose every pulse almost may be said to be published. They have no interior life. They never sit in the secret place and commune deeply with themselves, with nature, or with God. They are afraid of solitude. When they give, it is that they may be seen of men; when they pray, they speak loudly, that the world may pause and hearken; when they fast, they tell the story of their abstinence in shrivelled face or piteous tones. There is, however, a *public* side to the religious life. There are men whose right hand never tells the left any news of benevolence, simply because it has no such news to tell. These men are not unwilling to be credited with the possibility of having done a good deal in secret; and with many a sign they deceive the trustful and unwary.

### GENERAL NOTE.

Why should not the first verse in this chapter be regarded as common to all the directions respecting Giving, Praying, and Fasting? Let the word "righteousness" take the place of the word "alms," and then it will include the whole of the three religious exercises to which our Lord refers, and thus bring into special prominence the "righteous" side of giving, the "righteous" side of praying, and the "righteous" side of fasting, and by so much will increase the force of the command respecting *secrecy*.

19. Lay not up for yourselves treasures upon earth, where moth and rust doth corrupt, and where thieves break through and steal;

20. But lay up for yourselves treasures in heaven, where neither moth nor rust doth corrupt, and where thieves do not break through nor steal.

21. For where your treasure is, there will your heart be also.

The rich man reads these words, and then buys an estate; the incompetent man reads them, and pronounces the rich man unchristian. The meaning clearly is, that *the supreme attraction of the heart is not to be sought in material riches*. Christ is ever anxious about the "heart." The command may be justified on four grounds:—1. Material riches cannot satisfy the spiritual nature; 2. Material riches are less enduring than the spiritual nature; 3. Material riches are exposed to continual peril; 4. Material riches are excellent servants, but unworthy masters. Christ's ideal of spiritual strength is, that man should hold all material things, all temporary relations, and all accidental circumstances, in perfect subordination to his spiritual nature. The man may possess gold and silver to any extent, provided that his "heart" be above his property, evermore rising towards God. The true use of riches is indicated by Paul in 1 Tim. vi. 17. Christ's words may be paraphrased thus:—"You have a heart, a spiritual nature, of vast capability; it can lay hold of God and become like Him: it was made to keep His will, to enjoy His smile, and to live with Him for ever; see that it be not fixed on any inferior purpose; feed it not with husks, but give it bread from your Father's table; if riches increase, set not your heart upon them; be superior to all earthly attractions; set your affections on things above, and not on things on the earth; the thief may steal earthly comforts, but cannot deprive you of heavenly blessings."

22. The light of the body is the eye; if, therefore, thine eye be single, thy whole body shall be full of light.
23. But if thine eye be evil, thy whole body shall be full of darkness. If therefore the light that is in thee be darkness, how great is that darkness!

The eye of the "heart" should be upon God, and then it will be "full of light." While the eye is blinded with material riches the body necessarily stumbles, falls, or goes astray. What though a man be able to run quickly, if he be blind? Man has only one faculty by which he can communicate with the light, and if that one be incapacitated he must abide in darkness. The "heart" is the "eye" with which man sees God; if the heart be engrossed with earthly things it cannot enjoy the light of God's countenance; by long disuse it will eventually lose all power, and the man must wander in darkness for ever.

Christ is evidently continuing His discourse upon the heart in relation to secular things, and I take it that He regards the "heart" as the illuminating faculty, so to speak, of the spiritual nature, and points out the necessity of keeping this faculty "single" or "simple" (ἁπλοῦς) if man would walk in "light" and make his "whole body luminous" (φωτεινὸν).

24. No man can serve two masters; for either he will hate the one, and love the other; or else he will hold to the one, and despise the other. Ye cannot serve God and mammon.

1. Wholeness of heart is essential to all progress,—literature, art, commerce, as well as religion. 2. Division of heart is weakness. 3. All men *must* serve,—the choice is between God and mammon. 4. The true religious life is one of thorough identification with God, and all His purposes and works.

25. Therefore I say unto you, Take no thought for your life, what ye shall eat, or what ye shall drink; nor yet for your body, what ye shall put on. Is not the life more than meat, and the body than raiment?

26. Behold the fowls of the air: for they sow not, neither do they reap, nor gather into barns; yet your heavenly Father feedeth them. Are ye not much better than they?

27. Which of you by taking thought can add one cubit unto his stature?

28. And why take ye thought for raiment? Consider the lilies of the field, how they grow: they toil not, neither do they spin:

29. And yet I say unto you, That even Solomon in all his glory was not arrayed like one of these.

30. Wherefore, if God so clothe the grass of the field, which to day is, and to morrow is cast into the oven, shall he not much more clothe you, O ye of little faith?

31. Therefore, take no thought, saying, What shall we eat? or, What shall we drink? or, Wherewithal shall we be clothed?

32. (For after all these things do the Gentiles seek): for your heavenly Father knoweth that ye have need of all these things.

33. But seek ye first the kingdom of God, and his righteousness: and all these things shall be added unto you.

34. Take therefore no thought for the morrow: for the morrow shall take thought for the things of itself. Sufficient unto the day is the evil thereof.

The whole paragraph may be taken as showing the contrast between secular greatness and spiritual rectitude. 1. In their spirit. 2. In their aims. 3. In their destiny. Or it may be regarded as showing *Christ's method of interpreting the Book of Nature.* He interprets it :—1. So as to condemn all anxiety regarding physical sustenance. 2. So as to find everywhere indications of Fatherly presence and care. 3. So as to show the dignity and value of man in the sight of God. 4. So as to rise from the creature to the Creator. Christ is teaching trust in God in opposition to anxious care respecting physical wants, and His argument, direct and indirect, is four-fold :—1. That care of the "life" should take precedence of care of the "meat." 2. That care of the "life" will elevate a man above all sordid or anxious care for his inferior nature. 3. That the most anxious concern on secular affairs is useless. 4. That such concern is not Christian but Pagan. A man may commence from either of two points,—"the life" or "the meat;" according as one or other is the dominating consideration, will be the tone of a man's history.

The passage is not to be considered as forbidding the exercise of prudence or foresight, but as forbidding *atheism in secular affairs.* There are men who confine God to the sanctuary, and trust to themselves in all other places,—there are also men who are theologians, not Christians.

The Saviour next lays down the principle that *care of the greater secures the blessings of the inferior.* "Seek ye first," &c. The *inclusiveness* of the "kingdom of heaven" is often overlooked. Life's main business is to be *right*, all else will follow. Yet against this view may be set facts in Christian experience; good men are often in straits, while bad men often revel in prosperity. This is true; yet:—1. Difficulties are disciplinary. 2. God knows with how much men may be trusted. 3. Prosperity is fraught with peril.

4. Prosperity and adversity are modified by the moral nature,—a thankful, trustful spirit, multiplies the bounties of God.

Christianity heightens and refines man's view of secular life. The "Gentiles" take a low view; they believe in dust; they regard the hand as the only faculty of appropriation; they live within the narrow range of the senses. Christians, on the contrary, own "all things;" to them the universe is their Father's house, and all wheat-fields, olive-yards, and vine-yards, all cattle and gold, belong to Him whose love they trust.

Christ here presents:—1. The aim of true life,—the Kingdom of God. 2. The business of true life,—seeking this Kingdom. 3. The inclusiveness of true life,—"all these things shall be added." "'Seek first the kingdom of God, and all these things shall be added unto you.' He casts the latter into the former, as the tradesman does twine and paper into a parcel of rich goods. Suppose a child should ask his father for money to buy a bauble, but the father denies him; now, if the child should proclaim in the open street that his father never loved him, how would this be taken? Yet thus thou dealest with thy heavenly Father, if thou suspectest His love because He denies thee some earthly enjoyment."—(*Gurnall.*) "To do unnecessary things in the first place, and neglect those which are most necessary, and put them off to the last, is not this the part of a fool? If a man should go to London to get a pardon, or about some great suit at law, and should, in the first place, spend the most or chiefest of all his time in seeing the lions at the Tower, the tombs in Westminster Abbey, or the streets and buildings of the city, or in visiting friends, and put the other off to the last, would he not be a fool? Christ, who was wisdom itself, judged it folly in Martha to be busy about many things, and to neglect the main, that one thing necessary. It is not necessary to be rich, or learned, or great, though we have cause to bless God if we are so; but God's favour, and Christ, and grace are absolutely necessary. Therefore, says Christ, 'But seek ye first the kingdom of God and his righteousness, and all these things shall be added unto you.' So He, as wisdom, directs us."—(*T. Goodwin.*)

The last verse contains an expression which can be understood only figuratively,—"the morrow shall take thought for the things of itself." The verse may be homiletically used as showing :—1. The value of the present. 2. The bearing of to-day on to-morrow; postponement of duty on the part of man is not met by extension of time on the part of God. 3. The whole day is a type of the whole life,—its beginning, its progress, its noon, its decay, its evening hour. (There are many beginnings and endings in life; all these are spiritually suggestive.) He meets to-morrow best who uses to-day well; so he is best prepared for eternity who has wisely employed the talent of time. Think of the arrears of all our yesterdays being remitted to to-day!

The key-words in this discourse concerning secular things in their relation to spiritual realities, are—"life," "kingdom," and "Father." The words are immeasurably comprehensive; "life" stretching beyond the grave, which is only a comma in the punctuation of the soul's history; and "kingdom," including all the Divine empire, specially the government of all moral agencies by the Holy One; and "Father," gathering up all intelligences, and settling the races in a family relationship. Master these three words (life kingdom, Father), and Christian theology will be yours, in all its spiritual and intellectual wealth.

## CHAPTER VII.

1. Judge not, that ye be not judged.
2. For with what judgment ye judge, ye shall be judged; and with what measure ye mete, it shall be measured to you again.
3. And why beholdest thou the mote that is in thy brother's eye, but considerest not the beam that is in thine own eye?
4. Or how wilt thou say to thy brother, Let me pull out the mote out of thine eye; and behold a beam is in thine own eye?
5. Thou hypocrite, first cast out the beam out of thine own eye; and then thou shalt see clearly to cast out the mote out of thy brother's eye.

The meaning turns upon the first word — "Judge" (Κρίνετε). In the gospel by John we are told (vii. 24) to "Judge not according to the appearance, but judge righteous judgment." Men must, in a certain sense, judge (examine, estimate) one another. This practice penetrates the entire social system, and is, in fact, necessary to the equitable adjustment of human relationships. The element, however, which Christ condemns is *censoriousness*. The meaning is partially suggested by another use of the word κρίνω, as employed by Christ Himself—"For God sent not his Son into the world to *condemn* the world." (John iii. 17.) In the 12th chapter of John, Christ repeats this declaration thus, "I came not to *judge* the world." So far, therefore, as judgment is marked by bitterness, censoriousness, or prejudice, it is condemned by Christ. This condemnation does not interfere with—1. The honest critic; 2. The upright magistrate; 3. The sagacious and honourable citizen. The word (judge) is variously rendered in the New Testament; *e.g.*:—"Of the hope of the resurrection of the dead am I *called in question—κρίνομαι*." "One man *esteemeth* one day above another: another *esteemeth* (κρίνει) every day alike."

The whole passage may be used to show—1. That good men should guard against the perversion of the judicial faculty on all questions. 2. That specially on personal questions the judicial faculty should be purified and restrained (consider the sacredness of *reputation*, the consequences involved, &c.) 3. That personal judgments provoke reprisals, and reprisals often engender unholy desires for victory, &c. 4. That consciousness of our own imperfections should moderate our personal judgments.

The fact that a man with a "beam" in his eye may "judge" a brother whose eye is darkened by a "mote," strikingly illustrates the possibility of self-delusion. 1. We correct one another best by being personally pure. 2. Men may resent a word, when they might accept the silent rebuke of a deed. 3. The most influential judgment is that of a blameless life.

6. Give not that which is holy unto the dogs, neither cast ye your pearls before swine, lest they trample them under their feet, and turn again and rend you.

In this verse we are distinctly called to judgment. Men must judge both thought and character, otherwise they know not what is meant by "holy," or "pearls," or "dogs," or "swine." Yet there is no discrepancy between the first verse and the sixth, for into this latter judgment the element of censoriousness should not enter,—and *that* alone is the element which Christ condemns. The idea of the verse may be hinted at thus:—discriminate as to the character of the persons by whom you are surrounded; study adaptation in your speech, as the law of accommodation or adaptation must operate from the highest to the lowest, and not from the lowest to the highest, so you who are enlightened must adapt yourselves to the circumstances by which you are beset; bad men cannot understand sanctified affection, and if you expose yourselves to them you will be misinterpreted, misrepresented, and injured; for dogs and swine which cannot understand the value of precious things may turn and rend you: the lowest, basest things, being able do mischief.

Homiletically, the idea might be arranged thus :—1. Good men are enriched with precious spiritual treasures 2. Bad men are unable to estimate the worth of such treasures. 3. Good men should so study the judicial capability of bad men as to cause themselves not to be misjudged and injured. Adaptation to men, places, and things, requires consummate judgment; the savage might be more pleased with a brass button than with a thousand-pound note. He who would give a telescope to a wild barbarian would be deranging the true relations of things, as would he also who excluded all but the blind from the galleries of art. Men must be met on their own intellectual plane, and judgment must be so far exercised as not to confound fools with philosophers, or to regard the toys of children as the accoutrements of warriors. " Speak not in the ears of a fool, for he will despise the wisdom of thy words." (Prov. xxiii. 9.) We receive from men according to their peculiarity of nature. " Reprove not a scorner lest he hate thee: rebuke a wise man and he will love thee."

7. Ask, and it shall be given you; seek, and ye shall find; knock, and it shall be opened unto you:
8. For every one that asketh receiveth: and he that seeketh findeth; and to him that knocketh it shall be opened.

1. This law holds good not only in relation to what is distinctly termed prayer, but also to progress of every kind. 2. The highest blessings are contingent upon the simplest conditions. 3. Man must take the initiative. 4. Divine promises should be regarded not as sedatives, but as stimulants. Or thus :—

1. All these directions will be ineffective apart from *conscious want* on the part of man. 2. A right use of these directions will preserve the true relation between man and God. 3. These directions enable us to judge of the world's spiritual life. Where there has been much received there must have

been much asking; where there is little asking there can be but little receiving.

Is there anything suggestive in the grammatical form of the words in the original—αἰτῶν, ζητων, χρούων (χρουοντι)? The idea, from the literal rendering (asking, seeking, knocking), seems to be that while men are in the very act ("whiles they are yet speaking") the desired blessing is conferred. Thus we have immediate, not deferred, answers to prayer. "What things soever ye desire, when ye pray, believe that ye receive them, and ye shall have them." A man does not ask his friend a question and wait a week for an answer; nor does a man knock at his friend's door and return in a month to see if it be opened. But are we at liberty to reason thus analogically? Can we move in our inferences from the earthly to the heavenly? Let us see:—

9. Or what man is there of you, whom if his son ask bread, will he give him a stone?

10. Or if he ask a fish, will he give him a serpent?

11. If ye then, being evil, know how to give good gifts unto your children, how much more shall your Father which is in heaven give good things to them that ask him?

Then we *are* entitled to reason from the less to the greater. We have our own notions of fatherhood; with that holy relation we have associated ideas of care, strength, wisdom, love, benevolence; now God takes up all these ideas and magnifies them according to His infinite nature, so that the littleness of our petitions is lost in the vastness of the answer, for "he is able to do exceeding abundantly above all that we ask or think." Homiletically, the idea may be put thus:—

1. Man's capacity is the limit of man's prayers. 2. God's capacity is the measure of God's answers. 3. The relation of the suppliant to the Giver is filial. 4. Supplication (asking, seeing, or knocking) is true and influential, not in proportion to the multiplicity of words, but the intensity of the filial feeling.

Prayer is the rarest of all exercises,—that is to say, men seldom pray. We talk much, but pray little. Now and again there are pangs of the soul which bring us reverently to the Throne : when the shadow falls heavily, or even when joy prevails in the spirit, we come to know, in a partial degree, what prayer is; and it is most precious, and blessed beyond all words to tell. Man's life, indeed, is a continuous want, but the consciousness of that want is intermittent. The parent does much for the child which the child does *not* "*ask*," so also our heavenly Father does much for us apart from our prayers;—sun and rain, for example, shine and fall not in reply to our voice, yet in view of our necessities. There is, then, a great range of blessing opened to us apart from our prayers, yet it need not exist apart from our *thankfulness*. The morning shineth not because of my prayer, yet I can thank God for its light; my prayers bring not the flowers of summer or the fruits of autumn, yet they may " lead me to repentance," and excite the most devout and filial gratitude. Did we but know it, gratitude is truly prayer! Our very thankfulness enlarges our petitions. Is it not so in our walks of life ? When you bestow an alms upon a thankful fellow-creature your heart is kindled into generosity by the thankfulness of the receiver; and more than this, his gratitude causes you to feel kindlier towards all other men, and to distribute still more of your bounty. Who shall say that this same law, enlarged and sanctified by the Divine nature, does not prevail in heaven ?

12. Therefore all things whatsoever ye would that men should do to you, do ye even so to them: for this is the law and the prophets.

Is not this a side-lesson rather than direct? It reads as though the speaker had almost unexpectedly deflected from the main line to urge a conclusion which is hardly necessitated by the strain of his remarks, and yet it is in perfect keeping with one of their indirect bearings. The idea may stand thus: if you ask bread you would not like to receive a stone, or if you ask a fish you would consider yourself mocked if you were offered a serpent; therefore remember that you should do unto others as you would that others should do unto you, for the realisation of this idea is the fulfilment of the law and the prophets. Homiletically, the idea might be thrown into this mould:—1. The unity of humanity is attested by the sensibilities which all men have in common (all men may be pleased, grieved, disappointed, or satisfied). 2. Each man should consult his own sensibilities before making an experiment on the sensibilities of others. 3. This self-introspection would secure the most practical advantages to the individual and to society: (a) it would determine many a question in casuistry, (b) it would restrain much evil passion, (c) it would simplify human intercourse.

Eventually, men get from society what they have given to it. "With what measure ye mete it shall be measured to you again." He who gives a scorpion for an egg will in his turn receive the scorpion. "He shall have judgment without mercy that showed no mercy." The experience of Adonibezek is the experience of the whole world: "But Adonibezek fled; and they pursued after him and caught him, and cut off his thumbs and his great toes. And Adonibezek said, Three score and ten kings, having their thumbs and their great toes cut off, gathered their meat under my table: as I have done, so God hath requited me." (Judges i. 6, 7.) So true is it, that "The Lord of recompenses shall surely requite." (Jer. li. 56.)

The expression—"this is the law and the prophets"—is notable. Sometimes the agency employed seems greater than the result attained. Take a flower for example; "This is the soil, the dew, the light, the summer!" These agents are all required, not singly but unitedly, to produce a flower! They produced, indeed, a good deal *more* than the flower, but were all expressed in the flower. So with "the law and the prophets," while they are, in their moral effect and purpose, summed up in this word, yet they filled a wider range than it strictly indicated.

This decision, however, is remarkable for its comprehensiveness. "All the law is fulfilled in one word, even in this; Thou shalt love thy neighbour as thyself." The moral system is one. Duty may have many sections or ramifications, but truly it is one and indivisible. "Whosoever shall keep the whole law and yet offend in one point, he is guilty of all." To carry out Christ's idea, then, in this verse, is really not so simple and easy a matter as might at first sight appear. It demands a moral vitality and strength not to be realised except by Divine means and much patient waiting upon God. The artificial florist may make a flower in a day, but nature cannot. Nature is slower than art because it takes a wider sweep and carries forward a vaster design. Nature never makes a single flower only. The artist toils at a single leaf until he has approached the original as nearly as his limitations will allow; but nature works at particulars by working at generals; the impartial sun works upon the poor man's solitary flower and the rich man's gorgeous parterre at the same moment, with the same force, and with the same design. Now the moral constitution in its expansion under Christ, resembles rather the processes of nature than the operations of art. It does not produce a solitary grace, but being penetrated by heavenly fire it abounds with all the flowers and fruits and luxuriance of spiritual summer.

It is not so easy a matter, then, to do unto others as we would that they should do unto us. In carrying out this Divine law we shall again and again be thrown into difficulties which will show that Divine laws can only be carried out in Divine strength, and here the promise is full of encouragement—"Ask, and it shall be given you."

13. Enter ye in at the strait gate: for wide is the gate, and broad is the way, that leadeth to destruction, and many there be which go in thereat:
14. Because strait is the gate, and narrow is the way, which leadeth unto life, and few there be that find it.

The straitness of the gate and the narrowness of the way, are not peculiar to the kingdom of heaven. It is a common error to imagine that discipline, qualification, and self-denial are required alone at the door of God's kingdom. Look through life, and it will be found that in proportion to the importance of any "kingdom" which man wishes to enter is the stringency of the conditions of entrance. Look at the kingdom of learning: strait is the gate and narrow is the way, and few there be that find it! Look at the kingdom of wide intellectual influence: strait is the gate, &c. And so at the gate of all great kingdoms man has much to lay down at the outside. If such be the case, then, in the lower ranges of life, why should the Divine Kingdom, so awful in its spirituality, be an exception? Homiletically the form may be this:—1. The two gates,—only two. 2. The two conditions of entrance, —only two. 3. The two destinies,—"life"—"destruction,"—only two.

The word (ἀπώλεια) rendered "destruction" is variously translated in the New Testament, but always with terrible significations: it is rendered "perdition" (John xvii. 12); "damnable" (2 Peter ii. 1); "destruction" (2 Peter iii. 16.)

Reflect upon the overwhelming thought—"*many* there be which go in thereat." This reflection should:—1. Impress the Christian with the security of his position; and 2. Impel the Church to evangelistic labour. See how beautifully this command ("Enter ye in at the strait gate") is provided for by the preceding promise—"Knock, and it shall be opened unto you."

An awful difficulty has presented itself to many minds in connection with the collateral passage in the Gospel by Luke:—"Strive to enter in at the strait gate: for many, I say unto you, will seek to enter in, and shall not be able." (Luke xiii. 24.) It has been suggested that the explanation is to be found in the difference of intensity between Ἀγωνίζεσθε εἰσελθεῖν and Ζητήσουσιν εἰσελθεῖν; in the one case we have an exercise amounting to *agonising*, and in the other amounting merely to seeking, as if in a casual way, without any particular determination of purpose. In my judgment this solution is far-fetched and untenable; the explanation, I submit, turns entirely on the question of *time*. "When once the master of the house is risen up, and hath shut to the door,"—*that* is the explanation! The "seeking" begins too late! When the daylight is gone, no crying can bring back the sun. The men may seek, may seek earnestly, may agonisingly implore, but when the *opportunity* has passed no voice can recall the vanished angel.

15. Beware of false prophets, which come to you in sheep's clothing, but inwardly they are ravening wolves.
16. Ye shall know them by their fruits. Do men gather grapes of thorns, or figs of thistles?
17. Even so every good tree bringeth forth good fruit; but a corrupt tree bringeth forth evil fruit.
18. A good tree cannot bring forth evil fruit, neither can a corrupt tree bring forth good fruit.
19. Every tree that bringeth not forth good fruit is hewn down, and cast into the fire.
20. Wherefore by their fruits ye shall know them.

Beware of the *false*, in everything. The world had been saying this from the beginning: "beware of false coin, false medicine, false directions, false promises;" and now Christ takes up the world's own form of expression and says—"add the words *false prophets* to all the others which are covered by the word 'beware.'"

False prophets will allure men to the wide gate under pretence that it is strait:—1. The relation of truth to the corruptness of the age; good men always develop the bad elements in their contemporaries. 2. Prudence which is a general virtue is particularly required in connection with the religious life,—(*a*) from the nature of the heart; (*b*) from the fact of diabolic agency; (*c*) from the power of man to ruin man. This latter point is most solemn. It reveals the depravity and diabolism of *selfishness*. "False prophets" seek to make a gain of men whose minds are simple and credulous. They are ambitious; seeking influence, for sordid purposes: "also of your own selves shall men arise, speaking perverse things, to draw away disciples after them." "They that are such serve not our Lord Jesus Christ but their own belly; and by good words and fair speeches deceive the hearts of the simple." 3. False prophets are self-revealing. Give them time, and watch them closely. Test doctrine by example; narrowly scrutinise not the words only but the "fruits." God stultifies and paralyses the bad man simply by allowing him to reveal his corruptness.

This test of life may be employed beyond the case immediately cited. The appeal to "fruits" is practical, and may be conducted by such as have no skill in logomachy, casuistry, or theologic science. (Try this test in the family; in the church: in the social circle.) Christ exposed Himself to this test. "Many good works have I showed you from my Father; for which of those works do ye stone me?" "If I do not the works of my Father, believe me not. But if I do, though ye believe not me, believe the works:

that ye may know and believe, that the Father is in me, and I in him."

21. Not every one that saith unto me, Lord, Lord, shall enter into the kingdom of heaven; but he that doeth the will of my Father which is in heaven.
22. Many will say to me in that day, Lord, Lord, have we not prophesied in thy name? and in thy name have cast out devils? and in thy name done many wonderful works?
23. And then will I profess unto them, I never knew you : depart from me, ye that work iniquity.

1. Christian Life is not merely nominal. 2. Christian Life is not merely official (verse 22). 3. Christian Life is an expression of the Divine will in thought, feeling, and service.

Application : (*a*) How *nearly* men may come without being right ; (*b*) how terrible to know the name and yet be ignorant of the nature; (*c*) how awful to be disowned by Christ.

24. Therefore whosoever heareth these sayings of mine, and doeth them, I will liken him unto a wise man, which built his house upon a rock :
25. And the rain descended, and the floods came, and the winds blew, and beat upon that house ; and it fell not: for it was founded upon a rock :
26. And every one that heareth these sayings of mine, and doeth them not, shall be likened unto a foolish man, which built his house upon the sand :
27. And the rain descended, and the floods came, and the winds blew, and beat upon that house ; and it fell : and great was the fall of it.
28. And it came to pass, when Jesus had ended these sayings, the people were astonished at his doctrine :
29. For he taught them as one having authority, and not as the scribes.

The Sermon on the Mount may be regarded not only as an exposition of duty, but as an elaborate delineation of the spiritual life of Christ. By-and-bye we shall see Christ in miracle ; here we see Him in thought. This is the articulation of His interior (subjective) life, and by this we may test the man in His varied relations to society and God. As yet His works have been spoken of only in general terms, and His sermons have been brief and rousing. Here, however, we have a grand inaugural oration, a minute and magnificent programme, which we may accept not only for what it is in itself, but as a basis of inference, hope, and practical speculation. Christ has opened His heart, and told us all we can comprehend at present. There is in this sermon, in a negative point of view, one circumstance most remarkable, viz. :—

*The absence of what is now regarded as evangelical doctrine or sentiment.* Nothing could well be more unlike a modern sermon than this discourse. No reference is made to Eden. All the ages had been symbolising one great offering of blood, yet no reference is made to sacrifice in this discourse. The terms atonement, reconciliation, faith (the great watchwords of evangelism), are not to be found in this voluminous exposition. It reads rather like a modified Sinaic utterance than a Gospel proclamation; it is not like Calvary, rather like Sinai in summer. We have been wending our historic way through temple and altar and sacrifice, and sundry types and symbols, and now we have simply come to "these sayings of mine." True; but let it be remembered that there may be sacrifice in *teaching* as well as in *dying*. When the learned philosopher condescends to teach a child the alphabet, he developes, in a partial degree, the idea of sacrifice; that is to say, he does something for the sake of another, and the doing of it is out of the level of his own plane. I hold, therefore, that Christ's was a sacrificial life, as well as a sacrificial death. The Incarnation itself was a sacrifice. "When he made himself of no reputation and took upon him the form of a servant," He began the earthly part of His sacrificial work.

It is also to be considered that Christ's sacrifice, viewed

as a *death*, required for its full comprehension by the world a grand foreground of doctrine, teaching, or exposition. The death was to be retrospectively expository of the life. Many of "these sayings of mine" could not be understood until after "the decease which was accomplished at Jerusalem." Men saw other writing on the cross than Pilate's. They beheld there explanations of words which had been enigmatical. There is profound meaning in the expression, "These things understood not his disciples at the first; but when Jesus was glorified, then remembered they that these things were written of him, and that they had done these things unto him." (John xii. 16.) The "glorifying" casts light upon the doctrine and the miracle. Have we not an analogy in our own experience? Are not some men enigmas until they die, and is not death their expounder and friend? The grave is an interpreter. The Sermon on the Mount should be read at the foot of the Cross, or by the edge of the vacant rock.

But is not the absence of evangelical doctrine rather apparent than real? The very first word drives the heart beyond itself for help,—"Blessed are the poor in spirit, for their's is the kingdom of heaven." When a man grasps the meaning of this, he will find his need of a Saviour; the preacher who uttered the words must Himself lead the spirit into the poverty which He blessed. And what shall be said of "the pure in heart"? All movement in *this* direction requires an energy more than human. In the practical out-working, then, of these precepts, men will come perpetually upon difficulties which will force the soul far below the legal stratum, down to that evangelical grace purposed of God in Christ Jesus before the world began. It is to be remembered, too, that these precepts are not initial, but final: their fulfilment is the highest expression of spiritual life. Necessarily, therefore, they compel the spirit towards the grace without which they would be beyond the reach of the soul. Tell a man that in order to be a trustworthy naval captain he must be able to determine the latitude and longitude of a ship at sea ; in that case you have begun at the *end* of the qualification ! You might have said that in order to become a good captain he should study the first four rules of arithmetic, drill himself in the elements of geometry, pass on to trigonometry, and comprehend the processes of logarithmic calculation ; but all this was implied ; would any man, then, be justified in charging you with having ignored or undervalued the process simply because you announced the result ? The very announcement of the result drives the man into an inquiry respecting the process ; so when Christ says, " Blessed are the poor in spirit," He gives a result, a full analysis of which will disclose all the elements of evangelical religion.

I. This discourse reveals *Christ's relation to historical doctrine :*—1. He proclaims His superiority to all other teachers—" It hath been said . . . . but I say unto you." 2. He educates the world to an apprehension of the *spirituality* of life. 3. He makes human destiny turn entirely upon man's relation to "these sayings of mine."

II. This discourse shows *the essential importance of believing right doctrine :*—1. Opinion guides conduct. 2. Whatever guides conduct is immensely powerful. 3. Whatever is immensely powerful should be most carefully watched, trained, and directed.

1. All men are building. 2. All builders have a choice of foundations. 3. All foundations will be tried. 4. Only one foundation will stand.

" The people were astonished at his doctrine, for he taught them as one having authority." The Word was

His life; His preaching was part of Himself; He was not repeating a lesson which was given to Him, but His soul was in every articulation. As preachers become like Christ, they will speak with "authority." The pulpit loses much by its hesitation, and gains everything by confidence.

"Astonished at his doctrine." The excitement of wonder may be profitable to religious teachers.

"Astonished at his doctrine." There is an awful possibility of being "astonished" without being convinced, persuaded, saved!

The 28th verse seems to oppose the idea that the Sermon on the Mount was delivered to the disciples alone. The word (ὄχλοι) rendered "people," cannot be confined to the disciples, for it signifies crowds, and the same word is rendered "multitudes" in the first verse. A close examination of the phraseology will, however, favour the idea that the Sermon was addressed to the disciples, but certainly in the *hearing* of the "multitudes." The opening and concluding verses would read thus:—"And when he was set his disciples came to him, and he opened his mouth and taught them. . . . And the people were astonished at his doctrine, for he taught his disciples with authority, and not as the scribes teach their scholars." I think that the whole genius of the discourse confirms the idea of its having been delivered to a select auditory; especially such expressions as "ye are the light of the world," &c.

Christendom can never throw off the responsibility of being in possession of this discourse. We can never go back to an older standard of ethics, or pretend to be ignorant respecting the principles which should consolidate, direct, and dignify social life. The Sermon is in our midst, and we make ourselves so much nearer heaven or nearer hell by our treatment of it. The Sermon is of incomparably greater value than the miracle. It is remarkable how little reference is made in any of the epistles to Christ's miraculous works; they seem to have had little meaning for others than those who beheld them. We are carried forward from miracle to thought; our way is graduated from the outward to the inward, from the actual to the ideal; and this is God's plan of carrying the world forward; hence in our heavenly state we shall have no need of the "sun," for the Lamb will be the light, and no need of the "temple," for all heaven will be the sanctuary of God.*

## CHAPTER VIII.

1. When he was come down from the mountain, great multitudes followed him.
2. And, behold, there came a leper and worshipped him, saying, Lord, if thou wilt, thou canst make me clean.
3. And Jesus put forth his hand, and touched him, saying, I will; be thou clean. And immediately his leprosy was cleansed.
4. And Jesus saith unto him, See thou tell no man; but go thy way, show thyself to the priest, and offer the gift that Moses commanded, for a testimony unto them.

---

\* "Those who fix their eyes on the Sermon on the Mount, or rather on the naked propositions it contains, and disregard Christ's life, His cross and His resurrection, commit the same mistake in studying Christianity that the student of Socratic philosophy would commit if he studied only the dramatic story of his death. Both Socrates and Christ uttered remarkable thoughts and lived remarkable lives. But Socrates holds his place in history by his thoughts, and not by his life, Christ by His life and not by His thoughts."—*Ecce Homo*, page 96. Is this true? Christ Himself attaches all importance to "these sayings of mine," and in John's Gospel (vi. 63) He says, "The words that I speak unto you they are spirit and they are life." They are not "naked propositions" except in the sense that acorns are naked forests. Christ's "thoughts" were not a philosophic system which He had idealised, but were part of Himself, an expression of his very life; and so perfectly was Christ consistent with Himself that His "life" and His "thoughts" may be regarded as convertible terms. Most men are dualised; Christ was *one;* while other men's words gave instruction, Christ's gave life—Τὰ ῥήματα ἃ ἐγὼ λαλῶ ὑμῖν, πνεῦμά ἐστι καὶ ζωή ἐστιν.

"MULTITUDES," the same word rendered "multitudes" in chap. v. 1, and "people" in chap. vii. 28.

"Worshipped him:" this term means more than an offering of simple homage to a great character. The verb so translated occurs many times in the New Testament; for example, the wise men "fell down and worshipped" Christ. (Matt. ii. 11.) "Thou shalt *worship* the Lord thy God." (Matt. iv. 10.) "The Father seeketh such to worship him." "Let all the angels of God worship him." (Heb. i. 7.) In these cases the same word is used as in the text.

The Great Speaker is here the great Healer. 1. *Sorrow turns instinctively to the supernatural.* Leprosy was known among the Jews as "the finger of God." The removal of leprosy was always considered a Divine act. "Am I a god, that this man sends to me a man to be cured of his leprosy?" When Christ sent an answer to John, He bade the disciples tell their master that "the lepers are cleansed, the dead are raised." It is less easy to be an atheist in sorrow than in joy. Men are less courageous at midnight than noonday. 2. *Christ is never deaf to sorrow's cry.* "I will." Did His "will" ever run counter to the sinner's welfare? The will of man must concur with the will of God; he who would "find" must "seek." The great difficulty is to persuade (not logically but morally) men to have perfect faith in the Divine will, that it is not wise only but infinitely loving. When they feel this they will pray—"Thy will be done on earth, as it is done in heaven." 3. *Christ is superior alike to material contamination and legal restriction.* He could "touch" the leper, and yet feel no injury. Others touched, and the touch meant death; but He touched and yet was uncontaminated. This is a type of his relation to *sin*, &c. The ceremonial law forbade that the leper was to be touched. "And the leper in whom the plague is, his clothes shall be rent, and his head bare; and he shall put a covering upon his upper lip, and shall cry 'Unclean, unclean.' All the days wherein the plague shall be in him he shall be defiled, he is unclean: he shall dwell alone; without the camp shall be his habitation." "And Uzziah, the king, was a leper unto the day of his death, and dwelt in a several house, being a leper; for he was cut off from the house of the Lord." Such passages show how sublimely superior to plague and ceremonial limitation was the healing Christ. Mark the harmony between the Speaker and the Healer; the Speaker set aside much of what was "said by them of old time," and so did the Healer; Christ was thus consistent with Himself.

"Show thyself to the priest." Consider the grand moral effect which such an instance of healing was likely to produce upon the priest!

5. And when Jesus was entered into Capernaum, there came unto him a centurion, beseeching him,
6. And saying, Lord, my servant lieth at home sick of the palsy, grievously tormented.
7. And Jesus saith unto him, I will come and heal him.
8. The centurion answered and said, Lord, I am not worthy that thou shouldest come under roof: but speak the word only, and my servant shall be healed.
9. For I am a man under authority, having soldiers under me: and I say to this man Go, and he goeth; and to another, Come, and he cometh; and to my servant, Do this, and he doeth it.
10. When Jesus heard it, he marvelled, and said to them that followed, Verily I say unto you, I have not found so great faith, no, not in Israel.
11. And I say unto you, That many shall come from the east and west, and shall sit down with Abraham, and Isaac, and Jacob, in the kingdom of heaven.
12. But the children of the kingdom shall be cast out into outer darkness; there shall be weeping and gnashing of teeth.
13. And Jesus said unto the centurion, Go thy way; and as thou hast believed, so be it done unto thee. And his servant was healed in the selfsame hour.

I think that the word translated servant (παῖς) should be rendered "child." The same word is variously translated in the New Testament, "servant," "child," "men servants," and "young man." The rendering "servant" would show the centurion to be an excellent master, but the rendering "child" would better explain the pathos of the story. The narrative shows that *Christ's sympathy by being fundamental was inclusive.* He passes from the leper to the centurion with the utmost ease. In human relations we find that experience is the basis of sympathy; the leper can feel for the leper, the bereaved for the bereaved, the poor for the poor; but Christ feels for all, helps all, blesses all. How so? Because *His sympathy arises from moral causes.* He stands below the mere incident, and purifies the stream by purifying the fountain. A right view of sin gives a right view of suffering. Christ heals the body that He may heal the soul; where consciousness of want is *deepest*, Christ begins. This should be the great law of movement now. Men who cannot understand a sermon might well begin their studies by pondering some deed of mercy done to their lower nature. We may miss altogether by aiming too high. 1. The centurion shows *a beautiful combination of faith and modesty.* 2. The centurion *reasons from the lower to the higher:* a method of reasoning which would elucidate many a mystery. 3. The centurion's faith and modesty secure all the blessings required. This is an illustration of the word—"Ask and it shall be given you." Christ's method in this case shows:—1. His perfect mastery of physical causes; 2. His power to develop the human disposition, His answer to the application brought out the modesty of the appellant; 3. His interest in personal cases—no human want is trivial in his estimation; 4. His appreciation of faith wherever found—He loves *man* as man, not merely as Jew or Gentile; 5. His desire to turn all circumstances to a moral account.

The 11th and 12th verses suggest that there is a vital difference between nominal sonship and true kindred of the

92   HOMILETIC ANALYSIS.

soul by faith. 1. Some will be saved beyond our expectation; 2. Some will be lost beyond our fear.

Christ's exclamation gives a distant hint of the joy He will experience when His soul is "satisfied." There is a tone of rapture in this exclamation—one day the promise shall be redeemed which the prophets spoke, and He shall enter,into the gladness of perfect " satisfaction."

14. And when Jesus was come into Peter's house, he saw his wife's mother laid, and sick of a fever.
15. And he touched her hand, and the fever left her: and she arose, and ministered unto them.

Peter was a disciple, yet affliction was permitted to visit his domestic circle. Affliction at home :—1. Developes social sympathy; 2. Brings out family characteristics; 3. Unites the household circle in devotional exercises; 4. Evokes practical and affectionate gratitude.

16. When the even was come, they brought unto him many that were possessed with devils; and he cast out the spirits with his word, and healed all that were sick:
17. That it might be fulfilled which was spoken by Esaias the prophet, saying, Himself took our infirmities, and bare our sicknesses.

The mind and the body are alike under the control of Christ: He "cast out the devils" and He healed the sick. His own twofold nature has a bearing upon man's compound constitution. In what sense did Christ take our iniquities and bear our sicknesses? Not literally, in the sense of corrupting His own humanity with the plagues of His contemporaries; not merely sympathetically, else He would not differ in nature, though in degree, from ourselves. Peter's wife (verse 14) no doubt felt sympathetically for her fever-stricken mother;—how then? simply in the sense of removing them entirely out of the body. We never read of any merely partial cures being wrought by Christ. Men speak of physicians doing them " some good," or " much good," but in

Christ's cures there was perfectness. Still the element of sympathy is far from valueless. In a human physician it is highly estimated by the sufferer. As with the body so with the mind, the removal of sickness is entire, the cleansing of guilt is complete. "Who his own self bare our sins in his own body on the tree, that we, being dead to sin, should live unto righteousness; by whose stripes ye were healed" (1 Peter ii. 24.) The cured cripple could again break a limb, and the healed sufferer again experience paroxysms of agony; so the sin-healed man might again commit sin. This circumstance does not impair the argument that as Christ literally took away the sickness of the body, so He takes away the sickness of the soul. Did He remove all sickness? No. Only the sickness of such as applied to Him, and only on the condition of faith; He left multitudes of sick people unhealed; so with His spiritual work, He takes away the sin of such only as apply to Him and believe in Him, and He takes it away as completely as He took away the sickness of the body.

Here we have once more a clear indication of Christ's relation to the physical nature of man. He begins at the dust where He cannot get access to the soul. In the case of Nicodemus, having to deal with a master in Israel, he began at a high point, enunciated an abstruse and a most startling doctrine. Thus he took men according to their characteristics, and served his generation and ultimately the whole world, according as circumstances directed. His supreme object was, of course, to reach the soul, and he availed himself of every entrance to the inner nature.

18. Now when Jesus saw great multitudes about him, he gave commandment to depart unto the other side.

19. And a certain scribe came, and said unto him, Master, I will follow thee whithersoever thou goest.

20. And Jesus saith unto him, The foxes have holes, and the birds of the air have nests; but the Son of Man hath not where to lay his head.

The scribe uttered the language of impulse. He may have heard the "sayings" or seen the mighty works, and while he thrilled with wonder he extemporised a resolution which was marked rather by impulse than intelligence. We ourselves have been carried away with such stormy emotions, and as often, probably, have been stranded on some barren or dangerous rock. 1. Christ came to call men to follow Him; 2. Christian discipleship is to be founded in intelligence if it is to be permanent; 3. Men are not only to follow Christ the man, but Christ the Gospel. There is a possibility of following the speaker without "doing the sayings."

Christ's answer (verse 20), was accordant with the scribe's spirit. The scribe sought to follow the *man*, and therefore the mere man told him what to expect; had he prized the doctrine no chilling word would have fallen on his enthusiasm. This is a distinction not to be lightly regarded, forasmuch as its application is very extensive. Many an attendant in the sanctuary "follows" the preacher rather than the Gospel; it is a mere personal attachment; he admires the preacher's rhetoric, or pathos, or power, without caring as to the doctrine which his favourite orator is promulgating. When a crisis supervenes in the history of the Church such a person cannot be relied upon; he may go in quest of another charmer who can throw the wizard's spell over his fastidious ear. The scribe, in the text, gave expression to a merely personal attachment, and he was arrested by a merely personal reply.

21. And another of his disciples said unto him, Lord, suffer me first to go and bury my father.
22. But Jesus said unto him, Follow me; and let the dead bury their dead.

Here is a variation of feeling—a different type, indeed, of temperament. Christ's method in this case is perfectly consistent with His method in the other. In the first case His words amount almost to positive discouragement; in the second, they rise to the authority of a command; and the explanation of the difference is to be found in the temperament of the persons spoken to. There is an attachment to Christ which is merely impulsive; there is an attachment which is modified by inferior considerations. Christ will not accept unreasoning impulse; nor will He accept partial consecration. 1. This command does not contravene natural affection. 2. This command simply shows that where a distinct choice must be made, everything is to fall before the supremacy of Christ. This can be felt only by those whose Christianity is in the heart as a Divine inspiration; such as have realised the fulness of the blessing that is in Jesus Christ. Properly viewed, all that is strong in fatherliness, all that is tender in maternity, all that is charmful in sisterliness, all that is genial in brotherhood, is to be found in the Redeemer, and found in a degree superior to all earthly manifestations of the same. Christ is the up-gathering and perfect completeness of all that is divinely ideal in man. If, by accepting birth under conditions which are abnormal, He was as "a root out of a dry ground," yet He was the flower of Jesse and the plant of renown; and though He was "despised and rejected of men," yet He was "the desire of all nations." We are to grow up to this idea of Christ, and when we have attained it, we shall take such a view of the death of friends as will bind us to Christ in tenderer love by the very sorrow and tears which tend towards the earth, and the hope and triumph which aspire towards heaven. It will come to be understood, as men advance in spiritual life, that we truly love our departed friends most tenderly when we follow Christ most perseveringly.

## GENERAL NOTE.

The two men (verses 19, 21) suggest reflections upon the true place of Feeling in the Christian life. Feeling may be a mere sentiment, or it may be the attendant and exponent of intense intellectual persuasion. We are to love the Lord our God with all our *mind*. Sensibility is exposed to many perils. Frequent excitement, unbalanced by practical service, destroys the nerve on which it operates. The emotional nature may be well-nigh annihilated by excessive excitement, but where sensibility is associated with practical philanthropy, it becomes acuter and profounder, and yields a joy which is often unspeakable. We must establish a balance in our nature. Overindulged sensibility becomes fanaticism ; repressed feeling degenerates into the basest utilitarianism.

23. And when he was entered into a ship, his disciples followed him.
24. And, behold, there arose a great tempest in the sea; insomuch that the ship was covered with the waves; but he was asleep.
25. And his disciples came to him, and awoke him, saying, Lord, save us: we perish.
26. And he saith unto them, Why are ye fearful, O ye of little faith. Then he arose, and rebuked the winds and the sea; and there was a great calm.
27. But the men marvelled, saying, What manner of man is this, that even the winds and the sea obey him?

The *time* at which Christ answered the two men should be marked,—"He gave commandment to depart unto the other side." The scribe said, "I will follow;" the disciple said, "Suffer me first to go and bury my father:" —the one was ready, the other had family business on hand; the one was warned of consequences; the other was commanded to follow. Having treated both cases on their merits, Christ entered the ship, and sank into the oblivion of sleep. It was well-merited repose. It was the sleep of a philanthropist. Men may go down to sleep either (*a*) wearied by evil works, or (*b*) exhausted by services of mercy.

The scene on the water may be accommodated homiletically to show the perils of the Church, and how they may be controlled :—1. There are perils which are external,—storms, &c. 2. There are perils which are internal,—fear, misgiving, false interpretations of circumstances, &c. 3. The perils which beset the Church can be controlled by Christ alone. Or the scene on the water may be accommodated so as to suggest lessons of a wider range :—1. Here is an illustration of Christ's compound nature,—as man He sleeps, as God He commands. 2. Here is special appeal to Christ for aid : (*a*) Christ's life a proof of His benignity,—misery never appealed in vain to His compassion; (*b*) Christ is ever present to the prayer of faith. 3. Here is a type of men who invoke the aid of Christ at troublous times. 4. Here is an interposition of Divine assistance just where human power failed (refer to many *crises* for illustration). 5. Here is a proof that trials may arise, even in the discharge of duty,—the men went upon the sea in obedience to Christ's command! The whole subject may be applied thus :—

I. *Undertake no enterprise in which Christ does not accompany you.* Be sure that Christ is in the vessel.

II. *Distinguish between the storms which you have provoked, and the storms which God has appointed.* Trials are either punitive, or disciplinary.

III. *Be assured that all forces are under the control of Divine beneficence.*

28. And when he was come to the other side into the country of the Gergesenes, there met him two possessed with devils, coming out of the tombs, exceeding fierce, so that no man might pass by that way.

29. And, behold, they cried out, saying, What have we to do with thee,

Jesus, thou Son of God? art thou come hither to torment us before the time?

30. And there was a good way off from them an herd of many swine feeding.

31. So the devils besought him, saying, If thou cast us out, suffer us to go away into the herd of swine.

32. And he said unto them, Go. And when they were come out, they went into the herd of swine: and, behold, the whole herd of swine ran violently down a steep place into the sea, and perished in the water.

33. And they that kept them fled, and went their ways into the city, and told every thing, and what was befallen to the possessed of the devils.

34. And, behold, the whole city came out to meet Jesus: and when they saw him, they besought him that he would depart out of their coasts.

1. A picture of what *all* men would become under Satanic dominion. 2. The agony which the bad experience in the presence of the good. 3. A prophecy of the universal empire of the Son of God; the devils cringe when he approaches.

I shall not add to the innumerable speculations respecting the entrance of the devils into the herd of swine, but shall regard the circumstance as showing most impressively :— *The intolerableness of life in hell.*—The petition of the devils may be regarded as equivalent to,—" Send us anywhere, anywhere but to perdition; send us to the most shattered man; send us to the lowest creature, into man or beast, bird or reptile, anywhere but into hell ! "

The answer of Christ shows, in its results, that ruin always attends the presence of devils,—what they touch they destroy! The devil in trade, in amusement, in sensuous gratification, anywhere, simply means *ruin !*

The conduct of the people shows how secular considerations may be set against philanthropic service. The men were saved, but the swine were lost ! When society values its swine more than its children, it is enslaved by the spirit of secularism.

The expression,—" When he was come to the other side," is suggestive of the fact that on both sides, and on all sides, there are traces of diabolic malignity which Christ alone can obliterate.

### GENERAL NOTE ON THE EIGHTH CHAPTER.

In this narrative the deeds outnumber the "sayings." We have just concluded a sermon of words, and now we have a sermon of actions. These two sermons make up the sphere of Christian life. "As he was, so are we in the world." To-day, the Christian may be called to oral exposition of Divine things; he may stand on the mountain as the messenger of God, and pour his words to the flying wind that they may be borne everywhere: to-morrow he may be comforting a solitary heart, addressing himself to one poor leprous soul, or bringing the hope of heaven into the chamber of the dying. The work is one. A sermon of "sayings" is nothing, if it stir not the hand to noble effort on behalf of afflicted and perishing humanity.

### *CHAPTER IX.*

1. And he entered into a ship, and passed over, and came into his own city.

2. And, behold, they brought to him a man sick of the palsy, lying on a bed: and Jesus seeing their faith said unto the sick of the palsy; Son, be of good cheer; thy sins be forgiven.

Capernaum was Christ's "own city." Christ finds work to do everywhere,—in His "own city," and on "the other side." There is no charmed coast free from the presence of want and misery. The black flag of guilt flaps in every breeze. The earth groans under an all-including curse. The cure of the palsied man shows the place of "faith" in the mediatorial economy. " Seeing their faith," Christ said,

"Son, be of good cheer." How can faith bring such gladness? 1. Faith connects the lower with the higher,—the human with the Divine. 2. Faith expresses, in practical exercise, the most vital elements of human nature. In this particular it is with God as with men. When the child trusts you most, you do most for the child; in the very act of surrendering its will to yours the child puts the highest honour upon you. Can you prove false to the clinging grasping hand which commits everything to your strength and wisdom? Our heavenly Father turns our faith into gladness, so that not only have we victory, but all the joy and rapture of perfect triumph.

Christ strikes at the root when He says, "Thy sins be forgiven thee." The palsy was a mere accident; but the sin was in the very life. Any healing which is not moral, can be merely superficial and temporary.

3. And, behold, certain of the scribes said within themselves, This man blasphemeth.

This was the result of a false interpretation. By His perfect sympathy with the Father, by His own personal divinity, by the very nature of His mission among men, Christ could pronounce the forgiveness of sins. Take the matter of *presumption* among men: what would be natural to one man might be inexcusably presumptuous in another. Were an ordinary police-officer to occupy the judgment-seat and pronounce sentence upon criminals, the act would be deemed an outrage, and punished accordingly; but when the accredited judge pronounces sentence the act is accepted and esteemed. So, for a sinful man to pronounce forgiveness of sin is blasphemy, but for the Son of God to grant pardon of iniquity is a rightful and effectual exercise of the Divine prerogative. "Certain of the scribes" saw no further than the mere humanity of Christ, and thus ignorantly did they accuse him of "blasphemy."

4. And Jesus knowing their thoughts said, Wherefore think ye evil in your hearts?

There is a marked consistency between the power which pardoned the suffering sinner, and that which penetrated the evil thoughts of the accusing Scribes. These incidental illustrations of consistency are of immense value in estimating any character, and singularly so in the analysis of the dual life which was at once Divine and human.

5. For whether is easier, to say, Thy sins be forgiven thee; or to say, Arise, and walk?
6. But that ye may know that the Son of man hath power on earth to forgive sins, (then saith he to the sick of the palsy,) Arise, take up thy bed, and go unto thine house.

The one is as difficult as the other, but not so to human comprehension; in the one case there was no appeal to the senses, in the other the paralytic was before the eyes of the doubters. Spiritual processes are undervalued by the carnal judgment. In this case the spiritual was attested by the physical; the soul might have been healed and the body left untouched, but the paralysis, both moral and physical, was removed.

7. And he arose, and departed to his house.
8. But when the multitude saw it, they marvelled, and glorified God, which had given such power unto men.

Different classes view the same event with the most contrary feelings. Little cliques say one thing, and "multitudes" say another. A sectarian education separates man from the wide and deep sympathies of the world, and enslaves him by petty and most contracted prejudices.

In the case of the preaching, and in the case of the healing, the same ground is occupied by the multitudes; in the one instance we read "they were astonished at his doctrine, for he taught them as one having authority," and in the other, "they marvelled and glorified God, which had given such power unto men." The same word is rendered " authority " and " power," and may help to measure the moral stature of the " multitudes," at the time they employed it. The presence of wonder is one of the earliest intimations of consciousness; and the admiration of " power " is one of the first conditions of interest in a new teacher. Children take more notice of thunderstorms than of gradually lengthening days. The age of miracles was well adapted to the age of the world. As men become finer of nature they will be more deeply moved by a regenerated soul than by a re-invigorated body.

The incident, taken as a whole, shows:—1. How the strong may help the weak; 2. How ready Christ is to bless man alike for earth and heaven; 3. How independent Christ is of the opinions of objectors.

9. And as Jesus passed forth from thence, he saw a man, named Matthew, sitting at the receipt of custom : and he saith unto him, Follow me. And he arose, and followed him.

1. Christ calls all men from the secular to the spiritual. 2. Christ calls some men to the ministry of His word. 3. The man who is truly called of Christ should never go back; this applies (*a*) to individual consecration, and (*b*) to ministerial vocation. Retrogression implies:—1. A reflection upon Christ. 2. A preference of the secular to the spiritual. There may be difficulties in following Christ, but (*a*) they were foretold, (*b*) difficulties are incident to all life, (*c*) compensating grace is promised.

11. And when the Pharisees saw it, they said unto his disciples, Why cateth your Master with publicans and sinners?
12. But when Jesus heard that, he said unto them, They that be whole need not a physician, but they that are sick.
13. But go ye and learn what that meaneth, I will have mercy, and not sacrifice: for I am not come to call the righteous, but sinners to repentance.

1. Christ's protest against the exclusiveness of sectarianism. 2. Christ's immediate contact with the man he sought to bless,—He entered the social circle; He sanctified the breaking of bread, He identified Himself with the habitudes of the society of His day. All Christian ministers should know the advantage of the *personal* over the *abstract*,—" I am," is always better than " It is." The figure of the physician bears out this suggestion; *the physician comes into personal contact with the patient.* Let pastors learn a lesson !

Christ's identification of Himself (analogically) with a physician is suggestive of many reflections. The physician spends his life in going from sick-room to sick-room; he goes in the darkness of winter, and the brightness of summer; goes at noonday, goes at midnight; reads the secrets of the hearts as they are telegraphed by the truthful pulse; looks into the brightening or dimming eye ; and then does his little utmost for the healing of the sufferer. It was a beautiful appropriation on the part of Christ to take the physician's profession as illustrative of his own beneficent mission. Think of a physician being complained of for visiting the sick! Or, think of a physician who spent all his time in visiting the healthy and strong! It would be a falsification of his very name. Christ, then, is the heart's physician,—the healer of all human life. He knocks at the door of every dying heart, and offers blessed immortality.

Christ shows (verse 13) that God requires the spirit rather than the form,—mercy is better than sacrifice. He shows, too, the true mission on which He came, viz., to call sinners to repentance. This statement is not only gracious in itself, but suggestive of the true method and spirit of philanthropic service. Remedial measures should go to the roots of society, —the deepest strata out of hell. It is remarkable that while Christ spent so much time in *reproving* the Pharisees, He spent more in *saving* the fallen, the outcast and despised.

There is a philanthropic school whose creed is,—Save those who are about to fall, and leave those who are already fallen. Christ's practice is in direct contravention of this principle. He goes to the "lost," the "sick," the "sinners," and as He moves in His downward course, He scathes with lightning the pompous formalist who has virtue enough to keep a blameless outside while his heart is as a cage of unclean birds. The poorest woman, with shattered honour and hopeless heart, fared better at His hands than the learned Rabbi who had much knowledge, but no wisdom. The testimony of many philanthropists is that there is a deeper satisfaction in working for the lowest classes, than for those whose self-consciousness keeps them from full confession and penitence.

14. Then came to him the disciples of John, saying, Why do we and the Pharisees fast oft, but thy disciples fast not?

15. And Jesus said unto them, Can the children of the bridechamber mourn, as long as the bridegroom is with them? but the days will come, when the bridegroom shall be taken from them, and then shall they fast.

16. No man putteth a piece of new cloth unto an old garment, for that which is put in to fill it up taketh from the garment, and the rent is made worse.

17. Neither do men put new wine into old bottles: else the bottles break, and the wine runneth out, and the bottles perish: but they put new wine into new bottles, and both are preserved.

Here is another instance of sectarianism being thrown into disadvantageous contrast with the magnificence of Christ's Life. It is hard for the little sect to comprehend the universe, but easy for it to condemn all who are not enclosed in its shallow limits. Men are known by the inquiries they propound. Great men put great questions, tiny spirits perplex themselves with tiny riddles. The persons in the text put a question about "fasting,"—they were still in a very material and grovelling condition,—it is noticeable, however, that men who could abstain from food could not abstain from censoriousness; so true is it in all human experience that it is easier to restrain the bodily than the mental, easier to conquer dust than spirit.

Christ's answer to the sectarians left them without a word to say: from it we learn—1. That bodily penance should be the dictate of the heart's loneliness and want, not of a dogmatic formalism; and, 2. That men must be treated according to their moral age and stature. What was adapted to the ascetic John was inappropriate to the social Christ. Christ's religion was best figured by wedding feasts, wedding garments, and wine on the wedding table. Fasting was to be an expression of nature, not mere obedience to a dogmatic prescription. If a man feels that it would be well for him to fast, his abstinence will be acceptable to God, but if he fast simply because he has made a law to that effect, his soul may be guilty of gluttony and drunkenness, while his body is suffering from hunger.

Our spiritual life is not to be partly Christ and partly something else,—old and new,—but all Christ; independent, solitary, alone, because Divine. The Christian is free of the old law in its formality, but never free from law as an expression of love. We do not keep the decalogue because of its outward form and claim upon us, but we keep the commandments because we love the commander. "Love is the fulfilling of the law." We cannot "fast," because we are keeping the wedding feast with Christ; we are not in the desert, but in the bride-chamber; the prisoner of a sect may fast, but a freeman of the universe has "all things richly to enjoy." "Rejoice greatly, O daughter of Zion; shout, O daughter of Jerusalem; behold, thy king cometh unto thee." The chrysalis cannot understand the butterfly. Christ has taken us out of the legal dormancy of old formal observances, and given us wings by which we may mount into the high altitudes of the spiritual creation.

The 16th and 17th verses might be so accommodated as

106   HOMILETIC ANALYSIS.

to give a basis for a discourse upon *false and forbidden unions*.

18. While he spake these things unto them, behold, there came a certain ruler, and worshipped him, saying, My daughter is even now dead : but come and lay thy hand upon her, and she shall live.

19. And Jesus arose, and followed him, and so did his disciples.

20. And, behold, a woman, which was diseased with an issue of blood twelve years, came behind him, and touched the hem of his garment :

21. For she said within herself, If I may but touch his garment, I shall be whole.

22. But Jesus turned him about, and when he saw her he said, Daughter, be of good comfort; thy faith hath made thee whole. And the woman was made whole from that hour.

23. And when Jesus came into the ruler's house, and saw the minstrels and the people making a noise,

24. He said unto them, Give place: for the maid is not dead, but sleepeth. And they laughed him to scorn.

25. But when the people were put forth, he went in, and took her by the hand, and the maid arose.

26. And the fame hereof went abroad into all that land.

27. And when Jesus departed thence, two blind men followed him, crying, and saying, Thou son of David, have mercy on us.

28. And when he was come into the house, the blind men came to him: and Jesus saith unto them, Believe ye that I am able to do this? And they said unto him, Yea, Lord.

29. Then touched he their eyes, saying, According to your faith be it unto you.

30. And their eyes were opened; and Jesus straightly charged them, saying, See that no man know it.

31. But they, when they were departed, spread abroad his fame in all that country.

32. As they went out, behold, they brought to him a dumb man possessed with a devil.

33. And when the devil was cast out, the dumb spake: and the multitudes marvelled, saying, It was never so seen in Israel.

I.—CHRIST'S SIDE.

1. The speaker was called upon for *action*. It is a long way from eloquence to beneficence in the case of some speakers; in the case of Christ, speech and action were convertible terms.    2. Christ will interrupt an exposition for the sake of a man who mourns a little dead girl. (Luke viii. 42.)    3. It is more congenial to Christ to be binding

up a broken heart than to be debating with factious Pharisees respecting intercourse with publicans and sinners, or even to be explaining to sectarians the conditions which make "fasting" acceptable to God and useful to man. 4. Christ was ever equal to the call of the hour. Was exposition required? The living stream flowed from His gracious lips. Was a miracle required? The same voice had but to alter its tone, and the miracle was complete.

II.—THE HUMAN SIDE.

Here are four miracles: the raising of the dead; the healing of the issue of blood; the opening of the eyes of the blind; the cure of a dumb man possessed with a devil. These diversified cases reveal the human side of the transactions under several aspects: 1. The right spiritual state in which to approach Christ,—the ruler "worshipped Him:" the poor woman modestly and trustfully said, "If I may but touch his garment I shall be whole:" the blind men said "Have mercy on us:" the dumb man possessed with a devil found in his utter helplessness the best possible recommendation to Christ's mercy. 2. The indispensableness of faith in any transaction between the natural and the supernatural. Faith is the link: without *that*, connection is impossible. 3. This transactional faith can operate only in connection with profound consciousness of want. "To know ourselves diseased is half the cure."

[Many inquirers have found extreme difficulty in realising *the true relation of the human will to the work of the Lord Jesus Christ*. An examination of the Gospels will show that Christ demanded a condition on the part of those who applied to Him for aid: "*Believe* ye?" "What *will* ye?" "Ye will not come unto me." Call the condition "faith," or rectitude of *will*, it *was* a condition, and was constantly required. The youthful inquirer may catch a glimmer of the meaning by an illustration; the authorities of the city have laid immense water-pipes throughout all the thoroughfares; they have not entered a single house; the poorest man may close his door upon them, and forbid them to enter; all that the civic authorities have done is to make an ample provision of water : they say, however, to the inhabitants, "We have done this for you, and now, whosoever will, may have a supply of water in his dwelling-place." The inhabitants reply, " How can we connect those great main pipes with our houses?" The answer is, "If you want the water, say so, and all the work of connection shall be done for you." So far, then, the case is analogous to the provision of the water of life by the Lord Jesus Christ. He says, "If any man thirst, let him come unto me and drink," and it is said, "Whosoever will, let him take the water of life freely." The civic authorities force the water upon no man ; Jesus Christ forces the water upon no man. In the case of the civic authorities, however, an equivalent is demanded, and herein the analogy terminates, for the living water is to be had "without money and without price." The illustration may show, in one aspect, the relation of the *will* to that which is provided ; it may also show how the water may be pronounced as generally belonging to all, and yet particularly belonging to each individual ; hence, all Christians can say of Jesus Christ, he is " Lord, both theirs and ours."]

"The words, 'According to your faith be it unto you' (Matt. ix. 29), are very remarkable for the insight which they give us into the relation of man's faith and God's gift. The faith, which in itself is nothing, is yet the organ of receiving everything. It is the conducting link between man's emptiness and God's fulness ; and herein is all the value which it has. It is the bucket let down into the fountain of God's grace, without which the man could not draw up out of that fountain ; the purse, which does not itself make its owner rich, but which yet effectually enriches him by the treasure which it contains."—*(Trench.)*

GENERAL NOTE ON MIRACLES OF HEALING.

Miracles, as illustrative of a benevolent spirit towards man, were hardly known to the Olympian deities. "It does not appear that if we except the traditive ideas represented in Minerva and Apollo, they could either raise men from the grave, prevent their dying in the course of nature, heal their wounds or diseases, or set their broken limbs." Olympus was verily only *supposed* to reach unto heaven ; the Thessalian mount was still on earth, and its turbulent deities were restrained by all the limitations which bind the children of dust. God is *Love*. When He goes forth in His chariot of lightning, when He walks on the wings of the wind, when He speaks from the tabernacles of thunder, His great purpose is a revelation of His infinite *love*. The vulgar deities of Olympus revelled in their power of destruction; the true and only God has compassion on men, bears their infirmities and heals their sicknesses. "The Son of man came not to destroy men's lives, but to save them."

34. But the Pharisees said, He casteth out devils through the prince of the devils.

It is of more consequence to a sectarian to defend a prejudice than to rejoice over a recovered man. The Pharisees hated Christ, and what good can a hated man do? They hesitated not to trace a good effect to a bad cause. Sectarians are independent of logic and morality.

35. And Jesus went about all the cities and villages, teaching in their synagogues, and teaching the gospel of the kingdom, and healing every sickness, and every disease among the people.

The most powerful rebuke of His enemies. While they were uttering bad words, He was doing good deeds; while they were murmuring, He was working. Read the programme of the sectarians in verse 34, and compare it with the programme of Christ, in verse 35. It is easy to murmur; it is difficult to work. In these verses we have a picture of society in our own day. The narrowness of sectarian dogma is now set against the inclusiveness of the Divine purpose. The Pharisees loved *sect* more than *man*, and their vision was so disturbed that they saw the diabolic where they should have seen the Divine. "Blessed are *the pure in heart*, for they shall see God."

110                    HOMILETIC ANALYSIS.

36. But when he saw the multitudes, he was moved with compassion on them, because they fainted, and were scattered abroad, as sheep having no shepherd.
37. Then saith he unto his disciples, The harvest truly is plenteous, bu the labourers are few ;
38. Pray ye, therefore, the Lord of the harvest, that he will send forth labourers into his harvest.

The man who works most among the people sees most of their wants. Christ did not read the report of others, but came into actual contact with perishing men. A comprehension of the 35th verse will give its true force to this paragraph. Christ has been preaching and healing, through long hours and days, and still the needy throngs pressed upon him; from the east and the west they came, and from the north and south; the blind, deaf, dumb, idiotic, halt, maimed, paralytic, the ignorant, perverse, selfish, earnest, hypocritical; they came till the multitude was very great, and until He seems to have felt His loneliness amid the living mass of sinners and sufferers, and as cry after cry of distress broke upon His ear His heart yearned with compassion, and He spoke those words. We have here *Christ's view of human multitudes.* That view—1. Elicited His most practical sympathies; 2. Impelled Him to seek prayer on their behalf; 3. Led Him to announce the true method of evangelisation, viz., by human instrumentality. A right view of a multitude cannot but deeply affect a right-hearted man; (*a*) diversified histories; (*b*) conflicting emotions; (*c*) opposite relations to God and truth; (*d*) different destinies.

The great want of the world has been a want of *men;* Christ calls them "*labourers.*" The term is well selected ; the term, however, must not be limited. (*a*) Some men labour for the world by *thinking*, (*b*) some by *speaking*, (*c*) some by *giving*, (*d*) some by *suffering*.

## CHAPTER X.

1. And when he had called unto him his twelve disciples, he gave them power against unclean spirits, to cast them out, and to heal all manner of sickness and all manner of disease.

1. Disciples advanced to be apostles. First learners, then teachers; first near the person of the Lord, then evangelising those who are afar off. 2. He who calls to one position gives "power" to fill another. Power is not given at once. Even in the Church on earth it doth not yet appear what we shall be. Those who are now young in Christ may be called to apostleship, and great honour in evangelistic service. 3. As a perfect leader, Christ gave His servants power over the body, "all manner of sickness and all manner of disease." We have the *fact*, we cannot give the *explanation*. The principle, however, is of the utmost importance, viz., that the followers of Christ should concern themselves in *the physical welfare of society*. The Church should have its school, its orphan-house, its hospital, as well as its preaching-house. 4. Philanthropic labour should be *immediately identified with Christ's name*, not collaterally or incidentally, but vitally and directly. The apostles were wont to say, "in the name of Jesus Christ," we do this or that. Why should that solemn formula have fallen into disuse? Why not say, In the name of Jesus of Nazareth, we found this hospital, this orphan-home, this refuge for the destitute? If we thus honoured Christ would He not more abundantly honour us?

2. Now the names of the twelve apostles are these ; The first, Simon, who is called Peter, and Andrew his brother ; James the son of Zebedee, and John his brother ;
3. Philip and Bartholomew ; Thomas, and Matthew the publican : James the son of Alpheus, and Lebbeus, whose surname was Thaddeus ;
4. Simon the Canaanite, and Judas Iscariot, who also betrayed him.

"Names"? What have the ages to do with the "names"

of a dozen men? 1. Man employed to bless man. 2. A few sent to call the many. 3. Different types of men meet different types of the community. 4. Some famous, some unknown, but all useful. 5. Is every twelfth man a "devil"?

CHRIST'S CHARGE TO THE TWELVE APOSTLES.

This charge occupies the remainder of the chapter (verses 5—42), and presents some points of singular difference from the Sermon on the Mount.

There are peculiarities of expression in this charge :
Verses 5, 6. STIER'S observation upon the restriction is : "The first consideration of one who is sent of the Lord must ever be, that the immediate sphere of his activity should be accurately prescribed to him, and that he should know with precision whither he must not go, whither also he must."
Verse 23. STIER says : "Go ye whither I now send you forth ; perserve in patient performance of your duty in preaching and testifying through all persecution ; ye may comfort yourselves with the assured hope that *I Myself will come after* for salvation and separation." LANGE says: "Till the Son of man shall overtake you. The expression is, however, also symbolical, and applies to the Church generally. In this sense it points forward to the second coming of Christ ; including, at the same time, the idea, that their apostolic labours in Judea would be cut short by the judgment impending upon Jerusalem."
Verse 27. "What ye hear in the ear ;" what is communicated to you by the Holy Ghost.
Verse 28. "Fear him which is able to destroy both body and soul in hell ;" fear the devil, says STIER, but he has mistaken the meaning.
Verse 34. "I came not to send peace, but a sword,"—the sword prepares the way for peace. The surgeon gives pain that he may promote health.

The giving of charges to persons about to prosecute new and hazardous enterprises. Does not the anxious parent instinctively and pathetically charge the child who is about to leave home?

The twelve apostles went forth with this charge as their only inspiration. Mark this. They had the living word within them, and by its power they cleared their perilous way. A word may be as a pillar of fire lighting a man through the wilderness.

The very fact of undertaking such a mission empty-handed (verses 9, 10), supplies a vivid illustration of the social influence of the Gospel. The Gospel opens human hearts and human hands. They who preach faith should exemplify faith.

This method of encountering human voracity (verse 16) shows *the omnipotence of moral force.* Ideas are better than swords. Persuasion will conquer more than persecution.

He who labours for God is under the protection of God, and should, therefore, know nothing of fear. (Verses 28—31.)

The relation which men now occupy to Christ, is the relation which Christ will finally occupy towards men. (Verses 32, 33.)

The inspiration of moral labour is simply passionate love towards the Lord Jesus. (Verses 37—39.) This love is to transcend all other love, as appreciation of the sun exceeds our appreciation of all other light. We do not dislike a star because we admire the sun.

Christian labourers are vitally identified with their Master. (Verses 40—42.)

The 42nd verse may be used to show *God's recognition of the humblest service.* 1. God's intimate acquaintance with every member of His spiritual kingdom,—" *little* ones ; " " *one* of these little ones." 2. God's perfect knowledge of every transaction in His empire. This fact should (*a*) invest life with the profoundest solemnity; (*b*) inspire men with the holiest motives; (*c*) animate men with the noblest ambition. 3. God's special regard for all who are attached to Christ, "in the name of a prophet," "in the name of a disciple," "in the name of a righteous man." 4. God's pledge to reward the humblest good-doer. The practical application is five-fold. (*a*) There has been a fearful moral disruption in the social fabric; (*b*) a restorative economy has been established; (*c*) a retributional period will eventually supervene; (*d*) the feeblest power may be beneficently exerted; (*e*) in the vast economy of the universe nothing is lost.

## CHAPTER XI.

1. And it came to pass, when Jesus had made an end of commanding his twelve disciples, he departed thence, to teach and to preach in their cities.

2. Now when John had heard in the prison the works of Christ, he sent two of his disciples,

3. And said unto him, Art thou he that should come, or do we look for another?

4. Jesus answered and said unto them, Go and show John again those things which ye do hear and see :

5. The blind receive their sight, and the lame walk, the lepers are cleansed, and the deaf hear, the dead are raised up, and the poor have the Gospel preached to them.

6. And blessed is he, whosoever shall not be offended in me.

The spirit of this paragraph may be developed by a discourse upon *The Question of the Troubled Heart answered by the beneficent and patient Christ*. Recall the circumstances : (*a*) John was committed to a special identification of the Messiah ; (*b*) John had proclaimed judgment, under the figures of " fan," " ax," " fire ; " (*c*) John was, so to speak, an incarnation of the spirit of the Old Testament,—eminently judicial, demonstrative, stern in bearing, decisive in tone ; —(*d*) John had been imprisoned through the winter in consequence of his testimony on behalf of purity and honour. He was almost within hearing of the revels of the voluptuous court; the messenger of the Lord was in prison, while the debauchee was encircled by royal splendour. This problem in providence had perplexed the

Baptist as it had perplexed holy men of all ages. He was expecting the fires of judgment, but no fire fell; he listened for the coming of the judge, but no footfall broke the silence. Hope had almost expired; a strange, dark, heavy sorrow brooded over his spirit. He was now undergoing *his* temptation, as Christ had also done. In that hour of sadness he showed how the strongest man had seasons of weakness.

John's case, then, may be taken as showing *some phases of the troubled heart :*—1. The trouble which comes of measuring Divine progress by human impatience. 2. The trouble which comes of magnifying the personal over the universal,—each man considers his own case of the most urgent consequence. 3. The trouble which comes of not sufficiently discriminating between the *sinner* and the *sin;* the destruction of sinners (which would have been, physically, easy) would not have been the annihilation of *sin.* John would have smitten *Herod;* Christ would smite the *guilt.* 4. The trouble which comes of temporal difficulty or sorrow,—it requires a bright eye to see across the chasm which separates a prison from heaven.

Christ's answer may be taken as showing *some phases of the Divine government :*—1. The Divine government in its beneficent purpose towards the human *body.* 2. The Divine government in its beneficent relations to the human *soul.* 3. The Divine government as vindicating itself by *good works.* 4. The Divine government as administered by Christ, —all these works are but revelations of what was in the infinite heart of God from all eternity. 5. The Divine government as exercising human patience,—" Blessed is he whosoever shall not be offended in me,"—offended in my method of working, my longsuffering and patience; blessed is he who trusts and waits, even though he must trust in darkness and wait in a prison.

7. And as they departed, Jesus began to say unto the multitudes concerning John, What went ye out into the wilderness to see? A reed shaken with the wind?

8. But what went ye out for to see? A man clothed in soft raiment? Behold, they that wear soft clothing are in king's houses.

9. But what went ye out for to see? A prophet? Yea, I say unto you, and more than a prophet.

10. For this is he, of whom it is written, Behold, I send my messenger before thy face, which shall prepare thy way before thee.

11. Verily I say unto you, Among them that are born of women there hath not risen a greater than John the Baptist; notwithstanding he that is least in the kingdom of heaven is greater than he.

This is CHRIST'S DISCOURSE CONCERNING JOHN. This discourse is specially noticeable as showing Christ's spirit in relation to a *reverent doubter*. Lest the people should undervalue John's mission, or attach a false meaning to his momentary misgiving, Christ enlarges upon his personal dignity and official authority in this noble and defensive discourse. Christ was never harsh to devout doubters, yet he never failed to pronounce those "blessed" whose faith was unclouded. Witness the case of Thomas—"Blessed are they that have not seen, and yet have believed;"—and witness this case of John's—"Blessed is he whosoever shall not be offended in me." This was Christ's two-fold method, viz., to teach the Doubter, and "bless" the Believer; too often the so-called Christian Church hates the doubter or avoids him as a leper. That Church may well know the meaning of the declaration that this doubting forerunner of Christ was actually "*more than a prophet.*"

1. Some men require to be explained. 2. Some men are placed in circumstances which suggest a variety of false interpretations respecting their mission. 3. The true man will be finally explained and vindicated by God Himself.

Society has three methods of looking upon an extraordinary man:—1. As fickle, changeful, and uncertain,—"a reed shaken with the wind." 2. As self-seeking, loving ease and comfort,—"a man clothed in soft raiment." 3. As a true and well-credited man, who deserves attention,—"a prophet, and more than a prophet." The extraordinary man has generally to work his way to the third position. He is seldom looked upon as a prophet at first.

In this discourse Christ does three things:—1. He sets Himself forth as an interpreter of prophecy,—"This is he of whom it is written." Christ knew well all that the inspired records contained; look, *e.g.*, to the way in which He answered the tempter. 2. He determines the gradations of human eminence,—"there hath not risen a greater,"—(*a*) Men *do* vary in power; (*b*) Christ knows each man's capacity; (*c*) Variations of power do not impair moral claims,—the feeblest man may be *good*. 3. He asserts the superiority of the Christian life to every other,—" He that is least in the kingdom of heaven is greater than he." Not only do men differ, but eras, kingdoms, spheres differ. Men are affected by the dignity of the kingdom in which they live,—hence there is a greatness which comes upon a man from the outside; men are also partakers of the greatness of the kingdom which they voluntarily adopt. This is a greatness superior to the former, inasmuch as it touches the nature of the man rather than his mere circumstances. The 11th verse may be taken as suggesting, *The Responsibilities which attach to Relative Positions of Life*. The men of Tyre and Sidon will be judged by the light which they had; the men of Capernaum will be judged by a clearer light. Pagans will not be judged by Christian law. How can the least in one kingdom be greater than the greatest of another? John was the greatest man outside of Christianity, yet the least man in Christianity is greater than he. How so? The simplest flower of the field is greater than the most exquisite artificial flower; for nature is greater than art: the feeblest infant is greater than the most elaborate statue; for life is greater than marble:

the youngest son is greater than the oldest servant ; for love lies deeper than covenants and bonds.

This representation (verse 11) shows *the immense value which is attached by Christ to every member of His kingdom.* This idea runs through the whole of His discourses. He is ever jealously watchful of "one of these little ones," and "the least of these my brethren." Christ dwelt much upon the value of *individuals;*—one piece out of ten, and one sheep out of a hundred must be sought, found, and restored! Had the woman lost all the ten, and the shepherd all the hundred, they could not have done more than they did. These are hints of what Christ Himself attempted. Innumerable worlds kept their first estate, yet He came after the earth as if it were the only world.

12. And from the days of John the Baptist until now the kingdom of heaven suffereth violence, and the violent take it by force.
13. For all the prophets and the law prophesied until John.
14. And if ye will receive it, this is Elias, which was for to come.
15. He that hath ears to hear, let him hear.

This indicates the demonstrativeness which attended the ministry of John, and the ministry of Christ Himself. The idea may be paraphrased thus :—Up till the time of John the Baptist the kingdom of heaven was matter of prophecy ; men were hoping for it, and daily looking for it, but all was quiet, people were hushed by a great expectancy, but from the days of John the Baptist there has been much demonstration, there has been a call to repentance, there has been a call to baptism, John terminated the line of the prophets and the law, and the silence of the written word has been broken by a voice crying in the wilderness, and now the people who are most in earnest will take possession of the kingdom of heaven,—the victory, the honour will be given to enthusiasm, passion, violence,—" *Strive* to enter in at the strait gate ! "

Verse 14 shows that it is possible to miss a *fact* while looking for a *name*.

The people were looking for Elias, not knowing that he had already come in the person of John. The blessing is often near when we think it is distant. "There standeth one among you whom ye know not, he it is," &c.

16. But whereunto shall I liken this generation? It is like unto children sitting in the markets, and calling unto their fellows.

17. And saying, we have piped unto you, and ye have not danced; we have mourned unto you, and ye have not lamented.

18. For John came neither eating nor drinking, and they say, He hath a devil.

19. The Son of man came eating and drinking, and they say, Behold a man gluttonous and a wine-bibber, a friend of publicans and sinners. But wisdom is justified of her children.

1. A childish generation, like a childish man, necessarily takes a childish view of things. 2. The most extraordinary men have to undergo the judgment of the most childish judges. 3. Childish judges always determine by the accidental, not by the essential,—by eating and drinking, not by character or principles.

Christ wished men to become like children; why, then, did He complain of "this generation," when it was like unto children? The answer may be found in the difference between *childishness* and *childlikeness*.

The relation of Christ to the enjoyments of this life is shown in the 19th verse. Christ came eating and drinking; He enjoyed the gifts of God; He mingled freely with men. The Christian life does not forbid enjoyment: it allows a man to eat and drink freely, but gives him power to govern his appetite. The strong man is not he who avoids temptation, but he who meets it and vanquishes it. The man who fasts is under John's dispensation. In Christ men have liberty. Wisdom will be justified of her children in either case. Some men require to mortify themselves, others are stronger in moral power; the wisdom of each is to act according to his gift. The continent man may be trusted at any table; the incontinent man would gluttonise upon the poorest fare. Continence is entirely a question of the spirit.

20. Then began he to upbraid the cities wherein most of his mighty works were done, because they repented not:
21. Woe unto thee, Chorazin! Woe unto thee, Bethsaida! for if the mighty works which were done in you had been done in Tyre and Sidon, they would have repented long ago in sackcloth and ashes.
22. But I say unto you, It shall be more tolerable for Tyre and Sidon in the day of judgment, than for you.
23. And thou, Capernaum, which art exalted unto heaven, shall be brought down to hell : for if the mighty works, which have been done in thee, had been done in Sodom, it would have remained until this day.
24. But I say unto you, That it shall be more tolerable for the land of Sodom in the day of judgment, than for thee.

Then why were the mighty works not done? Why was Sodom destroyed when by a few mighty works it would have remained until this day? Was it not a waste of power to bestow miracles uselessly upon Chorazin, Bethsaida, and Capernaum, when, according to Christ's own statement, the very same miracles would have saved Tyre and Sidon and Sodom? In reply, three things may be suggested:— 1. God's plan requires time for its fulfilment. 2. In the days of the ancient cities the Christian miracles would have been premature. 3. God has acted as a Sovereign throughout the whole of His government. All this, however, is entirely unsatisfactory. If men have been lost when they might by a further disclosure of God's power have been saved, then God must be held accountable for the issue. The explanation is to be found in the expression, "more tolerable." The ancient cities will not be judged by modern advantages. God cannot judge the spring by the autumn. This lament on the part of Christ shows that *the moral is not co-ordinate with the miraculous.* The moral influence of miracles was comparatively limited. Upon the healed men, of course, it was often effectual, but how few of all the countless observers, professed change of heart simply in consequence of the miracles!

Christ's reproach of the cities shows:—1. That every worker should look for the results of his labour; and, 2. That the mightiest workers cannot command success. The world is not dying for want of good preaching, but for want of good hearing.

25. At that time Jesus answered, and said, I thank thee, O Father, Lord of heaven and earth, because thou hast hid these things from the wise and prudent, and hast revealed them unto babes.
26. Even so, Father; for so it seemeth good in thy sight.

This is a hint as to God's method of revelation. 1. The world's wisdom is ignored. 2. The simplest minds have the clearest disclosures. The history of civilisation, apart from evangelical truth, illustrates precisely the same fact. How much is secular civilisation indebted for discoveries and inventions to royal and aristocratic persons? Take from modern science and art all that such persons have contributed by way of direct discovery, and how much poorer would the world be? But take away the poor man's contributions, and modern civilisation would be annihilated. This arrangement (for so marvellous are the facts that they do constitute a plan) has three advantages:— 1. It shows that manhood lies deeper than the mere accidents of birth and station; 2. It preserves the balance of society, so that the power does not preponderate in one direction; 3. It shows that spiritual power comes from the root and core of society, and is not the property of any one section.

27. All things are delivered unto me of my Father: and no man knoweth the Son, but the Father; neither knoweth any man the Father, save the Son, and he to whomsoever the Son will reveal him.

Christ Himself was one of the "babes" to whom "these

things" were revealed. His contemporaries asked, Whence has this man this wisdom? He was more than simply one of the babes, He here claims to be the treasurer of all things. The important points in this statement are:—1. That the Father is not personally known; 2. That the Son personally knows the Father, and has, therefore, an advantage over all other men, for "no man knoweth the Father save the Son;" 3. That the Son is the only revealer of the Father to men,—" He to whomsoever the Son will reveal him." This places Christ in the most sublime relation to the human race. In every sense He is the *Mediator*. Through Him, as through an atmosphere, the glory of the Godhead descends upon the vision of men. His words have more in them than the meaning of common language; they shadow forth, as the ages may be able to bear, the purposes of the unseen but all-seeing Father.

28. Come unto me, all ye that labour and are heavy laden, and I will give you rest.
29. Take my yoke upon you, and learn of me; for I am meek and lowly in heart: and ye shall find rest unto your souls.
30. For my yoke is easy, and my burden is light.

1. Do you know what *weariness* is? Weariness of the *body*, weariness of the *mind*, weariness of the *heart*. 2. Rest? Body, mind, heart. 3. The "coming" is man's, the "giving" is Christ's,—we are co-workers. 4. The invitation is co-extensive with the distress.

What is the connection between "meekness" and "rest"? Christ says, " For I am meek and lowly in heart, and ye shall find rest," as if there was a logical connection between meekness and rest. So there is, undoubtedly,— *Passion* can never be at rest: rest expresses a *moral* condition. (*a*) *Selfishness* can never be at rest. (*b*) *Crime* can never be at rest. (*c*) *Ambition* can never be at rest.

Verse 30. 1. My yoke is easy,—then how men have

mistaken the Christian life! 2. My burden is light,— then all burdens may be avoided as unchristian. Some men's religion is a toil, a slavery, a perpetual gloom; it may be religion, but it is not the religion of *Christ*.

*CHAPTER XII.*

1. At that time Jesus went on the sabbath day through the corn; and his disciples were an hungered, and began to pluck the ears of corn and to eat.
2. But when the Pharisees saw it, they said unto him, Behold, thy disciples do that which is not lawful to do upon the sabbath day.
3. But he said unto them, Have ye not read what David did, when he was an hungered, and they that were with him;
4. How he entered into the house of God, and did eat the shewbread, which was not lawful for him to eat, neither for them which were with him, but only for the priests?
5. Or have ye not read in the law, how that on the sabbath days the priests in the temple profane the sabbath, and are blameless?
6. But I say unto you, That in this place is one greater than the temple.
7. But if ye had known what this meaneth, I will have mercy and not sacrifice, ye would not have condemned the guiltless.
8. For the Son of man is Lord even of the sabbath day.
9. And when he was departed thence, he went into their synagogue.

I. "His disciples were an hungered." All positive laws must yield to man's necessities. The law as a formal commandment may be broken, yet its spirit may be honoured. An illustration is supplied in this incident. Hunger must be appeased, else life would suffer; and throughout all the Divine economy the importance of life, specially of human life, is signally indicated. Life must be first satisfied, afterwards law may be observed, but law is nothing apart from life.

II. There is a relation of life to positive laws; there is a relation to moral law which is higher, and more exacting. The man who dies of hunger because some positive enactment binds him to a certain course, is guilty of suicide;

but the man who dies of hunger rather than break a moral law is the subject of martyrdom.

III. Christ shows that in all ages circumstances have arisen which have necessitated a violation of literal Sabbatism,—David ate the shewbread, and the priests profaned the temple, and yet were guiltless.

Christ's answer to the Pharisees shows:—1. That exceptional circumstances must be provided for under all dispensations; 2. That profanation of the Sabbath, as in the case of the priests, is blameless if it be the result of the necessities of life; and, 3. That the observance of all law is a question of the spirit rather than of the letter,—of " mercy " rather than " sacrifice."

Sabbath observance must be determined by the spirit. No man can literally, under all circumstances, keep the fourth commandment, yet all men may keep it in spirit. God " rested,"—man must rest. Whenever man rests from his usual occupation he admits the Sabbatic *principle*, whatever he may contend as to the details of the case. If man does *not* rest from his labours, he does not follow the example of God, and by so much he makes himself wiser than God, and so by a roundabout process he proves himself to be a fool. The fool always lives an expensive life,—he wastes his nervous force, he weakens his intellectual power, he diminishes his moral capacity, he rots away into the lowest degree of manhood, and only stops there because there is no deeper humiliation.

10. And, behold, there was a man which had his hand withered. And they asked him, saying, Is it lawful to heal on the sabbath day? that they might accuse him.

11. And he said unto them, What man shall there be among you, that shall have one sheep, and if it fall into a pit on the sabbath day, will he not lay hold on it, and lift it out?

12. How much then is a man better than a sheep? Wherefore it is lawful to do well on the sabbath days.

13. Then saith he to the man, Stretch forth thine hand. And he stretched it forth ; and it was restored whole, like as the other.

Christ adopts the analogical and cumulative method of argument : from the few points which His adversaries were prepared to grant, He reasoned to conclusions which they would gladly have escaped. He shows again and again that man does in *his* little sphere precisely as God does in the universe, and thus by a large concession to the rational element in man, He carries His hearers irresistibly to the results which He came to establish. The Pharisees allowed that it was right to save a *sheep*, yet they quibbled about the healing of a *man!* It was enough for Christ's purpose that they granted the first, and He consequently proceeded to show that the legitimate expansion of their own principle would involve the very act on His part of which they complained. The incident shows—1. That prejudice may restrain the exercise of benevolence; 2. That men (such as the Pharisees) may put religious inquiries in a very irreligious spirit; 3. That right-doing should be prosecuted in the very presence of the most resolute opposition ; 4. That well-*doing*, not well-*talking*, is the true method of keeping the Sabbath-day.

Dr. ADAM CLARKE has well said that "there are *four* ways in which positive laws may cease to oblige. First, by the natural law of *necessity :* Secondly, by *a particular law* which is *superior :* Thirdly, by the *law of charity* and *mercy :* Fourthly, by the *dispensation* and *authority* of the *lawgiver.*"

14. Then the Pharisees went out, and held a council against him, how they might destroy him.
15. But when Jesus knew it, he withdrew himself from thence : and great multitudes followed him, and he healed them all ;
16. And charged them that they should not make him known ;
17. That it might be fulfilled which was spoken by Esaias the prophet, saying,
18. Behold my servant, whom I have chosen; my beloved, in whom my

soul is well pleased : I will put my spirit upon him, and he shall show judgment to the Gentiles.

19. He shall not strive, nor cry ; neither shall any man hear his voice in the streets.

20. A bruised reed shall he not break, and smoking flax shall he not quench, till he send forth judgment unto victory.

21. And in his name shall the Gentiles trust.

Here is another instance of the Pharisees taking one course, and the multitudes another; the former were inspired with envy, the latter were conscious of most painful need. These two states of mind, with all the modifications which lie between them, explain the treatment which Christ has ever received at the hands of men. The whole paragraph may be used homiletically to show :—1. The action of the Pharisees: 2. The action of the multitudes : 3. The action of the Saviour. The action of the *Pharisees* shows the operation of an envious spirit :—1. It blinds the mind to a right interpretation of the prophetic and historic writings ; 2. It sets laws of arrangement above laws of life ; 3. It sacrifices human happiness to the dignity of effete dogmas ; 4. It hates and seeks to destroy every manifestation of God which does not comport with its own preconceptions. The action of the *multitudes* shows:—1. That bodily suffering may develop a courage superior to the tyranny of sectarian prejudice ; 2. That men are impelled to seek the Saviour more earnestly through suffering than through speculation ; 3. That suffering men are more anxious to follow a practical philanthropist than a conventionally recognised theorist. The action of *Christ* shows :—1. That prudence is an element of the highest courage ; 2. That the *prevention* of mischief was as much His business as its *cure ;* 3. That the foiling of an evil design need not prevent the fulfilment of a good one— " he healed them all;" 4. That the most vital and stupendous results may be obtained without vicious excitement ; 5. That the most exciting predictions may be fulfilled in the quietest life. Noise has never done much for the world. "The greatest objects in nature are the stillest."

22. Then was brought unto him one possessed with a devil, blind, and dumb : and he healed him, insomuch that the blind and dumb both spake and saw.
23. And all the people were amazed, and said, Is this the Son of David?
24. But when the Pharisees heard it, they said, This fellow doth not cast out devils, but by Beelzebub the prince of the devils.
25. And Jesus knew their thoughts, and said unto them, Every kingdom divided against itself is brought to desolation ; and every city or house divided against itself shall not stand :
26. And if Satan cast out Satan, he is divided against himself ; how shall then his kingdom stand?
27. And if I by Beelzebub cast out devils, by whom do your children cast them out ? therefore they shall be your judges.
28. But if I cast out devils by the Spirit of God, then the kingdom of God is come unto you.

The Pharisees are once more at their work. They knew of two causes to which great effects were commonly attributed—namely, God and the devil; and you have only to give some men the remotest possible opportunity of crediting the devil with any work, and they will, with the most indecent eagerness, avail themselves of it. The argument of the Pharisees was not devoid of ingenuity ; it seems to take some such turn as this,—"Christ and the devil are in league; they are, apparently, or even really, casting out devils now, so that they may attract attention and widen their influence; all this expulsion of devils seems very well at present, but by feigning to commit suicide the devil is actually getting men more entirely into his power, the whole thing is a deep-laid plot, he casteth out devils by Beelzebub, the prince of the devils." The reply of Christ struck at the root of this sophism, and His personal home-thrust covered them with confusion :—"And if I by Beelzebub cast out devils, by whom do your children, your associates, your recognised exorcists, cast them out ?" It is remarkable how in every case Christ found some point in the creed or life of His adversaries on which to base a defence of Himself; in every case He cut off the head of Goliath with Goliath's own sword. They who fight against God are whetting weapons for their own destruction !

This was an extraordinary case of healing; the man was possessed with a devil, blind and dumb. The human system could not have been more thoroughly despoiled. The man stood off at the extreme end of society,—as near death as a poor shattered life could be while yet numbered among men. Every human voice had failed to recall him to consciousness, or to give him completeness as a man. Christ came for the express purpose of seeking and saving the *lost*, and now a lost man, in a special sense, was before Him, a humiliating and saddening spectacle. A word was enough—"he healed him, insomuch that the blind and dumb both spake and saw." Christ was ever seeking the *completeness* of human nature,— the fulfilment of God's ideal; and in this case, as in every other, His power and His love prevailed against the devil. It was such an occasion as might have filled all hearts with holy joy, and brought all spirits in reverent and loving homage to the Saviour's feet, yet the Pharisees pronounced the cure a devil's trick, and blasphemed against God. The best protest which we can offer against the pharisaic spirit is—1. To remember that Jesus Christ is still the healer of humanity; and, 2. To make continual application to Him until the whole purpose of His redemption is complete in our nature,—body, soul, and spirit. It is not only possible but easy while denouncing the pharisaic *name* to be cultivating the pharisaic *spirit*.

So far as we have proceeded in this chapter, we have had repeated illustrations of the obstructiveness of the Pharisees. See how the case stands: the Pharisees complained of the disciples for eating the ears of corn; the Pharisees reproached

Christ for healing the withered hand on the Sabbath day; the Pharisees went out and held a council against Him; the Pharisees said that He cast out devils by Beelzebub the prince of the devils. Thus at every step they opposed Him; when He moved, He moved through the centre of an armed host. Nothing but infinite love could have carried Him through dangers so numerous and terrible; He went with His life in His hand,—His whole life was a lingering death,—His entire service was an atonement for the sins of the world.

29. Or else how can one enter into a strong man's house, and spoil his goods, except he first bind the strong man? and then he will spoil his house.

30. He that is not with me is against me; and he that gathereth not with me scattereth abroad.

The enemy of man is well represented as being "strong." There is this difference between the strength of God and the strength of the devil,—God's strength is employed in the salvation, and Satan's in the destruction of man. The work of destruction is always easy, so that a little strength goes a great way. The fact that the devil is strong should—1. Inspire men with continual fear of his temptations; and, 2. Impel them towards Christ to seek the only strength which can overcome them. In the thirtieth verse, Christ presents Himself as the man by whom all men should either rise or fall. He was the standard, so that men knew whether they were right or wrong according as they stood in an affirmative or a negative relation to Himself. These claims to priority are invaluable collateral illustrations of His divinity. They establish that marvellous *consistency* of His character which more than any mere statement or reasoning gives one to feel that He was not of the world, and that the world without Him would be a world without life or light. Men say that union is strength; this is true, but it should be remembered that *individuality* is also strength. The man who is divided against himself is weak ; the man whose convictions, sympathies, and actions all move in one direction is mighty either for good or evil.

The whole paragraph may receive fuller treatment thus:—
Imagine the spectacle—a *man* "possessed with a devil, blind, and dumb." Here is more of Satan's work. His way may be tracked by the ruins he has wrought. Blood-pools are his footprints. Darkness is his mantle. His whole force is directed against the temple of manhood. As I gaze on this melancholy sight, it speaks to me, saying, "I am but a picture of what Satan would make the whole world!" He would enthrone himself on every intellect. He would poison all love-streams. He would close the eye, that it might no longer dwell upon the glories of the universe. Every song of hope, every anthem of joy, he would silence; and when all men were fully under his dominion, he would announce his triumph with shouts of scornful laughter, and would gaze with pride on a universal hell. I wish you, then, to take this demon-bound, blind, dumb man, as a sample of Satan's work —as an indication of what he would make of yourselves but for the restraint of a merciful and omnipotent God.

I shall use this incident,—

I. TO SHOW THE GOOD MAN'S RELATION TO THE WORLD OF WANT.

This world is a wide one. It embraces the physical, mental, and moral nature of man. The world's great empty hand is evermore thrust out in token of deep and urgent necessity; and its imploring, want-revealing eye is ever looking for a Helper. You need not force your way to the abodes of poverty, squalor, and misery, to find lean, hungry, eager *want*. You may find it in every home, because you may find it in every heart. It has its manifold modifications indeed, but there it is—its bosom an aching void, its voice an everlasting appeal. Into this world of want the gentle

Saviour—the Good Man—came; and as I observe Him, with all the dignity of essential divinity, and yet with the tremulous tenderness of sympathetic manhood, walking up and down among the children of men—gazing upon them through His pure tears, shedding upon them His living smile, touching them with His brotherly hand, and speaking to them with His voice of love—I see in Him, and His work, the Good Man's relation to the world of want.

And around this relation many ideas—blushing with divinest beauty—cluster. Take three of them :—

First. *The Good Man is approachable.* He did not isolate Himself in gloomy grandeur, and do His deeds of mercy at an immeasurable distance. He might have done so. He might have hidden Himself, either in a pavilion of light or a tabernacle of darkness, and scattered His blessings thence. Instead of this chilling isolation, we find the holy Saviour mingling with men—communing with the inquirer, hearkening to the needy, feeding the hungry, and blessing all. Even little children could find access to the arms which were to be stretched in sacrificial death, and infancy was not too feeble to sustain the tender blessing of a tender Saviour. Do you ever find Him too weary to help the helpless? Does He ever plead His own indulgence as a reason for not receiving others? Never!—blessed be His sacred name—never!

Second. *The Good Man is sympathetic.* Jesus did not do His miracles as mere feats of power—as displays of proud ability. He often came to His work with tears. His sympathy trembled with compassion, and dissolved in showers, before He put forth the arm of His irresistible power! I have often been struck with the manner in which power was preceded by sympathy. It might have been otherwise. Miracles need not have been softened, mellowed, beautified by tenderness. The tear of sympathy need not have preceded the shout of power at the grave of Lazarus. But it did, and we thank God for it! God walked forth on the wings of the power, but man trembled in the tear. It was a glorious union. Power with a tear in its eye,—the eyelids of Omnipotence wet with the tears of sympathy. Ay, that is mystery—that is GOD!

Third. *The Good Man is unostentatious.* "And He healed him." Such is the simple phraseology in which this stupendous act is transmitted to posterity! What a mass of meaning is condensed into that little phrase! The devils banished—sight revelling in countless glories—mouth opened in song,—all wrapt up in that simple statement,—" And He healed him"! Many a man has made more demonstration in the simplest act of charity than Christ made in His sublimest, His world-amazing deeds. The angel named Charity, nightingale-like, sings her soft, rich, mellow song in the hush of midnight, with few listeners but the silent, bright-eyed stars. Love, charity, sympathy, and the other celestial sisters, run their errands noiselessly. They do not "strive or cry, neither doth any man hear their voice in the streets:" they are gentle-handed—"the bruised reed" they never broke; they are tender-hearted—"the smoking flax" they never quenched!

Such is the Good Man in his relation to the world of want. What Christ was, we should be in our degree. We must, indeed, move at a humble distance, but our business is to move in the same direction. We should be approachable, sympathetic, unostentatious, and thus reflect the splendour of a peerless example.

I use this incident,—

II. TO SHOW THE DEVIL'S RELATION TO GOOD MEN.

I take those captious Pharisees as a type of the devil; and I think not unjustly so, for they are doing the devil's work. Regarding them in this capacity, I am warranted in making this second use of the incident,—How did those devil's men use Christ?

First. *They resorted to personal abuse,*—" This fellow." Nothing easier than to use bad names; but bad names are bad arguments. When your opponent is driven to personal abuse he is driven to his wit's end, and you may safely leave him. Never throw mud. You *may* miss your mark, but you *must* have dirty hands. "This fellow" is no argument, it is scurrility—it is a faint spark of hell-fire; the man who throws that would throw something deadlier if he could.

Second. *They ignored the value of the greatest blessings.* They could not deny that the devil was gone, but were they *glad* that he was gone? So with the enemies of good men now. Good men are doing great deeds in the name of God, but there are many detractors. Even ministers are occasionally guilty of this habit of detraction in relation to their brother ministers. They cannot bear that their brethren should cast out *too many devils:* they don't care for an imp or two being expelled, but there is a point beyond which fraternal jealousy shows its glaring eyes, its clenched teeth, and its pitiless sword. Such men always endeavour to make a brother's success appear as little as possible. If, by changing an accent or modifying an emphasis, they can reduce a little, they are prone to avail themselves of these pitiful trickeries. Be it known, however, that such is not the Gospel spirit : it may be robed in the silk of orthodoxy, and bound with the purest white, but it is not heaven-born, and cannot be heaven-tending.

Third. *They insulted the plainest common sense.* Jesus knew their thoughts, and exposed the hollowness of their reasoning. He tore their sophistry to rags. "Every kingdom divided against itself is brought to desolation ; and every city or house divided against itself shall not stand. And if Satan cast out Satan, he is divided against himself; how then shall his kingdom stand?" In this pointed manner did Jesus show how common sense was outraged. But what is common sense to men who have an object to gain? They are determined to be at a certain point, and, if common sense stand in the way, cut it down—bury it beneath the most scornful insults, and gain their point. It is even so with the enemies of the Cross now; they can trample upon the simplest rules of argument, they can defame the holy name of reason, and turn the sacred temple of conscience into a place of fradulent merchandise.

Fourth. *They attempted to trace good results to a bad cause.* What do such men care for philosophy? It is nothing in their way to ascribe good to evil; they know that a corrupt fountain can bring forth pure streams,—they know that "cause and effect" is an old sophism, hatched by a school of sleepy-headed, brooding philosophers. It is the same with the enemies of Christ now. When a man is converted, and becomes a new creature, there are many ready to ignore the Holy Spirit, and the "precious blood" of Jesus, and to attribute the change to education, or example, or even to the devil himself,—to any one rather than to God.

Fifth. *They falsified the deepest and truest instincts of human nature.* "And if I by Beelzebub cast out devils, by whom do your children cast them out?" Still, you observe, they plunge headlong into ruin; they have overthrown common sense; they have laughed philosophy to scorn, and now let parental affection go too. The copestone once off, the wall soon disappears. They are quite willing that their children should be proclaimed the emissaries of Satan—anything; anything that Christ's honour might be smitten, and Christ's heart stabbed. They were bent on murder, and whatever or whoever stood in their way must bear the consequence of their fiery madness.

31. Wherefore I say unto you, All manner of sin and blasphemy shall be forgiven unto men : but the blasphemy against the Holy Ghost shall not be forgiven unto men.

32. And whosoever speaketh a word against the Son of man, it shall be forgiven him: but whosoever speaketh against the Holy Ghost, it shall not be forgiven him, neither in this world, neither in the world to come.

This doctrine will receive its true elucidation by reviewing the preceding verses. The climax of guilt had been nearly reached by the Pharisees, when they charged Christ with Satanic complicity in casting out devils. They had "spoken a word against the Son of man," and their madness was thereby nearly reaching the fatal point. Whether this extraordinary and much-controverted passage has yet received its true exposition may be doubted. The meaning seems to be this—"I am the Son of man; there are features about my method of revealing myself to the world which may stagger the prejudices of you Pharisees; I am poor, lonely, unprotected, and unpatronised by influential men; my incarnation has shocked all your anticipations; then be it known to you that though God may condescend to save you as parties belonging to the former dispensation, yet henceforth, after my ascension, I shall be revealed to men by the Holy Ghost, who shall take of mine and show it unto them ; and then whosoever shall speak against the Holy Ghost will speak against me, and having done so will have rejected the only method of salvation, and thus incurred a guilt which will cleave to him in all worlds, through all time."

This meaning:—1. Simplifies the expression; and 2. *Saves the co-equality of Christ with the Spirit.* Jesus Christ, not the Holy Ghost, is the Redeemer and Saviour of men ; our iniquities were laid upon Him, and by His stripes we are healed. The whole burden of redemption having been sustained by Him, it would, therefore, be inexplicable if the Redeemer could be dishonoured with impunity, and if the Holy Spirit, whose function is to reveal and glorify Him, could be spoken against in His simple individuality, without unpardonable guilt being the result. This interpretation degrades the person and work of Christ; but the meaning which had been suggested proceeds upon the ground that the Holy Spirit is the revealer of Christ, that Christ is the only way of salvation, and that by speaking against the Revealing Spirit men are also speaking against the Redeeming Son, and thus rendering themselves inexcusable and unpardonable. This meaning, and to it we attach immense importance, 3, gives us *a more hopeful view than any other of the fate of Christ's betrayers and murderers.* Christ Himself said—"They know not what they do:" the Holy Ghost was not then given in connection with His name; men saw only the Son of man according to the flesh, and in a mistaken zeal for God they put Christ to death. In our day, however, we stand on a different basis; the work of Christ has been completed; He is now represented by the Spirit, and to speak against the Spirit is to rebel against the whole economy of redemption, and he who does that cannot be forgiven.

Another interpretation is that the sin against the Holy Ghost is simply the sin of attributing Divine operations to Satanic agency. This view is supported by Mark's report of the discourse—"Verily I say unto you, All sins shall be forgiven unto the sons of men, and blasphemies wherewith soever they shall blaspheme, but he that shall blaspheme against the Holy Ghost hath never forgiveness, but is in danger of eternal damnation: because they said, He hath an unclean spirit." (Mark iii. 28—30.) This is in perfect harmony with the meaning which has been suggested, viz., that *the spiritual is inclusive:* Christ in the flesh was a link in a chain; Christ risen and glorified, and represented by the Spirit, is the fulness and glory of God.

He who seeks to turn God Himself into an unclean spirit can never be forgiven. As to persons frightening themselves lest they have committed the inexpiable sin, the old answer is still the best, viz., if they had done so they would have been totally indifferent to consequences.

33. Either make the tree good, and his fruit good; or else make the tree corrupt, and his fruit corrupt : for the tree is known by his fruit.

Christ demands consistency in every argument or imputation. He had been doing a good work, and the Pharisees traced it to a bad cause; He now rebukes them by saying: " Have some respect for your own consistency as reasoners —not only call me a bad tree but call that cured man bad fruit, for the tree is known by his fruit." Thus Christ stands or falls with His own works. Again and again He insisted on putting the works forward as a basis of faith in Himself. Christ abides by the simple law of cause and effect; a bad man may do an occasional good deed (good by the outside), but the life that is uniformly beneficent, being inspired by a good motive, is necessarily good. Christ, then, reduced the argument concerning Himself to the simplest possible limits—He pointed to a pure stream, and contended that such a stream could come only from a pure fountain.

34. O generation of vipers, how can ye, being evil, speak good things? for out of the abundance of the heart the mouth speaketh.

35. A good man out of the good treasure of the heart bringeth forth good things : and an evil man out of the evil treasure bringeth forth evil things.

He now retorts upon His accusers. He moves along the same line of argument, the line of cause and effect, and directly accuses them of bad-heartedness: from bad hearts bad words may be expected; where the heart is wrong the whole thought and speech and habit are wrong. Christ thus goes to the core of all mischief, and so proves that

He well understands the nature which He has come to redeem.

36. But I say unto you, That every idle word that men shall speak, they shall give account thereof in the day of judgment.
37. For by thy words thou shalt be justified, and by thy words thou shalt be condemned.

This gives us a most solemn view of *words*. Language is the principal medium of communication between man and man; by it thought is disclosed and purpose is stated; by it covenants are made, and upon its interpretation great speculations are based; if, therefore, language be vitiated, or used with double meanings, or anywise distorted, the most disastrous results may follow. It may seem an easy thing merely to *speak* against God or man, but there may be blasphemy in a word—there may be poison in a syllable. Solemn subjects demand solemn treatment. The Divine name is not to be profanely pronounced, and human character is to be treated as a sacred possession. Great destinies may hang upon a word; the peace of a day or of a lifetime may be broken by a harsh expression. This text has been quoted in condemnation of all pleasantry, but this is a perversion of its meaning—altogether a pointless and most absurd application of its import. The primary, and indeed exclusive, reference is to the most solemn subject that can engage human attention, and upon *such* a subject no idle word must be spoken; *men must not talk irreligiously about religion;* men may enjoy to the utmost all wit and laughter, but are forbidden to talk insincerely or ambiguously upon solemn subjects.

While bad speaking is thus condemned, good speaking is enjoined by implication. Bad men are not slow to show their corrupt spirit; nor should good men be too timid to bear their testimony in God's name. When the heart is right, the tongue will be eloquent for God.

38. Then certain of the scribes and of the Pharisees answered, saying, Master, we would see a sign from thee.

39. But he answered and said unto them, An evil and adulterous generation seeketh after a sign ; and there shall no sign be given to it, but the sign of the prophet Jonas.

40. For as Jonas was three days and three nights in the whale's belly ; so shall the Son of man be three days and three nights in the heart of the earth.

41. The men of Nineveh shall rise in judgment with this generation, and shall condemn it : because they repented at the preaching of Jonas ; and, behold, a greater than Jonas is here.

42. The queen of the south shall rise up in the judgment with this generation, and shall condemn it : for she came from the uppermost parts of the earth to hear the wisdom of Solomon ; and, behold, a greater than Solomon is here.

Bad-hearted people can never be satisfied with the amount of evidence which is placed before them in illustration of Christ's divinity. They don't *want* Him to be Divine, and they consequently turn the very light into darkness. The Pharisees had seen sign upon sign, yet they asked for another, as if none had ever been granted. Christ gave them to know that the only sign which should be shown unto them was *His own immortality;* out of His death He would come up clothed with "all power in heaven and on earth;" the momentary eclipse would be succeeded by eternal light.

Every age is responsible to its own prophet—Nineveh to Jonah, England to Christ. Men are to be judged according to the degree of light under which they have lived. What, then, must be the judgment of England ? This prediction respecting the ages confronting one another in judgment is most suggestive. 1. Here is the fact of human resurrection —"the men of Nineveh shall *rise;*" "the queen of the south shall *rise;*" 2. Here is the fact of human judgment— "the men of Nineveh shall rise in *judgment,*" "the queen of the south shall rise up in the *judgment.*" Take the startling announcement that Christ is greater than Solomon. How greater? 1. Not in the abundance of secular possessions; 2. Not in the extent of political influence. How then? 1. In His perfect familiarity with the future; 2. In the infinite purity of His character; 3. In the spiritual resources at His command; (*a*) Solomon appealed to the intellectual nature, but Christ to the depraved and ruined heart; (*b*) Solomon's gifts were compatible with his own selfish enjoyment, but Christ's involved a sacrificial life and death; 4. In the posthumous relation which Christ sustains to men; (*a*) Solomon has no power to condemn or acquit; (*b*) Solomon himself must stand at the common bar. From the whole subject we may learn:—1. That Christ demands the supreme attention of the world; 2. That man becomes great in proportion to his union with Christ; 3. That the most terrible guilt is involved in the neglect of this last and greatest of the prophets of God.

43. When the unclean spirit is gone out of a man, he walketh through dry places, seeking rest, and findeth none.

44. Then he saith, I will return into my house from whence I came out; and when he is come, he findeth it empty, swept, and garnished.

45. Then goeth he, and taketh with himself seven other spirits more wicked than himself, and they enter in and dwell there : and the last state of that man is worse than the first. Even so shall it be also unto this wicked generation.

Christ is still continuing His discourse occasioned by the charge of casting out devils by Beelzebub. That charge aroused Him to the very depth of His being, directed as it was against the very divinity of God. The cured man is still the text. In these words Christ shows the awful fate of those who have undergone a *merely negative change;* the unclean spirit has been expelled, but the Holy Spirit has not been besought to enter. The unclean spirit cannot find rest away from the human heart; no sea was ever so restless as the great deep of an unclean spirit. The consequence is that the unclean spirit returns to the heart out of which it had been driven, and, if that heart be not occupied with engagements worthy of its nature and destiny, its last state shall be worse than its first. The great appeal suggested by this text is to persons who have ceased to do evil, but have not learned to do well; and the solemn fact to be pressed home upon every man is that *Salvation is not only deliverance from the devil, but perfect union with God.*

46. While he yet talked to the people, behold, his mother and his brethren stood without, desiring to speak with him.

47. Then one said unto him, Behold, thy mother and thy brethren stand without, desiring to speak with thee.

48. But he answered and said unto him that told him, Who is my mother? and who are my brethren?

49. And he stretched forth his hand toward his disciples, and said, Behold my mother and my brethren!

50. For whosoever shall do the will of my Father which is in heaven, the same is my brother, and sister, and mother.

This declaration respecting His kindred would serve to show: 1. The intense spirituality of Christ's mission; 2. The comprehensive philanthropy of Christ's heart; 3. The true nature of man's union with Christ; 4. The high privileges secured by a living union with the Saviour. This statement further shows: (*a*) That connection with Christ is not determined by social position; (*b*) That connection with Christ is not a question of mere physical affinity. A chivalrous queen is reported to have said that her country was her husband. Christ says that all who do His Father's will are His brethren! 1. There is but one infallible will; 2. This infallible will may be disregarded; 3. This infallible will appeals for universal obedience.

### GENERAL NOTE ON THE WHOLE CHAPTER.

The whole chapter shows how mighty must have been the motive which controlled the life of Christ; otherwise, with so much that was discouraging on the outside, He would have thrown up His mission in anger and disgust. The *religious* people were against Him; and this fact is not sufficiently pondered by those who estimate the difficulties of His position, or by those who are often discouraged in the same way. The "sinners" were not Christ's opponents. The thieves and the harlots did not take up stones to stone Him; on the contrary, the chief priests, the Pharisees, the Scribes, the conservative theologians, were against Him to a man! This is a most extraordinary, but most impressive and suggestive fact, not only as a point in history, but as a principle in daily life. The fact is not only historic, it has all the newness of to-day upon it. Whoever shall arise to do any great work in the world will have the professedly religious people against him. The religion of some hearts appears merely to have increased their pugnacity and morbid sensitiveness, without working in them any breadth of holy charity or any power of self-reserve. They would fight Christ Himself, were He to reappear in any other form than that which would harmonise with their preconceived notions. This is proved by the rigour of their denominationalism. Christendom is divided as clearly into Pharisees, Scribes, and Sadducees, as ever the Jews were. The Christ who would be welcomed by one sect would be suspected by other sects. This must be so, for the sects suspect one another, and seldom forego an opportunity of inflicting mutual injury. Here, then, is a solemn and startling fact, that Christ was opposed by all the religious people of His day. Yet, with passion of love He toiled through all the trouble of His work! He never lost a moment through petulance or retaliation; He never said, "Well, die if you like, I shall care no longer for you;" but, with patience which put all other patience to shame, He worked until the time of His tarrying among men expired, and even then He shed tears where He might have hurled lightnings. His Life was

Love; no other word is deep enough to reach its mystery—to explain its meaning. Yet to-day He is the Rejected Man; society treats Him as an enemy; men speak of Him so seldom that one would deem His a shadowed name, not fit to be pronounced; yes, even now, in a land that is covered with churches, Christ stands on the outside waiting to be invited—eager to be loved—but the Pharisee knows Him not, and charges Him with blasphemy.

Christ's relation to "sinners" is, however, to be looked at in the light of the fact that they had no deep religious convictions to be shocked. In their case, Christ had no theological preconceptions to overget; they were cast out and despised, consequently any gleam of hope which fell on their darkness was magnified by their grateful surprise: they little expected it, and, when it came, it was inexpressibly welcome. Another fact to be noted is, that when sinners came to Christ, they abandoned their sinfulness. They did not love Christ on the ground that He was indifferent to sin, or that He was such an one as themselves; they loved Him for love, and, though incapable of arbitrating between Him and the Pharisees upon theological differences, yet they felt that His heart glowed with the most ardent and exalted affection towards guilty, abject, and friendless sinners. It is common in our day to talk of Christ's companionship with sinners as though He really enjoyed irreligious society. No blacker blasphemy can be spoken against His holy name. "He was separate from sinners;" He touched that He might heal; His companionship was as a fire which purified the heart.

*CHAPTER XIII.*

1. The same day went Jesus out of the house, and sat by the sea-side.
2. And great multitudes were gathered together unto him, so that he went into a ship, and sat; and the whole multitude stood on the shore.

3. And he spake many things unto them in parables, saying, Behold, a sower went forth to sow;

4. And when he sowed, some seeds fell by the way-side, and the fowls came and devoured them up;

5. Some fell upon stony places, where they had not much earth: and forthwith they sprung up, because they had no deepness of earth:

6. And when the sun was up, they were scorched; and because they had no root, they withered away:

7. And some fell among thorns: and the thorns sprung up and choked them;

8. But other fell into good ground, and brought forth fruit, some an hundred-fold, some sixty-fold, some thirty-fold.

9. Who hath ears to hear, let him hear.

The work of Christ and the general preaching of the Gospel are represented in this simple illustration. From it we learn—1. *That a general proclamation is attended by particular results.* This is notable, because one would have imagined that any declaration of God's will would have elicited an instantaneous, universal, and satisfactory response. The only difference which could have been supposed would be that each would be striving to excel the other in prompt and reverent obedience. 2. We learn, secondly, *that those particular results are not to be attributed to any special arrangement on the part of the sower.* The sower went forth to sow the whole field, at the same time, with the same seed, and with the same purpose; with entire impartiality he moved along the courses of the field, and scattered the grain on the right hand and on the left. Looking at the case from his point of view, we might have expected that his labours would have been productive of the most satisfactory results. Sowers cannot control harvests. They may sow well, and be mocked by a lean and withered harvest. This marks not only a limitation of power on the part of man, but on the part of God also in moral operations. No man can be compelled to bring forth fruit unto God. A man may receive the best seed and let it rot; he may live under the most fertilising influences, and yet be barren of all holy fruits.

The startling practical reflection suggested by this circumstance is, that *men are not saved by having opportunities, but by improving them*. It is no light consideration that with God Himself for a sower we may be disappointed in the fruitfulness and quality of the harvest. This refutes the sophism, that if the Gospel were properly proclaimed, men would yield to it. The fault is not in the instrumentality. The ministry of Jesus Christ was in certain aspects a failure; there were vast breadths of the field which He sowed with a liberal hand, which bore no trace of His service. The world is not perishing for lack of good preaching. Never was preaching so excellent and so abundant as it is to-day, yet hardly one token of harvest can be seen. We may learn—3. *That hearers must themselves supply the conditions of spiritual success.* Look at the particulars for illustration: The wayside hearer listens to the word, but understandeth (regardeth) it not, and from want of attention the enemy is suffered to "catch away that which was sown in heart." The condition which this hearer should have brought with him is *meditation*. The word touched him only by the outside; he gave it no lodgment in his heart, never watered the seed, never protected the fences, never opened his spirit to its power. The seed was good, the soil was bad; the sower was God, the enemy the devil. See how the case stands: the sower is God, the field is the heart, the destroyer is the devil; and in order to disappoint the enemy, the heart must co-operate with God. Take the stony-ground hearer. He listens to the word with gladness. He thinks it a pleasant sound, and while the music is in his ear, he resolves to profit by the Holy Word. What condition is wanting in his case? It is well named " root in himself;" no reality and depth of nature; empty, trifling, unreflecting; easily moved, self-indulgent, pliable; all right in sunshine, but cowardly in darkness; loving the Gospel sound, but lacking courage to endure anything for the Gospel's sake. Such a hearer brings much disappointment to his minister. The starting tear, the responsive gleam, the ready assent, are mistaken by being over-valued by the zealous preacher. No man can live to much purpose who has "no root in himself," nothing upon which even God can work. Mark the possibility of *exhausting one's manhood;* throwing away, or allowing to die out, the germ which was given to be cultured and expanded into fruitfulness towards God! Think of a *man* being dead at the *roots!* The thorny-ground hearer is represented in all congregations: the seed is good, the soil itself even may not be of the worst quality; the man is simply *preoccupied;* his idea is that life depends entirely upon his own exertions, and he consequently works as if he had no spiritual sources to draw upon. Give him a perpetual Sabbath, and he will be attentive, and perhaps partly religious; but as the working-week begins, the old tyrannous mammon spirit masters him. There is an influence which seems to be born, or at least revived, every Monday morning, which overpowers the partial religiousness of the Sabbath. It is not to be understood that religious men are exempt from the cares of this world, or even the deceitfulness of riches; they have them all, but the spirit that is in them is greater than the spirit that is in the world, and they thereby overcome.

[The expression — "the deceitfulness of riches" is an excellent text for a sermon to the busy. It may also be the foundation of a discourse to young merchants. The deceitfulness is shown in several ways, such, for example, as—"I am laying up for a rainy day;" "I care nothing for wealth, except to do good with it;" "when I have realised a sufficient sum, I shall spend the remainder in works of benevolence." All these are sophisms. The rainy day may never come; the rich man seldom does as much good as he did when he was not half so rich; money likes money, and the difficulty is to know when a man has "sufficient." The subject might then be viewed in a graver aspect, viz.:— *the power of riches to choke the Divine word in man.* Think of a man selling his aspirations, his faculties, his capacities, *selling his soul* for gold! This love of money does not come upon a man all at once, but "deceitfully," until a nature which might have been open and generous, becomes shrivelled and impenetrable.]

In the course of the parable Christ uses language which has often been perverted, by being made to support a theology which is anything but Christian. This language is as follows:—

10. And the disciples came, and said unto him, Why speakest thou unto them in parables?
11. He answered and said unto them, Because it is given unto you to know the mysteries of the kingdom of heaven, but to them it is not given.
12. For whosoever hath, to him shall be given, and he shall have more abundance; but whosoever hath not, from him shall be taken away even that he hath.
13. Therefore speak I to them in parables: because they seeing, see not; and hearing, they hear not; neither do they understand.
14. And in them is fulfilled the prophecy of Esaias, which saith, By hearing ye shall hear, and shall not understand; and seeing ye shall see, and shall not perceive;
15. For this people's heart is waxed gross, and their ears are dull of hearing, and their eyes they have closed; lest at any time they should see with their eyes, and hear with their ears, and should understand with their heart, and should be converted, and I should heal them.

From this language it has been inferred that Christ simply mocked His hearers, knowing that they could not apprehend His meaning or follow His counsel. The heart instantly rebels against so diabolic a doctrine. Christ had great disclosures to make; so great that even towards the last He felt that He could not make them without straining the capacity of His own disciples:—"I have many things to say unto you, but ye cannot hear them now." This was the case after He had been with the disciples a considerable time; how much greater, then, was His difficulty of revelation at an earlier period, and to a promiscuous auditory? His words may be thus paraphrased: You are my disciples, and as such you know the principles and purposes of my kingdom, but at present these mysteries are not generally understood; as you have been called to this discipleship you shall be led more and more into an understanding of the mysteries of my kingdom, but those who are afar off shall be afterward instructed, and according as they supply the right conditions of progress will be their destiny; if they prove to be wayside or thorny ground, or stony-place hearers, they shall suffer accordingly, for from him that hath not shall be taken away even that he hath; therefore speak I unto them in parables, because they seeing with their natural eyes will not see with their spiritual eyes, and though they hear the word, yet they will not regard it in their heart, and in them is once more fulfilled the words of the prophet Esaias. That this shutting-up of the faculties was not a Divine act may be seen from the expression—"Their eyes they have closed," showing that the act was entirely their own. This view of the doctrine is corroborated by the kind of hindrances which Christ specifies, viz., Satanic temptation, no root in himself, the care of this world, and the deceitfulness of riches. Here is nothing extraordinary; we have here only the common class of difficulties and hindrances, so that the contemporaries of Christ were just as we ourselves are, and therefore the suggestion of judicial blindness and Divine fate is inappropriate and untenable. The most of the thoughts suggested by the parable of the sower might be comprehended in a discourse upon *the history of the Divine Word among men*, and the outline might stand thus—1. The general distribution of the word—wayside, stones, thorns, good ground, all climates, temperaments, races, &c.; 2. The great purpose of the word *fruitfulness*—thought, action, family, business, nation, &c.; 3. The difficulties of the word—care, riches, superficiality, devil, &c.; 4. The results of the word—thirty, sixty, hundredfold; difference according to capacity, earnestness, opportunity, &c. The text suggests a cautionary word, viz., let not the thirty-fold producers imagine that they are hundredfold producers. There must be gradation in character, in position, in influence. The text suggests a word of encouragement, viz., the reward is not given for the mere *quantity* brought forth, but for the *fact* that there is a bringing forth. The same principle is illustrated in the parable of the talents; the reward was not in the ten and the four, but in the *doubling* of the original endowment.

24. Another parable put he forth unto them, saying, The kingdom of heaven is likened unto a man which sowed good seed in his field:
25. But while men slept, his enemy came and sowed tares among the wheat, and went his way.
26. But when the blade was sprung up, and brought forth fruit, then appeared the tares also.
27. So the servants of the householder came and said unto him, Sir, didst not thou sow good seed in thy field? from whence then hath it tares?
28. He said unto them, An enemy hath done this. The servants said unto him, Wilt thou then that we go and gather them up?
29. But he said, Nay; lest while ye gather up the tares, ye root up also the wheat with them.
30. Let both grow together until the harvest: and in the time of harvest I will say to the reapers, Gather ye together first the tares, and bind them in bundles to burn them: but gather the wheat into my barn.

Around this parable many curious interpretations have been gathered, in direct contradiction to Christ's own exposition as given in verses 36—43. From that exposition we learn—1. *That all good men are placed on the earth by the Son of man* ("the good seed are the children of the kingdom").

Good *men* come from the good *Man;* there is no germ of goodness, no hint or promise of good harvest that may not be traced directly to Jesus Christ. This fact is of great value as illustrative of His divinity. Nothing bad comes from Him; all good springs from His undefiled, His essentially holy soul. 2. *They are so placed as not to be beyond evil association.* They stand side by side with "the children of the wicked one." Proximity does not involve identity. Good men and bad men grow, so to speak, on the same earth, yet there is a difference of nature which cannot be mistaken. Time can never make the tares wheat, nor can time ever make the wheat tares. Time moulds the blossom into fruit, but time never brings figs out of thistles. The difference between good men and bad men is not a difference of position, a difference of circumstances, or a difference of opportunities, but a difference of *nature*. This fact must lie at the basis of all ameliorative schemes. We learn—3. *That physical force must never be used in uprooting vicious humanity.* The servants would have laid violent hands on the tares, but the master said, "Nay, lest while ye gather up the tares ye root up also the wheat with them." This circumstance explains the continuance of the present apparently anomalous economy of life; that is to say, all things are governed with a view to the development and the full ripening of good men: *they* are God's first consideration, and in caring for them many collateral, so to speak overflowing, advantages fall to the lot of bad men. The dew falls upon all plants, the light shines upon all fields. From this fact might be wrought out a powerful practical appeal respecting the indebtedness of bad men to good men. Take the doctrine into the *family;* the bad parent may be spared for the sake of the good child, or contrariwise: take it into the *nation;* five righteous men may be saving the land: take it into *business;* one true heart may be protecting an incompetent firm, &c. The great principle is that the present economy is upheld for the sake of the righteous, and that though it might appear to "servants" well to uproot the evil by violent means, yet the "master" says, Not so, lest ye injure the good. 4. *That difference of nature determines difference of destiny.* "The tares are gathered and burned in the fire,—the righteous shine forth as the sun in the kingdom of their Father." 1. Forcible separations are not to be effected by man; 2. Temporary associations are not to be mistaken for permanent fellowship; 3. Forbearance is not to be confounded with complacency.

There are two solemn considerations suggested by this parable respecting bad men. 1. They are the children of the devil; 2. They shall be cast into a furnace of fire, there shall be wailing and gnashing of teeth. Interpret these awful words as we may, we are driven to the conclusion that the wicked man's fate is one of inexpressible horror.

There is a peculiarity of expression in the 28th verse which cannot be seen apart from the original—'Εχθρὸς ἄνθρωπος τοῦτο ἐποίησεν. Literally, "A hostile man hath done this,"—not merely "an enemy," as it is rendered in the 28th verse, but a "hostile man," an enemy-man. The point to be noted is that suggested by the word "man." In the 39th verse this 'Εχθρὸς is declared to be Διάβολος. Bad men may hence learn how Christ identified them not only with the devil's service, but really with the devil himself.

A collation of the 38th and 41st verse suggests that Christ's kingdom is co-extensive with the world, and that *in this wide acceptation of the term* bad men may be in the good kingdom. This is no argument, however, for knowingly admitting bad men into the visible Church, or allowing them to remain when their characters have been disclosed. Apostolic authority is entirely in favour of marking them which cause divisions and offences, and avoiding them. (See particularly 2 Cor. vi. 14—18.) Still it must be remembered that the "things that offend and them which do iniquity" are said to be in "his kingdom" (τῆς βασιλείας αὐτοῦ),—not only in "the world" generally, but in "his kingdom" particularly. It is worth while starting the inquiry how far the language of the 41st verse may be held to apply to the weaknesses and errors which attach even to good men in the present sphere—weaknesses and errors which sustain the same relation to virtue that the chaff may sustain to the wheat. The grammatical construction of the original would seem to favour this suggestion. The angels are to gather out πάντα τὰ σκάνδαλα καὶ τοὺς ποιοῦντας τὴν ἀνομίαν. Literally, "all the scandals and the working the iniquity." Taken in this view we should have the idea of the entire purification of believers, rather than of the destruction of bad men. Both interpretations are correct; all men shall be tried, either in the winnowing fan or the furnace,—the chaff shall be taken from the wheat, and the dross shall be purged from the gold.

31. Another parable put he forth unto them, saying, The kingdom of heaven is like to a grain of mustard seed, which a man took, and sowed in his field :
32. Which indeed is the least of all seeds : but when it is grown, it is the greatest among herbs, and becometh a tree, so that the birds of the air come and lodge in the branches thereof.

The remarks of OLSHAUSEN on this parable are simple and decisive : "The idea which this parable is obviously designed to set forth is simply this—that in the manifestation of what is Divine, the beginning and the end of its development stand related to each other in an inverse ratio. Springing from invisible beginnings, it spreads itself abroad over an all-embracing field of operations." There have been a good many fanciful interpretations of this parable : such as that some men have mistaken a large shrub for a great tree, and that the fowls of the air represent the lodgment of worldly spirits in the Church. These seem to be entirely beside the mark. The simple purpose of Christ is to show that the day of small things may end in great glory. Homiletically, the idea suggests the following points :—1. That great movements may have small beginnings; 2. That the development of important purposes depends less on demonstration than upon a principle of vitality; 3. That the ideas of God often depend upon men for full evolution and consolidation: the mustard-seed must be *sown*, so the word of the kingdom must take effect in the heart ; 4. The power upon which the Gospel depends is the power of *Life*. STIER well says : " Trust not to anything great in this world which was not small in its beginning; for then it grows not from the kernel,—then in all probability the tree began from the branches before it had roots."

The parable may be used as an encouragement to those who are young in the Christian life, or to those who are feeling their first desires towards Christ. The law of growth in nature has its counterpart in the growth of the Divine word in the soul of man.

<small>33. Another parable spake he unto them ; The kingdom of heaven is like unto leaven, which a woman took, and hid in three measures of meal, till the whole was leavened.</small>

Having examined many interpretations of this parable, I have come to the conclusion that the common opinion is correct, viz., that it is intended to represent *the penetrating power of Divine truth*. It may be true that "leaven" is never referred to in the sacred writings except as a bad or forbidden thing, yet the *action* of leaven on meal may fittingly represent the penetrating energy of the Gospel in the individual heart, or in the world at large. HEUBNER, as quoted by

LANGE, puts the idea most concisely: "If the former parable presents the *extensive* power of Christianity, this exhibits its *intensive* force." LANGE himself says: "One of the main points in the parable is the 'hiding' or the mixing of the leaven in three measures of meal. This refers to the great outward Church, in which the living Gospel seems, as it were, hidden and lost. It appears as if the Gospel were engulphed in the world, but under the regenerating power of Christianity it will at last be seen that the whole world shall be included in the Church." By an unstrained accommodation the parable may yield the following homiletic reflections:—1. There is a vast mass of human nature to be brought under the influence of truth. 2. The relation between the means and the end is apparently disproportionate. "The expression, *three* measures, is not accidental, but intended to denote the large quantity which the leaven has to pervade. *Three* is the symbolical number for spiritual things." 3. The energy is in the *truth*, not in the nature on which it operates; yet 4. There is a similarity between the truth and the heart,—here is the Divine descent, the moral grandeur of man! The leaven would not operate upon stones, or upon any substance entirely foreign to itself; so the very fact that Divine truth operates upon human nature, with a view to its sanctification, is an illustration of man's high origin and sublime destiny.

34. All these things spake Jesus unto the multitude in parables; and without a parable spake he not unto them:
35. That it might be fulfilled which was spoken by the prophet, saying, I will open my mouth in parables; I will utter things which have been kept secret from the foundation of the world.

Great revelations must be made with special regard to the capacity of the hearers:—1. *Children are taught as children.* Sometimes the elders of the house speak to one another in the presence of their children in a parabolical manner, so as to avoid being understood except by one another. 2. *The gradual and reserved revelation of truth saves society from confusion, and deepens the attention of the world.* It is so in ordinary intellectual development. The scholar does not learn all at once, &c. Reserved revelation is itself an excellent discipline, when reverently accepted. 3. *Society gains much by the relation of teacher and learner.* (*a*) The necessities of different mental forces are provided for; (*b*) men learn to esteem men; (*c*) a deep common sympathy is engendered and sustained.

All that the ancient prophets had foretold of Christ had been dictated by Christ Himself; hence the ease and naturalness with which He took up their words and fulfilled their meaning. He was Himself a fulfilled prophecy. The ages were gathered up in Him, so that though He was young according to the flesh, yet according to the spirit He was "the ancient of days." All the ages had themselves been mysterious parabolic signs, and Christ was the answer of their enigma; yet the answer itself was a parable, as if the world could not be educated but by riddles and pictures. His parabolic method of teaching is not to be regarded as an attempt to bewilder and mislead His hearers; it was a continuance of the Divine method from the beginning,— a collateral and most invincible argument on behalf of His deity. We are now, individually and nationally, in the very midst of a parable. "We know in part and we prophecy in part." We are not without light, yet we see through a glass darkly. The Divine Parabolist is proceeding with His mysterious, half-explained utterances, and we shall have to follow Him, as did the disciples, into "the house," which in our case means into the heavens, in order to know the meaning of His solemn and far-reaching words.

36. Then Jesus sent the multitude away, and went into the house : and his disciples came unto him, saying, Declare unto us the parable of the tares of the field.

This should be turned to practical account. In this verse we have two points :—1. Men anxious for the interpretation of Divine words; and 2. Such men making appeal to the Divine Interpreter. No object should awaken such deep solicitude as the attainment of a right idea of Christ's utterances, for they were "the words of eternal life;" and this object can be realised only by communion with Christ,—this union suggests the following subject :— *Prayer in its relation to a right understanding of the Scriptures.* The reasonableness and consequent profitableness of such prayer may be maintained on the following grounds :—1. He who wrote the Scriptures is the object of prayer. 2. The Scriptures are addressed to the human mind and heart. 3. He who wrote the Scriptures bestowed also the faculty of interpretation. 4. He who bestowed this faculty has promised to renew and enrich it in answer to prayer. "If any man lack wisdom," &c., "If ye being evil," &c., "Ask, and it shall be given you," &c.

As we have already referred to Christ's exposition of the parable of the tares (37—43), we may proceed to the next parable :—

44. Again, the kingdom of heaven is like unto treasure hid in a field ; the which when a man hath found, he hideth, and for joy thereof, goeth and selleth all that he hath, and buyeth that field.

1. The kingdom of heaven is *precious*. 2. What is precious must be *sought for*. 3. All other possessions must be appropriated to the securing of the kingdom of heaven. Or thus :—1. All men value *treasure*. 2. Treasures are of *different value*. 3. The treasures which are most valuable are *spiritual*. 4. The highest of spiritual treasures is the *Gospel of Christ*. 5. The attainment of this treasure should

be a secret joy, and should necessitate a continual surrendering of inferior possessions.

But how is the kingdom of heaven like unto treasure hid in a field? 1. Because it is in the world as an *unknown thing*. 2. Because when discovered it attracts and absorbs the deepest attention of the world.

But why should the finder of this treasure-field hide it as if to keep other persons from it? Is it not the nature of the Gospel to expand and liberalise the heart? Truly, and the "hiding" of the treasure is referred to simply to show the eagerness, the intensity, and determination of the finder; if it is pressed farther it is pressed entirely out of its meaning.

45. Again, the kingdom of heaven is like unto a merchant man, seeking goodly pearls:
46. Who, when he had found one pearl of great price, went and sold all that he had, and bought it.

The same idea is contained in this parable as in the foregoing. 1. Here is a man *seeking*,—all men *seek*. 2. Here is a man seeking *good things*,—he is not merely an accumulator, but an accumulator of valuable possessions. 3. Here is a man finding *unexpected treasures*. 4. Here is a man who decides that *one* may be more than *many*,—*quality* is better than *quantity*. The great object of life should be *much* not *many*.

47. Again, the kingdom of heaven is like unto a net, that was cast into the sea, and gathered of every kind:
48. Which, when it was full, they drew to shore, and sat down, and gathered the good into vessels, but cast the bad away.
49. So shall it be at the end of the world: the angels shall come forth, and sever the wicked from among the just,
50. And shall cast them into the furnace of fire: there shall be wailing and gnashing of teeth.

1. The visible kingdom of heaven is not secure from the intrusion of unworthy men. 2. A period of discrimination

will supervene in the history of God's kingdom on the earth. 3. In that period nothing will avail but the highest excellence of character.

51. Jesus saith unto them, Have ye understood all these things? They say unto him, Yea, Lord.
52. Then said he unto them, Therefore every scribe which is instructed unto the kingdom of heaven is like unto a man that is an householder, which bringeth forth out of his treasure things new and old.

Understanding should express itself not merely in sentiment, but in persevering and generous service. 1. Christ's ministers should be instructed; 2. Their instruction should not be enjoyed for selfish purposes; 3. Their instruction should express itself in divers methods and ranges, according to the capacities of the hearers. The material will be old, the illustration may be new. Truth is venerable as eternity; its phases may bloom with the freshness of summer. Christ himself uttered no new truth; He only "uttered things which had been kept secret from the foundation of the world," yet every parable was a new aspect of the eternal truth, adapted to the state of contemporary thought. The fifty-second verse gives the teacher his range of liberty, and that range includes both "old and new." Can any liberty be greater? Civilization, in which term I include all the higher life as well as all that is refined and elevated in material progress, is continually being set at different angles, and the wise scribe is commanded to watch all such variations that he may adopt the presentation of the truth accordingly. The age that would reject a dogma might accept a parable. The entire history of Religious Thought might be written under the twofold division of DOGMA˚ and PARABLE. This is emphatically the PARABOLIC ERA, taking its tone, and order of development, from the transitional state of the intellectual world, as represented by Science and Philosophy. In periods of intellectual quiescence we find that the religious world is settled firmly upon its theological Dogmas, but in periods of great intellectual excitement the religious world passes into what may be termed its *Parabolic phase*. Not that Dogma is destroyed, any more than mountains are annihilated by the luminous mists which are often seen upon them on autumnal mornings. The true power of religious teaching is best shown in following the order which Christ Himself followed in the ministry. He gave Doctrine, and He gave Parable; the first met the positive want of the *religious* nature, and the second encouraged all that was best on the speculative side of the *intellectual* nature. Thus Christ avoided the cold and stern *finality* which is characteristic of formal Dogma. There was always something beyond; some opening in the golden clouds of the horizon which invited the spectator to go in and behold yet brighter visions: the Dogma was decisive, but the Parable set the heart longing for closer intercourse with the Parabolist; hence we find the disciples following Christ and pressing for further explanation. The Dogma marked the distance that had been travelled; the Parable pointed to the distance which lay far ahead: Dogma was finished like *Yesterday*, Parable had about it all haze, yet all the promise and allurement, of *Morrow*. It was thus that in an unequalled, or rather unique, degree, the teaching of this Scribe "instructed unto the kingdom of heaven," combined "things new and old," and thus that He has maintained His hold upon the ages, filling and satisfying their entire capacity of vision and desire. The Parable takes the enquirer farther along the line of truth than Dogma does; it stands in relation to Dogma as poetry to prose. Even the arithmetician calls in the aid of the algebraist at a certain point of the science of numbers, and thus gets upon what may be called the Parabolic side of truth. When he says "let $x$ represent the unknown quantity," he means, in his particular sphere of enquiry, what Christ meant when He said, "the kingdom of heaven *is like* —." Dogma is the known; Parable the unknown: hence there is not a little reality in the bold saying of the ancient Sophists that "probabilities were more to be valued than truths."

53. And it came to pass, that when Jesus had finished these parables, he departed thence.
54. And when he was come into his own country, he taught them in their synagogue, insomuch that they were astonished, and said, Whence hath this man this wisdom, and these mighty works?
55. Is not this the carpenter's son? is not his mother called Mary? and his brethren, James, and Joses, and Simon, and Judas?
56. And his sisters, are they not all with us? Whence then hath this man all these things?
57. And they were offended in him. But Jesus said unto them, A prophet is not without honour, save in his own country, and in his own house.
58. And he did many mighty works there because of their unbelief.

The Truth subject to the evil influences of prejudice, is the topic suggested by this paragraph. The attention is not so much fixed upon "this wisdom, and these mighty works" as upon the low origin of the man. The subject suggests:—1. A *possibility*,—that of being overcome by prejudice even in the most momentous pursuits. 2. *An admonition*,—that truth is independent of accidental circumstances. 3. *A warning*,—that unbelief may deprive us of the presence and service of Christ.

Among the general remarks which may be made on this paragraph are such as:—1. Foolish notions about ancestry. 2. Forgetting that the trade does not make the man. 3. Keeping men down because their parents were not eminent. 4. The fate of great souls is to be misunderstood. 5. If nothing can be brought against a man himself, he may be reproached with the obscurity of his parentage. On the other side, Christ's, it may be seen:—1. That man has more fair play to expect from strangers than from so-called friends. 2. That blessings are not to be forced upon unwilling hearers. 3. That discouragement in one direction need not terminate the purposes and labours of a good man.

### GENERAL NOTE.

This chapter is largely occupied with parabolic illustrations of "the kingdom of heaven." By that expression is to be understood the *Theocracy*,—including all the purposes and providences of God in relation to the human world. Whenever anything is found that is truly loving, beautiful, valuable, or exalting, there is an aspect of God's kingdom upon the earth. There is a contention between two kingdoms,—the kingdom of heaven and the kingdom of hell; the latter is "like unto" death, corruption, darkness, tumult and kindred terrors; the former is like unto life, progress, light, peace, and all that goes to make up heaven. Whenever man feels lifted up towards better life, or enkindled by pure and elevating hope, he is under the influence of the heavenly kingdom; and whenever his lower nature dominates over his soul, beclouding his intellect, and rousing into flames his vilest passions, he is under the power of the kingdom of darkness. A wide and fertile field of illustration is opened by a contrastive statement between the parables of Christ in regard to the kingdom of heaven, and what is known of the Satanic kingdom. For example, "the kingdom of heaven is like unto a man which sowed good seed in his field;" the contrast of this would be, "the kingdom of hell is like unto a man which sowed bad seed in his field:" again, "The kingdom of heaven is like unto treasure hid in a field;" the contrast would be, "the kingdom of hell is like a deceitful and worthless bubble floating in the air." Thus, as the light gives the shadow, so the parable, which represents the kingdom of heaven, also sets forth the spirit and features of the kingdom of darkness.

## CHAPTER XIV.

1. At that time Herod the tetrarch heard of the fame of Jesus,
2. And said unto his servants, This is John the Baptist; he is risen from the dead; and therefore mighty works do shew forth themselves in him.
3. For Herod had laid hold on John, and bound him, and put him in prison for Herodias' sake, his brother Philip's wife.
4. For John said unto him, It is not lawful for thee to have her.
5. And when he would have put him to death, he feared the multitude, because they counted him as a prophet.
6. But when Herod's birthday was kept, the daughter of Herodias danced before them, and pleased Herod.
7. Whereupon he promised with an oath to give her whatsoever she would ask.
8. And she, being before instructed of her mother, said, Give me here John Baptist's head in a charger.
9. And the king was sorry: nevertheless for the oath's sake, and them which sat with him at meat, he commanded it to be given her.
10. And he sent, and beheaded John in the prison.
11. And his head was brought in a charger, and given to the damsel: and she brought it to her mother.
12. And his disciples came, and took up the body, and buried it, and went and told Jesus.
13. When Jesus heard of it, he departed thence by a ship into a desert place apart: and when the people had heard thereof, they followed him on foot out of the cities.

Man may be slain, but truth cannot be annihilated. John was buried, but the Gospel was still making way in the world. It has been thought that Herod Antipas (son of Herod the Great) was a Sadducee, and that this exclamation respecting Jesus testified in a remarkable manner to the power of conscience in relation to theological belief. The Sadducees denied the resurrection of the dead; yet conscience rebelled against the theory, and forced the superstitious tetrarch into this confession. Whether it be true or not that Herod was a Sadducee, it is certainly true that the moral nature does, on great occasions, clear its way through all fanciful theories and speculations, and become authoritative as the voice of

God in the soul. Man overlays his spiritual constitution, so to speak, with creeds which flatter his vanity and give false peace to his conscience; but crises supervene which affect a moral resurrection, and give man to feel the discrepancy between the wants of his nature and the promises of false creeds. There is a great quickening and educational force in the *exceptional* circumstances of life. Crises make history. Man cannot tell what he is until some special event makes his soul quake with fear, or brings upon him the light of a great joy. As with individuals, so with nations; monotony would kill them; all enthusiasm would die out, and corruption would become universal. God has so arranged His government that monotony is broken up by startling events,—the thunderbolt, the pestilence, the mildew, come suddenly upon us,—death teaches life, and the grave calls to heaven. In all great crises, both in individual and national life, there is an instinctive movement of the soul towards God. The temporary creed is subordinated to the normal constitution; and it is most solemn to watch the soul in its resurrectional moods how impatient it is of mere speculation, and how anxious for positive doctrine and assurance. It then lives double life; with frightful energy it clears the field of false friends, and with startling rapidity passes over the chasms of the past and brings up all the sins which have weakened and deformed itself. When Herod heard of the fame of Jesus a species of resurrection occurred. The night of bacchanalian revel came back; the holy prophet's blood dripped upon the palace floor again; and the soul said, This Jesus is the man whom I murdered! There is, so to speak, a moral memory as well as a memory that is merely intellectual. Conscience writes in blood. She may brood in long silence, but she cannot forget. All the universe helps her recollection. Every leaf of the forest contains her indictments, and every voice of the air prompts her remembrance. The revel passed, the dancing demon-hearted daughter of Herodias went back to her blood-thirsty mother, the lights were extinguished, and the palace relapsed into its accustomed order ; but the prophet's blood cried with a cry not to be stifled, and angels with swords of fire watched the tetrarch night and day. All men are watched. The sheltering wing of the unseen angel is close to every one of us. The eye sees but an infinitesimal portion of what is around,—we are hemmed in with God ! This great truth we forget ; but exceptional circumstances transpire which for a moment rend the veil, and give us to see how public is our most secret life, how the angels hear the throb of the heart, and God counts the thoughts of the mind.

In this paragraph we have glimpses of three men and two women. The men are Herod, John, and Jesus ; the women are Herodias and her daughter. The special characteristics of all are indicated very concisely but very vividly.

Take Herod : 1. Here is *abused power*. Government is of God, but not *bad* government. 2. Here is a *time-serving policy*. In the first instance Herod " feared the people," and in the next he killed John because his courtiers, who hated the prophet, where round about him when the daughter of Herodias asked for the Baptist's head. All bad men "fear the people." No one man in the crowd was so mighty as Herod ; but the crowd, as a whole, held him in subjection. Even kings cannot afford to ignore public sentiment,—it is a law which makes all outward laws, and only as outward laws shape themselves to the educated sentiment of the age are they likely to be useful or permanent. The people when taken in detail may be insignificant, but when taken in combination, they are as the sand-built shore which shuts in the billows of the great deep. 3. Here is a *perverted conscientiousness*,—" nevertheless for the oath's sake." Conscience founded on vanity is a false monitor ; conscience founded on reason is a light from heaven. Men often blunder when talking of conscience. Some men confound the subtle interplay of honour and courtesy with moral instincts, and serve the published conventional creed rather than the directions of unsophisticated nature. Herod sacrificed conscience to courtesy; he immolated Right on the altar of Pride. No man has a right to swear to another man's hurt. God never delegates the proprietorship of human life. John the Baptist was God's property, not Herod's; and Herod sinned in overlooking this fundamental truth. Every man is bound to recall foolish, false, impracticable, or unwarranted words and oaths. It is not his conscience that will be injured, but his pride will be wounded, and his selfish vanity will be cut up by the roots. Conscience is not a flower to be planted on its own grave. Conscience was violated in the *promise;* the "oath" itself was the crime; and no cure could be applied but to the error itself, as Herod had committed it.

So much for Herod; now look at John the Baptist. 1. Here is *injured innocence*. The prophet of God in prison; the prophet of the devil on the throne! This is among the paradoxes which make up the mystery of Providence. God is not to be judged by isolated acts. Providence is a *system*. The light makes the shade. 2. Here is *moral courage*. John was in prison because he had condemned Antipas for marrying the wife of his half-brother, Herod Philippas. Princes must be reproved by prophets. The religious element should dominate in society. Godly men should make their influence felt in all movements; for "the kingdom of heaven is like unto a net which gathered of every kind." Many men lecture the poor, but who will rebuke the rich? The prophet of the Lord has a right everywhere, specially where the devil is spreading his snares or rioting in the destruction of man. True godliness holds in reverence all social rights.

It holds the marriage bond to be sacred. It smites the wicked king; it comforts the dishonoured husband. All reforms are partial that do not begin with the moral nature. When man is harmonised with God, society will move with ease towards its great destiny, developing ever-increasing power and ever-heightening dignity. 4. Here is *temporary defeat*. John was beheaded; the royal murderer was triumphant. So much for *to-day*; but *to-morrow* will come!

Turn now from John, and look at Christ. John's disciples went and told Jesus. How plaintive and touching the scene! *Jesus, the hearer of all human woe.* Picture Him in a listening attitude, hearkening to the long sad wail of misery,—the cry never ceases, the listener is never released! Do we not need such a listener, and does not the fact of His existence suggest the Divinity of His person? When Jesus heard the saddening narrative "he departed thence by ship into a desert place apart." *Jesus turning away from the haunts of wicked men.* He wanted rest after hearing such a story. There are recitals which make a heavy drain on one's very life. They make us faint and weary, as if we had undergone a personal affliction. There is something profoundly suggestive in this keen susceptibility on the part of Christ. Who shall say what tears of blood He shed in the "desert place apart?" The good man is sickened every day by some sight of wickedness; and as he is like Christ in spiritual sensitiveness, he will live a martyr's life. The sight of wantonness, oppression, misery, is such as to make one seek "a desert place apart,"—it sends a shock of disappointment on the soul as if all labour were vain, as if heaven itself were weak in contest with hell. This going away is solemnly prefigurative of *Christ's final withdrawment from His mediatorial work.* There is a point at which He will leave wicked men to themselves. He will take from them all the good, and in mutual hatred they will spend the ages that have no end.

Christ shows *that the fate of good men should be interesting to Christians*. Great spaces are left vacant when good men die. The *young* should be fired with holy ambition to take up the positions of those who have ascended to heaven.

Look to Herodias and her daughter. 1. *A bad mother;* 2. *A child willing to follow bad instructions*. Is there a more terrible designation known in all the language of men than a *bad mother?* Here is wickedness at the very roots of society, or poison at the very fountain-head of life. The lesson to be learned from this womanly hatred of the Baptist is *the tendency of hatred in the direction of murder*. People often hate those who expose and rebuke their sins. There is nothing out of hell so virulent as the hatred of a woman. It never rests; nothing can appease its thirst but the hot blood of its victim. As woman on one side is nearest God, on the other she is nearest the devil. There is no love like hers, there is no hatred like hers. If she cannot operate directly, she will work indirectly. She will not hesitate to make her own child an instrument of hell. A mother putting murderous desires into her daughter's heart!—to such lengths will hatred drive all who submit to its malignant rule.

The incident is fruitful of suggestion as to life generally. 1. Bad men may have great power. 2. The season of intoxication, the season of temptation. 3. Reason extinguished by voluptuousness. 4. Opportunities to wreak their vengeance will always occur to those who are watching for them. 5. Great faith has great trials. 6. The most honoured men put to the greatest extremities,—" among men that are born of women there hath not appeared a greater than John the Baptist." 7. The man who preached the baptism of water, sealing his testimony with the baptism of blood. 8. This closing of a dispensation with the blood of a *martyr*, a very fitting introduction to a dispensation which was to be closed with the blood of a *Saviour*. Thus one dispensation is graduated into another, the cry of the old prophets is taken up by the voice of John, and the blood of martyrdom is carried into the deep meaning of the blood of sacrifice: the old prophetic mantle has its counterpart in the leathern girdle, the block is elevated into the Cross; savage hearts gloat over the blood of the martyr, guilty hearts will find purity in the blood of the Redeemer. Thus the dispensations are graduated,—all the purposes of God are carried forward to the climacteric point, "the Lamb slain" seated in the midst of the throne.

14. And Jesus went forth, and saw a great multitude, and was moved with compassion toward them, and he healed their sick.

Though Christ had upon receiving intelligence of John's murder, retired into "a desert place apart," as if sickened with the signs of depravity which were thickening around Him, yet His Divine philanthropy overcame the momentary depression, and impelled Him once more to mingle with the society which needed Him so much. The 13th and 14th verses represent the two aspects of Philanthropic Life; the aspect that is shadowed with failure, shocked by a terrible disappointment, and almost darkened into despair; and on the other hand the aspect which attests the immortality of love, the all-enduring patience of a great purpose. These verses supply the basis of a discourse upon *The Retreating and the Re-appearing Christ*. 1. The circumstances under which He retreats,—unbelief; misapprehension; ingratitude; disappointment; &c. 2. The circumstances under which He re-appears,—human sin; necessity; misery; penitence; helplessness; &c. Conceive the pictures,—Christ *going*, and Christ *coming!* Have not all philanthropists passed, according to their degrees, the very experience related in these verses?

Imagine the result if Christ had *not* re-appeared! Think of society being governed by such men as *Herod*, &c. Under

Herodic government three results would obtain: 1. Free speech would be stifled; 2. The holiest social obligations would be dishonoured; 3. Good men who speak the word of a pure and happy future would be silenced or murdered.

15. And when it was evening, his disciples came to him, saying, This is a desert place, and the time is now past; send the multitude away, that they may go into the villages, and buy themselves victuals.
16. But Jesus said unto them, They need not depart: give ye them to eat.
17. And they say unto him, We have here but five loaves, and two fishes.
18. He said, Bring them hither to me.
19. And he commanded the multitude to sit down on the grass, and took the five loaves, and the two fishes, and looking up to heaven, he blessed, and brake, and gave the loaves to his disciples, and the disciples to the multitude.
20. And they did all eat, and were filled: and they took up of the fragments that remained twelve baskets full.
21. And they that had eaten were about five thousand men, beside women and children.

Here we have a special exemplification of the philanthropic spirit of Christ. In Christ, philanthropy was not a sentiment but a controlling power, not a dream but a fact. Some of the more striking suggestions of this paragraph are these: 1. *Two different methods of dealing with social problems,—* "send the multitude away;" that is *one* method,—"give ye them to eat;" that is *another*. We often have the remedy at hand while we fruitlessly seek it afar off. No man knows the range of his resources. This applies to *mind, money, influence*,—to all the aspects of life. A man's resources, looked at from the outside, may be as a grain of mustard seed; but *planted, used*, put into *right conditions*, &c. The disciples took an insufficient view of their resources,— taking the account from the various evangelists, they said, "We have five loaves, we have *but* five loaves, we have but five *barley* loaves; we have but *two* fishes, we have but two *small* fishes." Lower and lower they sink in their representation of their resources,—*a picture of men who have no faith.* The life that is *in* a man multiplies the resources that are *outside.* 2. *The entire fulness of Christ in relation to all human need.* He said, " Bring them hither to me." Christ cared for the bodies of men; and *His religion* can never be unmindful of social, secular, commercial, and physical questions. The *whole man* came originally *from God,* and to the end of time the whole man must be *profoundly interesting to God.* All our resources must be taken to Christ if we would make them truly availing to the necessities of men. We hardly yet understand Christ's relation to material questions. " Let the people praise thee. . . *Then shall the earth yield her increase."* Man loses no bread by praying over it. The principle may be extended—*no life spent in true devotion is wasted.* If *Christ* " looked up to heaven " while using the things of earth, shall *we* use the things of earth as though there were no heaven ? 3. *The compatibility of carefulness with the greatest bounty,*—" They took up of the fragments that remained twelve baskets full." God will not suffer loss. He makes use of every sunbeam now that fell upon the first morning of time, and the dew which glittered in Eden sparkles in the rainbow of to-day. God is the most exacting of economists.

Among the miscellaneous remarks suggested by this paragraph may be named:—1. Christ's power in all the wildernesses of time. 2. The impossibility of loneliness or want in fellowship with Christ. 3. The union of religious exercises with daily engagements. 4. The Giver of earthly bread is also the Giver of heavenly bread. 5. The man who is prepared to give *himself* is prepared to give all lower property.

There need not be any difficulty in receiving this statement. If a man will closely examine himself he will find that in his own life there have been interpositions and deliverances, unexpected and thrilling manifestations of bounty which verify this narrative, and show that *in every life the miraculous element is most positive and influential.*

22. And straightway Jesus constrained his disciples to get into a ship, and to go before him unto the other side, while he sent the multitudes away.
23. And when he had sent the multitudes away, he went up into a mountain apart to pray: and when the evening was come he was there alone.

Christ's power over men,—He sent away the disciples and He sent away the multitude. There is something mournful about this idea of Christ "sending away,"—every step from Christ is a step into darkness. In this case Christ wishes not merely to check the enthusiasm which the idea of a temporal kingdom excited, but to renew His strength in devout retirement. The 23rd verse shows :—1. That the holiest life requires periods of prayerful repose. 2. That the busiest life can secure such periods if so determined. That the shortest life can spare such periods, and in sparing them increase its faculty and range of usefulness. Or thus :—1. Christ's example refutes the sophism that special seasons of communion with God are not required by good men ; 2. Christ's example shows that devout and reflective exercises are only part of the Christian life. Jesus came back again ; He built no tabernacle on the mountain ; He went only as a man might go to fetch water from a pure stream. Taking the miracle and the retirement together, a discourse might be founded on *the reciprocal action of service and contemplation in the Christian life.*

24. But the ship was now in the midst of the sea, tossed with waves : for the wind was contrary.
25. And in the fourth watch of the night Jesus went unto them, walking on the sea.
26. And when the disciples saw him walking on the sea, they were troubled, saying, It is a spirit ; and they cried out for fear.
27. But straightway Jesus spake unto them, saying, Be of good cheer ; it is I ; be not afraid.

The ship had been driven from the shore where it was to have waited for Christ, so that when He came down from the mountain He had to walk upon the sea in order to join the disciples. This appears to be the most sensible suggestion yet offered upon the incident by many of the best expositors. The suggestion is important as showing that Christ never performed a miracle merely for the sake of performing it; the power was always associated with a purpose. By a slight accommodation, the incident may yield several points of remark :—1. The winds which baffle the servants cannot baffle the master (apply this to all the circumstances of human life). 2. An absent Christ always means a present storm. 3. A returning Christ always means a returning peace. Or the incident may be thrown into this homiletic form. 1. In doing their duty men may be exposed to storms (Christ bade the disciples go); 2. Storms which come in the course of duty are not to be regarded as tokens of Divine displeasure; 3. Jesus Christ never allows any storm to separate Him from His Church. By another accommodation the incident may be taken as the basis of a discourse upon *mistaken interpretations of Divine Providence*. 1. The disciples evidently thought that Christ *could not* walk on the sea. 2. Circumstances often obscure the Divine presence—night, storm, perplexity, &c. 3. Results do not turn upon human interpretations, but upon Divine purposes,—men may mistake God for a phantasm, but He is God still! 4. The weakness of human faith is not always punished by a withdrawment of the Divine favour; Jesus announced Himself; He knows what human nature is, and how to meet its moods of doubt, and its poverty of faith and hope. The incident might be further used to show the *influence of Christ's presence upon a troubled life :*—1. That presence dispels *fear*. 2. That presence inspires *joy*. 3. That presence secures *safety*. In the history of war we often read of the effect of one man's presence, or one man's courage; all such instances feebly represent the effect of Christ's presence in the Church.

28. And Peter answered him and said, Lord, if it be thou, bid me come unto thee on the water.
29. And he said, Come. And when Peter was come down out of the ship, he walked on the water, to go to Jesus.
30. But when he saw the wind boisterous, he was afraid; and beginning to sink, he cried, saying, Lord, save me.
31. And immediately Jesus stretched forth his hand, and caught him, and said unto him, O thou of little faith, wherefore didst thou doubt?
32. And when they were come into the ship, the wind ceased.
33. Then they that were in the ship came and worshipped him, saying, Of a truth thou art the Son of God.

I. Peter's action shows:—1. The worthlessness of a faith that is merely *impulsive*. 2. The worthlessness of a faith that looks to *circumstances* rather than to *Christ*—He saw the wind boisterous! 3. The worth of a faith that looks to *Christ* rather than to *circumstances*—Jesus saved him.

II. Christ's action shows:—1. His perfect power over nature. 2. His benevolence under the most extreme conditions of human weakness. His constancy to great principles; He ever set *Faith* against *Doubt*.

III. The disciples' action shows:—1. The tendency of men to believe in *power*. 2. The tendency of men specially to believe in power that *preserves*. 3. The tendency of men to worship the power that has saved their lives.

Application:—1. We are all in storms. 2. We may all mistake presumption for faith. 3. If salvation be the basis of worship, what homage will be rendered to Christ by a rescued world!

34. And when they were gone over, they came into the land of Gennesaret.
35. And when the men of that place had knowledge of him, they sent out into all that country round about, and brought unto him all that were diseased;
36. And besought him that they might only touch the hem of his garment: and as many as touched were made perfectly whole.

Christ wanted on the land as well as on the sea. Every place has its own history of sin and woe; so has every family; so has every man. Christ equal to all the calls made upon Him. He who prays on the mountain may save on the sea; He who saves on the sea may heal in the city. Christ's was not a local power or a special skill; His energy was universal as the light or air. 1. The blessed privilege of having an opportuity of being healed by Christ. 2. The tremendous responsibility of neglecting that privilege.

### CHAPTER XV.

1. Then came to Jesus Scribes and Pharisees, which were of Jerusalem, saying,
2. Why do thy disciples transgress the tradition of the elders? for they wash not their hands when they eat bread.
3. But he answered and said unto them, Why do ye also transgress the commandment of God by your tradition?
4. For God commanded, saying, Honour thy father and mother: and, He that curseth father or mother, let him die the death.
5. But ye say, Whosoever shall say to his father or his mother, It is a gift, by whatsoever thou mightest be profited by me;
6. And honour not his father or his mother, he shall be free. Thus have ye made the commandment of God of none effect by your tradition.
7. Ye hypocrites, well did Esaias prophesy of you, saying,
8. This people draweth nigh unto me with their mouth, and honoureth me with their lips; but their heart is far from me.
9. But in vain they do worship me, teaching for doctrines the commandments of men.

A new kind of service required at the hands of Christ. He saves life, and He saves truth. As He gave human life greater scope, so He gave truth wider and more spiritual interpretations. The Scribes and Pharisees were punctilious; anxious about an unwashed hand, yet careless about an impure heart. Jesus Christ here adopts an argument which is not usually considered of much value; He says, *tu quoque;* He recriminates. The argument, however, has infinite value in Christ's case, for it lays down a principle of universal and everlasting application, viz., that *the heart is to rule the life*. A man may make a pastime of washing his hands; a man may follow the tradition of the elders through the most sinister motives; but he cannot purify his heart without undergoing processes which are vital and acceptable to God. In this rebuke Christ sets the commandment of God against the tradition of the elders, and in so doing He gives the absolute standard of all judgment. On the peculiar expression of the 5th and 6th verses, Dr. ADAM CLARKE makes this sensible observation: " It is sacrilege to dedicate that to God which is taken away from the necessities of our *parents and children;* and the good that this pretends to will, doubtless, be found in the catalogue of that unnatural man's crimes, in the judgment of the great day, who has thus deprived his own family of its due. To assist our *poor* relatives is our first duty, and this is a work infinitely preferable to all *pious legacies and endowments.*" OLSHAUSEN says: " The idea is that the parents are making a request, and the children are refusing it, with the explanation that the thing which it would have been becoming in them to grant they had already decided to give to the temple." By a legitimate accommodation the paragraph may be made the basis of a discourse upon *Technical Fault-finding* :—1. Technical fault-finding is always *punctilious and trivial.* The charge here is that certain men did not wash their hands before eating. 2. Technical fault-finding is always *external and superficial.* The hand! Appearances, ceremonies, ritualism, &c. The technical fault-finder would rather be out of the world than out of the fashion. 3. Technical fault-finding is always *associated with a wrong condition of heart.* The fault-finders set the tradition (παράδοσις) of the presbytery against the commandment of God; ritual over-rode principle; ceremonialism destroyed the instincts of nature. Bad men are always the most censorious critics. 4. Technical fault-finding is always *opposed to the spirit of Jesus Christ.* " Ye hypocrites," &c. Jesus begins at the heart, &c. 5. Technical fault-finding is always *a vain service in the sight of God.* " In vain they do worship me," &c. Acceptable service is based on fundamental truth, not on empty ritual. Fault-finding is forbidden by the spirit of the Gospel, except it is occasioned by conduct which endangers the soul or pollutes society. The whole paragraph may also be used to expose the worthlessness of ritualism.

10. And he called the multitude, and said unto them, Hear, and understand :
11. Not that which goeth into the mouth defileth a man ; but that which cometh out of the mouth, this defileth a man.
12. Then came his disciples, and said unto him, Knowest thou that the Pharisees were offended, after they heard this saying ?
13. But he answered and said, Every plant which my heavenly Father hath not planted, shall be rooted up.
14. Let them alone : they be blind leaders of the blind. And if the blind lead the blind, both shall fall into the ditch.
15. Then answered Peter and said unto him, Declare unto us this parable.
16. And Jesus said, Are ye also yet without understanding?
17. Do not ye yet understand, that whatsoever entereth in at the mouth goeth into the belly, and is cast out into the draught?
18. But those things which proceed out of the mouth come forth from the heart ; and they defile the man.
19. For out of the heart proceed evil thoughts, murders, adulteries, fornications, thefts, false witness, blasphemies :
20. These are the things which defile a man : but to eat with unwashen hands defileth not a man.

The ideas suggested by this paragraph may be classified under some such heading as *Man's Morality not affected by Man's Receptivity.* This fact—1. Refutes the sophism that crime is necessitated by *circumstances;* 2. Charges upon men the responsibility of his own words ; and 3. Shows that every man is the source of his own character and influence. The subject admits of powerful application to those who are thrown into unpleasant positions in life, where they must hear and see much that is offensive. The third point is supremely important,—man the arbiter of his own destiny! Under this head may be described the limitation of diabolic power. Even the devil cannot enter a man without the man's own consent. While the hearer may not be defiled by evil speech, the evil speaker proclaims himself a polluted man.

The answer to the statement that the Pharisees were offended is significant (verse 13); it shows:—1. The fate of bad men; and 2. The fate of untrue doctrine; both bad teachers and bad teaching shall be rooted up—$εκριζωθησεται$—every fibre torn up; not a trace left! Great teachers must often speak the word that may offend: their business is not to study what is popular, but what is true. All truth has one aspect that is offensive, but few men are brave enough to press that aspect upon the attention of their age.

21. Then Jesus went thence, and departed into the coasts of Tyre and Sidon.
22. And, behold, a woman of Canaan came out of the same coasts, and cried unto him, saying, Have mercy on me, O Lord, thou son of David; my daughter is grievously vexed with a devil.
23. But he answered her not a word. And his disciples came and besought him, saying, Send her away; for she crieth after us.
24. But he answered and said, I am not sent but unto the lost sheep of the house of Israel.
25. Then came she and worshipped him, saying, Lord, help me.
26. But he answered and said, It is not meet to take the children's bread, and to cast it to dogs.
27. And she said, Truth, Lord: yet the dogs eat of the crumbs which fall from their masters' table.
28. Then Jesus answered and said unto her, O woman, great is thy faith: be it unto thee even as thou wilt. And her daughter was made whole from that very hour.

This incident may be used to show *the might of earnestness in relation to Divine purposes*. Christ's plan did not, at the time of this event, comprehend the heathen; it was limited to the lost sheep of the house of Israel. This woman was a member of the heathen community, and was therefore placed beyond the then line of Christ's action. There is nothing in the circumstance to oppose the idea that Jesus Christ was the Saviour of the whole world. His life was a development. From the beginning He moved into vision and service gradually; first to a few, then to many; first privately, then publicly; always advancing, always enlarging, until He comprehended "all the world" and "every creature" in His benevolent designs.

The woman of Canaan came upon Him, as it were, before His time. Her soul was charged with a great passion, and with its inseparable impatience and urgency. A terrible battle was proceeding in her house,—a devil was vexing her child; and now she sought to enlist the might of God on behalf of the sufferer. She had heard of others receiving blessings at the hands of Jesus Christ, why should she forbear to plead where others had prevailed? This question starts the subject just specified, *the might of earnestness in relation to Divine purposes.* From the general tenor of Christ's life, as well as from this special incident, it may be inferred :—1. *That God has no purposes which are inconsistent with the well-being of every creature.* Behind the darkest cloud the light of love is shining. Under His profoundest thought there is an unchangeable resolution to consult the best interests of the universe. For a moment hesitate on this point, and all that is attractive in God vanishes for ever! If one cruel thought could live in God, the heart could no longer trust Him, even under His most gracious aspects. This, then, should be made the fundamental idea, that God works by a plan, and that His plan is never inconsistent with the happiness of every human being. 2. *That the most benevolent purposes of God have always been developed gradually.* The whole current of Biblical history proves this,—the promise in Eden; the types and the prophecies; all show this. This is not an incident standing alone; it is part of the whole plan. It is important to remember this, in order to save ourselves from far-fetched interpretations. 3. *That man's earnestness has always been honoured in connection with the purposes of God.* Jacob wrestling with the angel, Abraham pleading for the cities, Nineveh, and many other instances may be cited from the Old Testament. Christ's conduct at Emmaus ("they constrained him"), an instance from the New. All such instances show the place and power of *Prayer.* Provision is evidently made for prayer in all God's arrangements. The mother may be working by a plan in her household affairs, but the cry of her necessitous child may modify her purposes; so with God, &c.

Among the general remarks which may be made are—1. Christ tests faith; 2. Earnestness is not deterred by silence or rebuke; 3. The crumbs of Christ's table are better than the luxuries of any other; 4. The kingdom of heaven may still be taken by the violent; 5. The exercise of faith is not a question of nations, but of hearts. "In every nation he that feareth God, and worketh righteousness, is accepted of him."

29. And Jesus departed from thence, and came nigh unto the sea of Galilee; and went up into a mountain, and sat down there.

30. And great multitudes came unto him, having with them those that were lame, blind, dumb, maimed, and many others, and cast them down at Jesus' feet; and he healed them:

31. Insomuch that the multitude wondered, when they saw the dumb to speak, the maimed to be whole, the lame to walk, and the blind to see: and they glorified the God of Israel.

We now approach incidents which may be regarded as repetitions. We have read such words as these before; why read them again? *Because God's government is a great repetition of love!* There is, however, a marked discrepancy between the freshness of His mercy and the responsiveness of man's heart. His "mercies are new every morning"—

literally "new,"—fresh from His heart, never specifically given before, and yet they have virtually been all given in the gift of Jesus Christ! Is there no lesson in the fact that we have now come to what may be termed a commonplace in Christ's history? There is this lesson at least—*The possibility of being accustomed to favour until we receive it without emotion.* Let it be supposed that this paragraph alone contained all that was known of Jesus Christ; into what enlarged proportions it would rise! Is it, then, the less important because it is one of many? The practical lesson is, that familiarity with God's great gifts may induce carelessness as to their value and purpose.

The paragraph, by an easy accommodation, shows:—1. *A marvellous combination of Separateness and Sympathy on the part of Jesus Christ.* He is seated on the mountain, or throne of His own making, and by so much is separated from society; yet He is accessible—He may be tracked by His footprints—men may go after Him. So He is now in heaven, &c. 2. *A marvellous combination of Suffering and Hope on the part of the people.* All kinds of sufferings were represented by the "great multitudes," and all the sufferers had hope, as they were borne towards the Man seated on the mountain. Think of the ministry of *Hope* in the sick-chamber! 3. *A marvellous combination of Delight and Reverence on the part of the observers.* Delight and reverence are not always associated. (*a*) Some delight would be incompatible with reverence; (*b*) The measure of reverence determines the true nature of the delight. Worship should always be associated with personal and public benefactions,—"they glorified the God of Israel."

32. Then Jesus called his disciples unto him, and said, I have compassion on the multitude, because they continue with me now three days, and have nothing to eat: and I will not send them away fasting, lest they faint in the way.

33. And his disciples say unto him, Whence should we have so much bread in the wilderness, as to fill so great a multitude?
34. And Jesus saith unto them, How many loaves have ye? And they said, Seven, and a few little fishes.
35. And he commanded the multitude to sit down on the ground.
36. And he took the seven loaves and the fishes, and gave thanks, and brake them, and gave to his disciples, and the disciples to the multitude.
37. And they did all eat, and were filled: and they took up of the broken meat that was left seven baskets full.
38. And they that did eat were four thousand men, beside women and children.
39. And he sent away the multitude, and took ship, and came into the coasts of Magdala.

Another repetition. We have already remarked on the miracle of feeding; we propose therefore to look at this incident as furnishing five points of contrast with the immediately preceding miracle of healing. 1. In the case of feeding the multitude, the desire originated on the part of Christ; in the case of healing the multitude, the desire originated on the part of the sufferers. This double demand (if the expression may be allowed) upon the resources of Christ is being constantly repeated. Christ gives innumerable blessings that *are not asked for*, and, in addition, answers innumerable *prayers*. How could He be satisfied with doing merely what He was asked to do! "He is able to do exceeding abundantly above," &c. 2. In the case of disease there was a great illustration of Christ's power to *cure;* in the case of feeding, there was a great illustration of Christ's power to *prevent*. The reason which He assigned shows this,—"lest they faint in the way." This consideration introduces us to the boundless sphere of Christ's *preventive ministry*, and taken in connection with the other miracle, shows that Christ's service covers the *whole ground* of human necessity. 3. In the case of healing, the multitudes showed no want of confidence in Christ; in the case of feeding, the very chosen men started a difficulty. It is so to-day. Most of the difficulties are inside, not outside the Church; where faith should be the strongest, there is sometimes hardly any faith at all! 4. In the case of healing, Christ worked without intervention; in the case of feeding, Christ availed Himself of instrumentality,—"He gave to his disciples, and the disciples to the multitude." So to-day, there is a ministry in which He serves alone; there is also a work in which He employs servants. His difficulty is, that some of the servants wish to help Him in His peculiar work;—they are not content to *dispense* the bread, they must try their skill at a *miracle*. 5. In the case of healing, there was a human declaration of reverence; in the case of the feeding, there was a Divine reproof of unbelief,—"they took up of the broken meat that was left seven baskets full." Compare the different endings of the two incidents; in the one case "they glorified the God of Israel," in the other not a word was spoken, but every crumb was a witness against the unbelief of the disciples! God rebukes His people constantly in precisely the same way. The *abundance* of His gifts is a reproof of distrust. With how many blossoms He fills the trees; with how many flowers He beautifies the garden, the field, and the way-side; there is superabundance everywhere —baskets of fragments on every hand! Nothing is done in weakness, or by constraint; He is as mighty at the end as at the beginning,—"He fainteth not, neither is weary."

The two cases give two points of application :—1. To the suffering; 2. To the hungering.

### CHAPTER XVI.

1. The Pharisees also with the Sadducees came, and tempting desired him that he would show them a sign from heaven.
2. He answered and said unto them, When it is evening, ye say, It will be fair weather: for the sky is red.
3. And in the morning, It will be foul weather to-day: for the sky is red and lowering. O ye hypocrites, ye can discern the face of the sky ; but can ye not discern the signs of the times?

4. A wicked and adulterous generation seeketh after a sign; and there shall no sign be given unto it, but the sign of the prophet Jonas. And he left them, and departed.

LANGE says: "We would suggest that the Lord attached a symbolical meaning to what He said about the signs of the weather. The red at even of the Old Testament betokened fair weather at hand. Similarly, the red sky at the commencement of the New Testament indicated the storm about to descend on Israel." This appears to be strained. STIER says: "Had He even done as many signs in the heaven as He did on earth they would assuredly have impudently come forward still more with the objection, —' What good is to be done to us by all these appearances and spectacles, which dazzle the mob, and which aërial spirits may produce for Him by magic? Let Him, instead of this, heal our sick, the lame, and the blind, as it is written in the prophets, that we may know that it is He!'" This interruptive interview shows:—1. *The difficulty of satisfying impracticable people.* They always want something which lies beyond the point which has been attained. They are "ever learning, yet never able to come to a knowledge of the truth." The impracticability of the enemies of Christ arose from moral eccentricity. 2. *The dangers of a half-educated sagacity.* The opponents of Christ could read the signs of the weather, but not the signs of the times. Sharp people in one direction may be very obtuse in another. This should restrain those who have partially exercised their sagacity; because a man can foretell a storm, it does not follow that he can predict a revolution. 3. *The right application of hard names.* Hear what Christ calls these men,—" Hypocrites, wicked and adulterous generation." An inquiry may be good, though the inquirer is bad. Let us beware of fair questions propounded with bad motives. Christ discerned the spirits of the inquirers; but we have not His penetration, let us therefore withhold the epithets until we acquire the discernment. 4. *The demand of Christianity to be judged by a wide induction of facts.* Christ points to "the signs of the times." He saw Himself everywhere. The appeal of Christianity is the same to-day,—look at literature, science, politics, national development, and in all there are symptoms of a profound Christological influence. This is still an available plea on behalf of Christianity, viz., *Look at men! Look at events!*

Christ explains His own meaning about Jonah in chapter xii., 40th verse.

5. And when his disciples were come to the other side, they had forgotten to take bread.

6. Then Jesus said unto them, Take heed and beware of the leaven of the Pharisees and of the Sadducees.

7. And they reasoned among themselves, saying, It is because we have taken no bread.

8. Which when Jesus perceived, he said unto them, O ye of little faith, why reason ye among yourselves, because ye have brought no bread?

9. Do ye not yet understand, neither remember the five loaves of the five thousand, and how many baskets ye took up?

10. Neither the seven loaves of the four thousand, and how many baskets ye took up?

11. How is it that ye do not understand that I spake it not to you concerning bread, that ye should beware of the leaven of the Pharisees and of the Sadducees?

12. Then understood they how that he bade them not beware of the leaven of bread, but of the doctrine of the Pharisees and of the Sadducees.

1. An instance of giving superficial interpretations of deep words. Christ's thoughts have always been exposed to this peril; they have either been made so personal as to lose much of their comprehensiveness and dignity, or they have been so generalised as to lose all practical worth. 2. This incident shows the danger, too, of finding personalities where no personalities were intended. "It is because we have taken no bread," say self-conceited men, even when the remotest personal reference is out of the question!

The spirit that is willing to apply truth to personal circumstances ought to be cultivated; but the spirit that narrows everything to insignificant ends is to be avoided. 3. The danger of *literalising* is also pointed out. The figure is not to be mistaken for a reality; when Christ says, "leaven," He may mean "doctrine." What need, then, of reflection, comparison, and devout inquiry !

13. When Jesus came into the coasts of Cæsarea Philippi, he asked his disciples, saying, Whom do men say that I the Son of man am?

1. CHRIST CAME TO BE THE CENTRAL SUBJECT OF HUMAN INQUIRY. Compared with Him all other themes are trifles, 2. BEING THE CENTRAL SUBJECT OF HUMAN INQUIRY, EACH MAN MUST HAVE AN OPINION ABOUT CHRIST. *Must* have. Not to have any opinion is to have the opinion that other subjects have priority of claim, or superiority of fascination. 3. AS EACH MAN MUST HAVE AN OPINION ABOUT CHRIST, CHRIST'S MODE OF REVELATION MUST HAVE BEEN ADAPTED TO ALL CLASSES OF INTELLECT. *How* did He reveal Himself? In the *flesh;* as Son of *man;* as Son of *God;* as a *Teacher;* as a *Sacrifice.* 4. AS CHRIST'S REVELATION WAS ADAPTED TO ALL CLASSES OF INTELLECT, HE WILL ULTIMATELY DEMAND A VERDICT FROM EVERY MAN. "Whom do ye say that I am?" On the answer, what issues hang!

14. And they said, Some say that thou art John the Baptist; some, Elias; and others, Jeremias, or one of the prophets.
15. He saith unto them, But whom say ye that I am?

No being has so challenged the speculative faculties of men as Jesus Christ. All great natures excite speculation. A great man is a great problem. We naturally wish the wonder-worker to tell us his secret. While, however, Christ has awakened so much speculation, about no man have so many mistakes been made as about Himself,—witness the different answers just given.

16. And Simon Peter answered and said, Thou art the Christ, the Son of the living God.

17. And Jesus answered and said unto him, Blessed art thou, Simon Bar-jona: for flesh and blood hath not revealed it unto thee, but my Father which is in heaven.

18. And I say also unto thee, That thou art Peter, and upon this rock I will build my church: and the gates of hell shall not prevail against it.

19. And I will give unto thee the keys of the kingdom of heaven: and whatsoever thou shalt bind on earth shall be bound in heaven: and whatsoever thou shalt loose on earth shall be loosed in heaven.

20. Then charged he his disciples that they should tell no man that he was Jesus the Christ.

Peter representative of *inspired* men. We cannot see the point of contact between Peter and God, yet by his words we know he had received a revelation from heaven. This circumstance shows:—1. There *is* a communication between God and the human mind. 2. That special men are chosen for special communications. 3. That such chosen men are "blessed." The practical lesson is, That though all may not be immediate *receivers* of the word, yet all may be *doers* of the word. Peter was *one*, but the Church is *many*.

The first man who was "called" gave the first complete statement of the person of Christ. Why should we hesitate to acknowledge the position which Jesus Christ Himself assigned to Simon Peter? A *man* was needed to stand first and highest among men as Christ's representative; why should not Peter be that man? If Christ's Peter fell, so did God's Adam; what if this should but show the utter dependence of the highest forms of humanity upon Divine support? Was it more to be Peter than to be Adam? A beginning must be made somewhere; if Adam was to be the father of all living, why should not Peter be the rock on which the Church was to stand? God has built the whole human family upon Adam; and Christ proposed to build the whole human Church upon Peter;

where is the incongruity? It is said that some men pretend to be successors of Peter; but are not all men successors of Adam? All who cherish the spirit and do the work of Peter are undoubtedly Peter's successors, and will have the " power of the keys " quite as much as Peter had. There need not be any more difficulty in accepting Peter as " the rock " than in accepting Adam as the federal head of the world; no physical inconvenience arises from the latter; no spiritual inconvenience need arise from the former.

In the 17th verse Peter stands before his brethren as an *inspired* man; σὰρξ καὶ αἷμα οὐκ ἀπεκάλυψέ σοι ἀλλ' ὁ πατήρ μου, ὁ ἐν τοῖς οὐρανοῖς. Flesh and blood (σὰρξ καὶ αἷμα, a Hebrew idiom signifying *man*, generally) cannot reveal the higher truths; man, in other words, is not the source of his own highest conceptions. *How* the Father can communicate truths to the human mind is not revealed. " The wind bloweth where it listeth," &c. Paul prays " that the God of our Lord Jesus Christ, the Father of glory, may give unto you the spirit of wisdom and revelation " (Eph. i. 17); and James says that God giveth " wisdom liberally and upbraideth not." The fact is stated, the process is unrevealed. God's relation to the human mind will probably remain a mystery; but the instance now under notice, and others given in the Scriptures, show that God *does* communicate directly with men, and that not unfrequently He communicates to the most unlikely men His highest revelations. " Base things of the world, and things which are despised, hath God chosen, yea, and things which are not, to bring to nought things that are." " Thou hast hid these things from the wise and prudent, and hast revealed them unto babes." In the inspired man we have:—1. A correct reader of human character; and 2. A fearless speaker of

Divine convictions. Other men had been making mistakes respecting Christ; calling Him John the Baptist, Elias, Jeremias, or one of the prophets; but Peter announced Him by His true name. Peter was not pronounced an inspired man until he had pronounced inspired words: " By their fruits ye shall know them."

In the 18th verse we find words which some have dreaded to interpret in a plain and natural way. Christ does not put Peter before Himself. He says, "*I* will build," and He calls the Church "*my* church." Did God put Adam before Himself when He constituted him the father of all living? God is still the Creator of the human family; and Christ is still the Founder and Foundation, the Redeemer and Builder, of His Church. Our Christian relation may be the same to Peter that our physical relation is to Adam. Adam was the first man, Peter was the first Christian. Adam stands next to the Creator, Peter stands next to the Redeemer. Christ builds the Church upon Peter, and Peter is founded upon Christ; "for other foundation can no man lay than that is laid, which is Jesus Christ;" and Peter himself describes Christ as the "living stone, disallowed indeed of men, but chosen of God, and precious" (1 Peter ii. 4).

"The gates of hell" (πύλαι ᾅδου), "the gates of Hades," is an expression which may signify all the forces of evil. 1. The Church is opposed to evil. 2. Evil will be opposed to the Church. 3. In the contest the Church will not be injured.

The 19th verse sets forth the transcendent dignity of the inspired man. A new era opened upon the disciples at the moment that this confession was made—the era of immediate communication with Christ's Father. Heaven and earth were felt to be in closer connection.

The inspired man, *so long as he keeps up to the level*

*of his inspiration*, cannot do wrong:—what he binds on earth is bound in heaven,—what he looses on earth is loosed in heaven. This must be so; for, *being inspired*, he is in communication with Christ's Father; the words that he *hears* he speaks,—the visions which he sees he reveals. Every inspired man has "the keys of the kingdom of heaven" by virtue of his inspiration; he is so far free of the dominion of the senses as to have distinct visions of truth which are not revealed to men who walk after the flesh. The Church need not have any fear of men who associate Peter's inspiration with Peter's authority; and as for those who boast his authority without his inspiration, they need not be feared, for their influence is comprehended under the expression "gates of hell."

Figurative expressions are, of course, to be explained as such. In the case under review there is considerable mingling of figure; for example, in one place Christ is called the *foundation*, and in another He is called the *builder;* He is said to be "the chief corner-stone," and yet in the 18th verse He says, "I will build my church;" how can the chief corner-stone build the Church? Manifestly the expressions are figurative, and must be explained accordingly.

Peter was confessedly the most inconstant disciple, yet the frailest man becomes a rock by Christ's gracious influence! He may be cast down, but he shall not be destroyed; he shall stand the shock of the gates of hell. In making this promise Christ does two things:—1. He asserts a *moral* power quite equal to the *miraculous* power which He had so often displayed. He says He will defend His Church, and defend it against enemies invisible, insidious, and persistent. 2. He specifies a body of men between whom and Himself the most vital association subsists: that body of men is called "my church." In the expression, "I will build my church," there is great sublimity. How little prospect there was of building a community; how few and poor the materials; how scanty the apparent resources of the builder! Speaking of the ἐκκλησία, LANGE says: "The Church is not the kingdom of heaven itself, but a positive institution of Christ by which, on the one hand, the kingdom of heaven becomes directly manifest in the world by its *worship*, while, on the other hand, it spreads through the world by means of its *missionary* efforts. The Church bears the same relation to the kingdom of heaven as the Messianic state under the Old Testament to the theocracy, the two being certainly not identical." LANGE's observation on "the gates of hell" is striking: "Throughout Scripture Hades means the kingdom of death; which is, indeed, connected with the kingdom of Satan, but has a more comprehensive meaning. Hades is described as having gates; it is figuratively represented as a castle with gates. These gates serve a hostile purpose, since they opened, like a yawning abyss of death, to swallow up Christ, and then Peter, or the apostles and the Church, in their martyrdom. For a long time it has seemed as if the Church of Christ would become the prey of this destroying Hades. But its gates shall not ultimately prevail,—they shall be taken; and Christ will overcome and abolish the kingdom of death in His Church." STIER has some bold statements on the passage. He says, on verse 18th, "That *this* applies to Peter no longer merely in the name of all the apostles, but with a certain preference of his *personality*,—which the Protestant Church ought never to have denied to its own hurt, by an unnatural explanation of the words."

Great fear has been expressed lest Peter should seem to have any supremacy, but the fact is, that supremacy is a law of life; men cannot all be first; men cannot all be equal; in the Church, as in common society, there must be gradation. With regard, however, to the supposed supremacy of Peter, it should be remembered—1. That after the resurrection the disciples were invested with equal authority—"Receive ye the Holy Ghost: whose soever sins ye remit, they are remitted unto them; and whose soever sins ye retain, they are retained" (John xx. 22, 23); and even before the crucifixion a promise of the same import was given to the disciples collectively—"Whatsoever ye shall bind on earth shall be bound in heaven: and whatsoever ye shall loose on earth shall be loosed in heaven" (Matt. xviii. 18). Why not? The Holy Ghost directs the man, gives the man his power, and saves the man from committing blasphemy. The deed has no validity apart from the Holy Ghost. This fact is the explanation of the mystery. It should be remembered—2. That Peter himself makes no undue assumptions of power; he recognises Jesus Christ as "the living stone," "the chief corner-stone, elect, precious." His sermons and letters contain many proofs of his humility and unpretending fellowship with the apostles (Acts xv. 7; x. 43, 44, 45).

On a review of the whole subject five things are evident: 1. That a right apprehension of the Person of Christ is associated with "blessedness;" 2. That whoever has the clearest apprehension of the Person of Christ has a corresponding supremacy among men; 3. That supremacy among men is dependent entirely on the continuance of the inspiration which originated it; 4. That where the inspiration is equal the authority is equal; 5. That as all Christians are promised the Spirit of inspiration if they will "ask" for it, all Christians may, according to their personal capacity, share the spiritual authority which was first given to Peter.

This should be the basis of all power in the Church—viz.,

*Inspiration.* The man who walks most closely with God should wield, and will ultimately wield, the profoundest influence in the Church.

21. From that time forth began Jesus to show unto his disciples, how that he must go unto Jerusalem, and suffer many things of the elders and chief priests and scribes, and be killed, and be raised again the third day.

22. Then Peter took him, and began to rebuke him, saying, Be it far from thee, Lord: this shall not be unto thee.

23. But he turned, and said unto Peter, Get thee behind me, Satan: thou art an offence unto me: for thou savourest not the things that be of God, but those that be of men.

24. Then said Jesus unto his disciples, If any man will come after me, let him deny himself, and take up his cross, and follow me.

25. For whosoever will save his life shall lose it: and whosoever will lose his life for my sake shall find it.

26. For what is a man profited, if he shall gain the whole world, and lose his own soul? or what shall a man give in exchange for his soul?

These words may be used as the basis of a discourse on *Great Purposes and Interruptive Voices, or the Profound and the Superficial in human life.* Christ says, "I must go to Jerusalem,"—that is a *Great Purpose.* Peter said, "Not so; be it far from thee,"—that is an *Interruptive Voice.* We see how necessary Inspiration is to Authority by comparing Christ's address to Peter in this case with his address to Peter given immediately before. Put the two together:—

"Blessed art thou, Simon Bar-jona" (ver. 17).
"Get thee behind me, Satan" (ver. 23).
"Flesh and blood have not revealed it unto thee" (ver. 17).
"Thou savourest not the things that be of God" (ver. 23).

How the inspired man may fall!

Looking at the words homiletically, they suggest the following points:—1. THE GREATNESS OF A PURPOSE GIVES ITS POSSESSOR CORRESPONDING TRANQUILLITY IN ANTICIPATION OF THE SEVEREST TRIALS. As Christ uttered this "must go," He embodied the greatest purpose that ever actuated human life; and how calm He was! 2. SUPERFICIAL NATURES CANNOT COMPREHEND GREAT PURPOSES. Peter said,—" Be it far from thee." Great ideas have always had to struggle for existence; they have been encountered by Peters who could not see through death to resurrection. Every man has a tempter on his way! 3. GREAT PURPOSES ARE NECESSARILY ASSOCIATED WITH SELF-SACRIFICE. " If any man will come after me," &c. These words acquire their true significance when regarded as the continuation of the discourse concerning what was awaiting the Saviour at Jerusalem. Thus the 21st and the 24th verses might be read without any break, and the sense would be this:— "From that time forth began Jesus to show unto his disciples how that he must GO . . . . then said Jesus unto his disciples, If any man will COME AFTER ME." First, *Whoever follows a great leader must expect great sacrifices.* Second, *The spirit and example of a great moral leader must ever be reproduced by faithful followers.* 4. GREAT PURPOSES ALWAYS CORRECTLY ESTIMATE THE VALUE OF MATERIAL POSSESSIONS. " What is a man profited," &c. What may the word "soul" be taken to signify in this connection? It is equivalent to *great purposes*. Peter wished Christ to forego his great plan of life; and Christ asks, What shall it profit me if I gain the whole world and stifle my convictions, falsify my vows, quench my aspirations? 5. SUPERFICIAL NATURES ALWAYS PROCEED UPON A SELF-DEFEATING POLICY. " Whosoever will save his life shall lose it: and whosoever will lose his life for my sake shall find it." Look at Lot as an illustration. Peter wished for present ease, Christ showed him that the "soul" was of the first importance, and all else secondary or trivial.

27. For the Son of man shall come in the glory of his Father with his angels; and then he shall reward every man according to his works.
28. Verily I say unto you, There be some standing here which shall not taste of death, till they see the Son of man coming in his kingdom.

1. Exaltation after crucifixion; 2. The good man cannot

be kept in the grave; 3. The man who has done most for the race will be its judge—service is the best qualification for criticism; 4. Dark sayings keep the mind from stagnation— how the 28th verse would startle the disciples! Why "some," and not "all"? What is the " kingdom" of the Son of man? Hard words for ignorant men, yet much calculated to excite the mind in a course of devout and practical inquiry.

*CHAPTER XVII.*

1. And after six days Jesus taketh Peter, James, and John his brother, and bringeth them up into an high mountain apart,
2. And was transfigured before them: and his face did shine as the sun, and his raiment was white as the light.
3. And, behold, there appeared unto them Moses and Elias talking with him.

The Transfiguration, like the revelation of the Church, marks a distinct epoch in Christ's life. *What is the place of the Transfiguration in the Messianic development?* It would seem that from the time of our Lord asking, "Whom do men say that I the Son of man am?" he called particular attention to his own Person. Up to that time He worked as it were simply as a public benefactor, a great philanthropist, who lived expressly for the purpose of doing good: but the time had come for showing that He was *more* than was generally understood by a public benefactor, and there was a difficulty in getting men to understand what *more* He was. With infinite wisdom He collected public opinion through His disciples; having ascertained what "men" said, He asked the disciples their own opinion; thus, by two steps, He came forward towards a full disclosure of His Personal dignity; it was not hurried upon the disciples; the revelation was graduated; and, lest the light should be too intense for their vision, the great shadow of the *Cross* was thrown over it,—He must " suffer many things of the elders and chief priests and scribes, and be killed, and be raised again the third day." The apprehension of the Person of Christ on the part of the disciples, was associated with a sublime *moral* revelation on the part of Christ. The disciples were now to be taught something of *sacrifice;* and in order to have a true idea of sacrifice they must have a true conception of Christ's *person*. If He was only a common man He could only be "killed;" if He was more than a common man He could "be raised again the third day." The question, then, was, "Who am I?" The answer given by inspiration of the Father was, "Thou art the Christ, the Son of the living God." This character separated Him from all other men. *Now*, when He spoke of being "killed," the word had an application which it could not otherwise have had. How could the *Son of the living God* be killed? How could the very fountain of immortality be affected by death? A spark may be quenched, but the sun can only be eclipsed,—a momentary darkening, and then the great brightness! At this point may be seen the use of a Divine revelation of the *Person* of Christ. Everything turned upon the *quality* of that Person. Hence the joy, the exultancy, of Jesus Christ when He found that the *Father* had told what He Himself could hardly express,—told the disciples that their Master was His own Son! Here, then, so much is gained; the Person has been revealed, the Cross has been hinted at. Meanwhile the intelligence was to proceed no further,— "Tell no man that I am Jesus the Christ; let me work for some time longer, just as I have been working; the plan must be disclosed gradually: you, as my disciples, shall hear about it first; but even *you* must restrain your curiosity, and do your daily work in all quietness and patience."

The Transfiguration showed another phase of the Person of Christ. Hitherto He had dwelt secretly in the flesh, and was not physically distinguished from other men. How little did observers know the *interior* life of Jesus Christ! What awful force was beating in His heart! What light was shaded by His eyes! He could not tell all, or show all; the sun is lighting more worlds than ours; what if he were to turn his concentrated splendour upon the earth? Jesus Christ was the brightness of the Father's glory, and the most He could do was to shed a few broken rays on the weak vision of the world. On the "high mountain apart" He showed more of His glory than He had before disclosed. There are exceptional hours in human history, when men utter words which attest the grandeur of the human mind, when the countenance burns with the fire of intelligent enthusiasm, and the voice reaches a tone of purer music than is born of earth; and in those exceptional hours we see somewhat of the dignity of human nature. Multiply this by infinitude, and we shall know something of what the disciples saw when Christ's "face did shine as the sun, and His raiment was white as the light." The Transfiguration completed the revelation of the Person of Christ,—the Father had revealed Him to the *mind*, now the Father reveals Him to the *sight*.

What was the meaning of Moses and Elias talking to Christ? Moses represented the law; Elias represented the prophets; Christ was the fulfilment of both. Many incidental points of importance might be inferred from this appearance of Moses and Elias: it shows—1. That departed men are still living; 2. That death does not destroy the individuality of men; 3. That the *greatest* of departed men are interested in the work of Christ; 4. That immediate personal communication between departed spirits and men yet in the flesh is possible.

4. Then answered Peter, and said unto Jesus, Lord, it is good for us to be here: if thou wilt, let us make here three tabernacles; one for thee, and one for Moses, and one for Elias.

Peter has apparently recovered himself from the effects of the error recorded in ch. xvi. 22; yet his proposition, though well intended, was unheeded. Soon, therefore, do we come upon instances of fallibility, which show that the moment a man loses his *inspiration* he loses his *authority*. It is characteristic of partially developed natures to wish to build and rest on the very first appearance of anything like comfort or peace. Peter had seen no such sight before; weary of the world, he desired a resting-place; excited by religious impulse, he wished to build three tabernacles. A very fallible Peter, truly! One day, close to God; another, rebuked as the medium of the devil! There is something beautiful, too, in Peter addressing *Jesus* particularly; *Moses* was there; *Elias* was there; great names to every Jew! Yet Peter overlooked all the history and tradition associated with their illustrious names, and addressed *Jesus* as the Lord. Was there anything in this prefigurative of the perfect homage which the Church, throughout all time, should render to the Son of the living God? The point need not be pressed; yet, as a matter of fact, Moses and Elias must decrease, while of the increase of *Christ's* government there shall be no end.

5. While he yet spake, behold, a bright cloud overshadowed them; and behold a voice out of the cloud, which said, This is my beloved Son, in whom I am well pleased; hear ye him.

Up to this time little has been said of the Miraculous Conception of Jesus Christ; now God declares Himself, in the hearing of Moses the lawgiver, Elias the prophet, and the disciples who formed the nucleus of the Church, Jesus Christ's Father. He had declared this to the general multitude at the baptism; now He declares it on a "high mountain apart," and adds, "hear ye him." The command means that Jesus Christ had something particular to say; had, in fact, a new revelation to make, the making of which would mark an epoch in His ministry. The words, "Hear ye him," are very emphatic: 1. Christ's authority Divine; 2. Christ's authority undivided; 3. Men are to be "heard," only so far as they repeat Christ's words.

6. And when the disciples heard it, they fell on their face, and were sore afraid.
7. And Jesus came and touched them, and said, Arise, and be not afraid.
8. And when they had lifted up their eyes, they saw no man, save Jesus only.

There are experiences which cast men down with a view to their being lifted to a higher and firmer elevation than they have yet attained. When the disciples "fell on their face, and were sore afraid," they little understood how God was conducting them to a fuller knowledge of the purposes which had been kept secret from the foundation of the world. Review life, and say how much we owe to having been cast down and sore afraid? We truly need to be struck with the higher light, and thrust down by the higher power, before we can be much or do much in life. The Saul who is blinded for three days may become a Paul. Looked at homiletically, this portion of the narrative suggests:—1. The *mercifulness* displayed in a *graduated revelation*; 2. Our dependence upon *Christ* through all the crises of our spiritual development (ver. 7); 3. The glorious *issue* of some of the most *mysterious circumstances* of life,—" they saw no man, save Jesus only."

9. And as they came down from the mountain, Jesus charged them, saying, Tell the vision to no man, until the Son of man be risen again from the dead.

1. Christ's life not to be told in *fragments*; 2. The parts of Christ's life are mutually explanatory; 3. The resurrection of Christ, the great reconciling and all-explaining fact in His ministry. His profoundest words would have had no meaning had He not known that He would rise again from the dead.

## MATTHEW XVII.

10. And his disciples asked him, saying, Why then say the scribes that Elias must first come?
11. And Jesus answered and said unto them, Elias truly shall first come, and restore all things.
12. But I say unto you, That Elias is come already, and they knew him not, but have done unto him whatsoever they listed. Likewise shall also the Son of man suffer of them.
13. Then the disciples understood that he spake unto them of John the Baptist.

The disciples now begin to put deeper questions than they had ever put; now they want explanations of prophecies and criticisms upon current theology; and from Christ's method of meeting their inquiries, we may learn:—1. That prophecies may be fulfilling while men are *unaware* of the fact; 2. Consequently, that men may be proceeding on *miscalculations as to time;* 3. That God is responsible for the *facts,* not for the *interpretations* of prophecy; 4. That all prophets may expect *maltreatment* at the hands of *dogmatic or technical interpreters* (ver. 12). All these considerations impart a profound solemnity to life!

The command—"tell the vision to no man, until the Son of man be risen from the dead"—which is given again and again in various forms, proceeds upon a principle, with whose operation society is well acquainted; that principle is that *no man can be fully understood or appreciated while he is living.* Many circumstances combine to conceal his réal stature. Specially are the "*visions*" of living men apt to be misconstrued and misapplied; their common daily history may be lived in the presence of the world, but if they are favoured with visions and dreams, with inspirations and prophetic foresights, let this higher life be kept a secret until death has supplied the chief condition of a just judgment. This hiding of the higher life will be in proportion to its compass and elevation. The young Christian talks more of his experience than the old Christian, just as a rill may make more noise than a river. An *ordinary* mother talks much of her child; but the mother of *Christ* "kept all these things, and pondered them in her heart."

14. And when they were come to the multitude, there came to him a certain man, kneeling down to him, and saying,

15. Lord, have mercy on my son: for he is lunatick, and sore vexed: for ofttimes he falleth into the fire, and oft into the water.

If the "tabernacles" had been built according to Peter's suggestion, what would have become of those who were hoping in Christ for help? Seasons of rapture should prepare for seasons of service. Compare the scene on the top of the mountain with the scene at its base; this comparison will show:—1. The great *contrasts* of human life; 2. The condition of society in the *absence* of Christ; 3. The *highest function* of man—to *save* (physically, mentally, spiritually, men may do much to save one another); 4. The *practical aspect* of the sublimest realisations of life,—what a realisation Christ had, yet how practical was the after-work! It is better to heal a *man* than to dwell in a tabernacle on the high mountain.

16. And I brought him to thy disciples, and they could not cure him.

This verse, by a natural accommodation, shows:—1. That the disciples are powerless *without Christ.* 2. That the powerlessness of the disciples is likely to bring *discredit upon Christ.* 3. That the powerlessness of the disciples is entirely *their own fault,* because they need never to be without Christ.

17. Then Jesus answered and said, O faithless and perverse generation, how long shall I be with you? how long shall I suffer you? bring him hither to me.

18. And Jesus rebuked the devil; and he departed out of him: and the child was cured from that very hour.

19. Then came the disciples to Jesus apart, and said, Why could not we cast him out?

20. And Jesus said unto them, Because of your unbelief: for verily I say unto you, If ye have faith as a grain of mustard seed, ye shall say unto this mountain, Remove hence to yonder place; and it shall remove; and nothing shall be impossible unto you.

21. Howbeit this kind goeth not out but by prayer and fasting.

The last point is proved by these words, which, taken by themselves, show:—1. That the inefficiency of the Church is a source of grief to Jesus Church. 2. That what is wanting on the part of the disciples is made up by the power and grace of the Master. 3. That different diseases require different treatment,—"this kind goeth not out but by prayer and fasting." Illustration may be found in common life; among diseases of the soul may be set down—Pride, Lust, Covetousness, Self-confidence, &c., the cure of which may require variations of treatment. 4. However many and subtle the variations, Christ's power is available for all.

On the expression, "This kind goeth not out," &c., LANGE remarks: "It were a mistake to regard this demoniacal possession as different from others in kind, and not merely in degree, and hence as constituting a peculiar kind, for which specific prayer and fasting were required. The Lord rather conveyed to His disciples that they had not preserved or cultivated the state of mind and heart necessary for the occasion, that they were not sufficiently prepared and collected to cast out so malignant a demon. . . . The demons of such complete melancholy could only be overcome by most earnest prayer and entire renunciation of the world." STIER says: "Our Lord says two things in the *But*: first, that He had meant the casting out of devils by the similitude of removing mountains; and, secondly, that to control spirits, to break the evil will, the wicked power in the kingdom of sin, and of rebellion against the Almighty, who tolerates it according to the law of freedom, and even only thus removes it, is, indeed, another and greater thing than the simple working of miracles on helpless nature." OLSHAUSEN says: "The immediate connection of the words, with the reproof administered to the apostles, leads obviously to this meaning—'this obstinate enemy was not to be overcome in the same way that many others are. It was needful for you, with prayer and fasting, earnestly to strive after more of the power of faith, and then might you have been victorious.'" Speaking of the same verse (21st), ADAM CLARKE says: "I strongly suspect it to be an interpolation; but, if it be, it is very ancient, as Origen, Chrysostom, and others of the primitive Fathers, acknowledge it."

22. And while they abode in Galilee, Jesus said unto them, The Son of man shall be betrayed into the hands of men :
23. And they shall kill him, and the third day he shall be raised again. And they were exceeding sorry.

What had Jesus Christ done that He should be condemned to death? Could He not interpose the power with which He had worked His miracles, and so save Himself from such a betrayal as that spoken of? The understanding of the idea depends upon a proper criticism of the word παραδίδοσθαι; instead of being rendered " shall be betrayed," the expression should be, "is about to be *delivered*," the word "delivered" having a wider meaning than the word "betrayed,"—embracing the principal idea of the latter, but extending further. The word παραδίδωμι is variously rendered in the New Testament; for example, John was (παρεδόθη) cast *into* prison (Matt. iv. 12); and in Mark iv. 29, it is rendered "*brought forth*" (παραδῷ); in Acts xv. 26, we have παραδεδωκόσι rendered "*have hazarded;*" and, in 1 Peter ii. 23, the word is translated "*committed.*" It is important to note the various senses in which the word is used, so as to escape the idea that Jesus Christ was simply overpowered by superior force, and so made a victim or a martyr. The betrayal of our Lord was not a merely human deed; was not Jesus Christ mightier than

Judas Iscariot? He offered, or gave, or delivered himself; no man took His life from Him; He surrendered it, not as a martyr, but as a sacrifice.

About this announcement there are two things remarkable:—1. Christ's care in *preparing* His disciples for the Cross. 2. The confidence with which Christ affirms His own *resurrection*,—"the third day he shall be raised again." To have spoken of the betrayal alone, would have been to have put before His disciples a fragmentary truth; over the darkness of death, Christ sheds the light of resurrection. The disciples saw the fragment, they could not see the whole; hence they were ἐλυπήθησαν σφόδρα, "grieved exceedingly." The revelation of Christ's purposes can occasion grief only when it is incompletely apprehended; sorrow attaches to some of the intermediate points, but never to the issue: "the Lamb *slain*" is a part of the process; the Lamb slain, but seated *in the midst of the throne*, is the sublime consummation.

The change of subject is startling; we pass from the great sacrifice for sin to the payment of tribute money:—

24. And when they were come to Capernaum, they that received tribute-money came to Peter, and said, Doth not your master pay tribute?
25. He saith, Yes. And when he was come into the house, Jesus prevented him, saying, What thinkest thou, Simon? of whom do the kings of the earth take custom or tribute? of their own children, or of strangers?
26. Peter saith unto him, Of strangers. Jesus saith unto him, Then are the children free.
27. Notwithstanding, lest we should offend them, go thou to the sea, and cast an hook, and take up the fish that first cometh up; and when thou hast opened his mouth, thou shalt find a piece of money: that take, and give unto them for me and thee.

On this passage LANGE says: "DE WETTE regards the passage as involving some difficulties, since Jesus had disowned every outward and earthly claim in His character as Messiah, and had become subject to the law. Accordingly, this critic suggests that Jesus had only intended to prove the rashness of Peter's promise, and to suggest the thought to him (as he was still entangled with Jewish legalism) that, in point of law, the demand made upon him was not valid. On the other hand, OLSHAUSEN maintains that Jesus asserted His exaltation above the temple ritual (as in chap. xii. 8). MEYER reminds us that although, as Messiah, Jesus was above the law, in His infinite condescension He submitted to its demands. This explanation is, so far, more satisfactory. But commentators seem to forget that the breach between the ancient theocracy and the ἐκκλησία had already begun in Judæa and Galilee, and that Jesus had entered on His path of sufferings. It was inconsistent to reject, and virtually (though perhaps not formally) to excommunicate, Jesus, and yet, at the same time, to demand from Him the temple-tribute. And, in this sense, the apostles themselves were included among the υἱοί (in the plural). They were to share in the suffering and in the excommunication of their Master."

The circumstance may be paraphrased thus: We are now called upon to pay tribute, not to the Roman government, but in support of the temple. But I am the Lord of the temple, and consequently am free from its law of offerings and tributes and taxes; and my disciples, by reason of their vital union with myself, are also free. We might, therefore, resist all demands, and thus bring into stronger contrast than ever the old temple and the new church; but let us give none offence, neither to the Jews, nor to the Gentiles, nor to the Church of God; even as I please all men in all things, not seeking mine own profit, but the profit of many, that they may be saved. Go, therefore, and cast an hook, and take up the fish that first cometh up; and when thou hast opened his mouth, thou shalt find a piece of money: that take, and give unto them for me and thee.

The last expression, viz., "for me and thee," is remarkable; why Peter alone? Why were not the other disciples included? "All the disciples were young, and had a long earthly course before them. Zebedee and Salome, the parents of James and John, were still living. This must be well kept in view in study of the Gospel history. . . . Peter had a family, the other disciples formed that of Jesus. For this reason they that received tribute-money asked, 'Doth not *your*,' not 'Doth not *thy*, Master,' &c. It may be that the other disciples had not passed their twentieth year, and were not yet liable to the rate." (*Critical English Testament*, vol i.) " Every one that passeth among them that are numbered, from twenty years old and above, shall give an offering unto the Lord " (Ex. xxx. 15).

Viewed homiletically, the incident suggests the following points:—1. Christians may do some things which are *expedient*, though not demanded by law. 2. In doing things which are expedient, Christians should be governed by a desire *not to offend*. 3. In being anxious to avoid offence, Christians should not be *unfaithful to God and conscience*. 4. In avoiding unfaithfulness to God, Christians will not create a conscience that is not founded on *reason*. Unreasoning conscientiousness leads to a most unhealthy morality—a morality which expresses itself in bigotry and intolerance. A modern homilist suggests, among many others, the following general points:—1. That it is highly politic for the Christian man to fall in, as much as possible, with the institutions of his country. 2. That it may be sometimes necessary to waive a personal privilege, in order to avoid collision with existing institutions. 3. That Christ's disciples can afford to be generous in their concessions to public sentiment (*The Genius of the Gospel*, pp. 452-4). No doubt this passage may, by a fallacious interpretation, be much abused. The desire of avoiding *offence* is very liable to misapplication. In referring to Christ's case it should be remembered :—1. That the tribute was required for *the temple.* 2. That the temple was a *Divine institution*, and 3. That the Divine institution of the temple had not then been *superseded by the Christian Church*. Christ's act was the last expression of veneration for an institution which was about to pass away; that institution having been instituted by God Himself. No argument can be legitimately drawn from this circumstance in favour of extortions on behalf of Pagan or politico-religious institutions.

GENERAL NOTE ON THE TRANSFIGURATION.

In the course of this mysterious incident we often feel quite at a loss to interpret its purpose, but when we take Christ's own standard of interpretation, viz., the Resurrection, there is less difficulty in seeing its profounder significations. Read in the light of the Resurrection, then, we have the following points :—1. *The human body is capable of the most glorious transfiguration.* It is promised that Christ shall change our vile or common body, &c. 2. *Not until after the Resurrection was the Church entirely liberated from the ancient dispensations.* As with Christ, so with men; the law has dominion over us until we are crucified; the only way into life is through death. 3. What was told to a *few* before the Resurrection, was to be preached *to every creature after the Resurrection.* We have nothing now to wait for. The *disciples* had to keep silence for a time; *we* may teach all nations. We may reverse the Saviour's words, and say,—Tell the vision to *every* man, for the Son of man *is* risen from the dead !

## CHAPTER XVIII.

1. At the same time came the disciples unto Jesus, saying, Who is the greatest in the kingdom of heaven?

2. And Jesus called a little child unto him, and set him in the midst of them,

3. And said, Verily I say unto you, Except ye be converted, and become as little children, ye shall not enter into the kingdom of heaven.

4. Whosoever therefore shall humble himself as this little child, the same is greatest in the kingdom of heaven.

Questions of gradation arise naturally in the working of human associations. There must be diversity of position, and diversity of position necessitates diversity of influence. There is, then, nothing unnatural in the inquiry which the disciples propounded; nor is there anything presumptuous in it, viewed simply as an inquiry. From the other evangelists we learn that the question became a controversy, and then the mischievous element was imported into it. "Being in the house he asked them, What was it that ye disputed among yourselves by the way? But they held their peace: for by the way they had disputed among themselves, who should be the greatest?" (Mark ix. 33.) "There was a strife among them which should be accounted the greatest" (Luke xxii. 24). The inquiry was not confined to the earliest days of the Church; even now it is uppermost, and its settlement is impeded rather than facilitated by the complications of an artificial civilisation. We know nothing of pristine simplicity: the age is laden with decorations, certificates, and double-class honours; so that there is an earnest thronging towards the chief seat. It may be well in the midst of this excitement to consult Jesus Christ upon the question; to look at the principle which regulates position and authority in the Church.

The answer which Jesus Christ returned strikingly illustrates His method of putting the last first, and the first last. Who could have conceived that the least was the greatest? Who, but God Himself, dared have likened the kingdom of heaven unto the least of all seeds? Jesus Christ said, "Except ye be converted;" the word is very emphatic; it is equivalent to μετανοῆτε, repent; except ye *turn back*, except ye take a directly opposite course, ye cannot so much as enter into the kingdom of heaven, much less have any position in it! Whoever shall humble (ταπεινώσῃ) himself, shall be greatest in the kingdom of heaven.

From this answer we learn that *the conquest of self is the indispensable condition, not only of authority in the Church, but of actual entrance into the Church*. In this, as in all else, Christ himself is the example: "He made himself of no reputation," "He humbled himself," He washed the disciples' feet. The Christian is a man in whom the dominion of self is broken; so long as the fraction is held to be greater than the integer, the heart is at a great distance from Jesus Christ. This principle has important practical applications in all the relations of life. The man who works only for himself may be a theologian, but he is not a Christian; he is not working on the line which terminates in the Cross; the spirit of self-crucifixion is not in him. Christ will excuse ignorance, and will pity weakness; but He is indignant with vanity, with self-satisfaction, with self-worship. "Take my yoke upon you; learn of me; for I am meek and lowly in heart." "Though the Lord be high, yet hath he respect unto the lowly; but the proud he knoweth afar off." "He hath showed thee, O man, what is good; and what doth the Lord require of thee, but to do justly, love mercy, and walk humbly with God?" The difficulty to be overcome in this movement towards a childlike spirit, is the difficulty of *affectation*. A simulated amiability is the most plausible of hypocrisies.

The wolf may appropriate the sheep's clothing. On few practical subjects are greater mistakes made than on *Christian temper.* Christ was meek and lowly in heart, yet He sent a sword upon the earth; it should be said, however, that He never fought for the selfish, but for the universal; when He slew men, it was that He might heal them again.

> 5. But whoso shall receive one such little child in my name receiveth me.
> 6. But whoso shall offend one of these little ones which believe in me, it were better for him that a millstone were hanged about his neck, and that he were drowned in the depth of the sea.

This is somewhat of a deflection from the original line of illustration. *Christ identifies Himself with the child-like man.* To-day the world applauds the men who can show great results, not the men who exemplify a great spirit. A successful soldier excites greater enthusiasm than a patient sufferer, and is everywhere " received " with keener interest. It is now thought better to divide the spoil with the proud, than to be of a humble spirit with the lowly. One of the gravest complaints which Jesus Christ will urge against society, will be its neglect of modest men; not men of feigned modesty, who trifle away their lives in religious coquetry, but men who await encouragement, as folded flowers await the morning.

To offend the modest man is to offend Christ. In Greece and Syria, criminals were drowned; hence the force of the figure which is employed in the 6th verse. Truly the meek and quiet spirit is an ornament of great price in the sight of God! Society admires power, faculty, mastery of affairs, and richness of resources; but how little it cares for the modest man, the gentle spirit, the frail child! In this it is unlike Christ; He allies Himself with the " least of His brethren," and sees Himself in a little child, as the sun might see himself in a drop of dew.

The whole paragraph—1. Supplies a new standard of

*authority;* 2. Furnishes a crucial test of *temper;* 3. Shows Christ's interest in those who to the faculties of men add the simplicity of children; and 4. Points out as a crime what might have passed as a feature of manliness.

> 7. Woe unto the world because of offences! for it must needs be that offences come; but woe to that man by whom the offence cometh!

LANGE: "The world, as such, does not *give*, but receive offences from false disciples; and that in what may be designated its border-land, where it is represented by the little ones. The offence of these little ones would accumulate to such an extent as to bring woe upon the whole world." ADAM CLARKE gives it as the opinion of some eminent critics, that our Lord ever used the word *Woe*, or *Alas!* (Οὐαί) to express *sympathy* and *concern*. "*It must needs be*," &c. (ἀνάγκη γὰρ ἐλθεῖν, &c.), is a difficult expression. The word ἀνάγκη occurs eighteen times in the New Testament, and is always rendered as implying irresistibleness or unpreventibleness, or great stress in one direction; for example, the unwilling guest who bought the ground said, "I *must needs* go and see it;" of Pilate it is said (Luke xxiii. 17), "For of *necessity* he must release one unto them at the feast;" and Paul, speaking of his preaching, said, "*Necessity* is laid upon me" (1 Cor. ix. 16). LANGE says that the reference is not to fate, or to a metaphysical, but to a historical ἀνάγκη, or the necessary connection between guilt and judgment; and in this sense not merely allowed by God, but "ultimately traceable to the Divine counsel" (MEYER).

The general meaning may be taken as,—It must be, in a fallen world where the spirit is at war with God, and all original relations are dislocated, that scandals, persecutions, offences of every kind, will arise; depravity will express itself in action; but the consequences are bad,—bad to the doers and bad to the sufferers are the results of such action; however stormy, however tumultuous and chaotic the process, the retributive element is always asserting the honour and righteousness of God; the devil is represented by the "offences," God by the penal "woe."

> 8. Wherefore if thy hand or thy foot offend thee, cut them off, and cast them from thee: it is better for thee to enter into life halt or maimed, rather than having two hands or two feet to be cast into everlasting fire.
> 9. And if thine eye offend thee, pluck it out, and cast it from thee: it is better for thee to enter into life with one eye, rather than having two eyes to be cast into hell fire.

Let every individual do the work of reformation upon himself, then the world will be saved from offences! A most practical "wherefore"! There are many persons who are ready to cut off other people's offending hands and feet, forgetting that the command is to cut off their own (see the Analysis of chapter v. 29, 30). At all costs save the life! Hands, feet, eyes, may be cast away, but let the soul be held in godly discipline. As it must needs be, in a fallen world, that offences come, let every man watch himself, and reduce the extent of bad nature upon which such offences operate most disastrously; when the storm threatens, the mariner takes in his sail. The verses suggest as a subject—*Individual discipline the best protection against social offences.* Man can do more injury to himself than society can do to him. Not that which is without, but that which is within, defileth a man.

> "To thine own self be true;
> And it must follow, as the night to day,
> Thou canst not then be false to any man."

ALFORD'S remark on the text is—"*Wilt thou avoid being the man on whom this woe is pronounced?—then cut off all occasion of offence in thyself first.*" OLSHAUSEN says: "The cutting off of hand or foot can, as is self-evident, be only taken as denoting something spiritual, since the outward act were meaningless unless the inward root of sin were destroyed. Hand, foot, eye, here appear to be used by the Saviour to denote mental powers and dispositions; and He counsels their restraint, their non-development, if a man finds himself by their cultivation withdrawn from advancing the highest principle of life. The *every-sided* development of all our faculties, the inferior as well as the more elevated, is certainly to be regarded as the highest attainment; yet he who finds by experience that he cannot cultivate certain faculties —the artistic, for example—without injury to his holiest feelings, must renounce their cultivation, and make it his first business, by painstaking fidelity, to preserve entire the innermost life of his soul, that higher life imparted to him by Christ, and which, by the dividing and distracting of his thoughts, might easily be lost; nor must it give him any disturbance if some subordinate faculty be thus wholly sacrificed by him." LANGE gives a somewhat fanciful symbolism to the various bodily members: "The hand here designates special aptitude and inclination for ecclesiastical *government;* the foot for ecclesiastical *exertion* and *missionary undertakings;* the eye for ecclesiastical *perception* and *knowledge.* All these gifts should remain in subjection to the Spirit of Christ, and serve for the advancement and edification of the little ones, instead of inducing pride or contempt of inferiors."

10. Take heed that ye despise not one of these little ones; for I say unto you, That in heaven their angels do always behold the face of my Father which is in heaven.

Why deny the doctrine of angelic tutelage? The "little ones" is an expression which includes not only children in the proper sense of the term, but children in the heart-sense; the humble, the lowly. Christ distinctly states that such children have guardian angels, who through all time (διαπαντὸς) stand in His Father's presence. How this idea unites the worlds! The poet says that "star unto star speaks light; world unto world repeats the password of the universe;" but there is a closer connection still,—a connection between human and angelic *life*. How many a man, weary with long sinfulness, has said—

> "I could have turned
> Into my yesterdays, and wandered back
> To distant childhood, and gone out to God
> By the gate of birth, not death."

It is for us to remember that the oldest man may even now sit at Christ's feet like a little child! It is not a question of age, it is a question of spirit. If any man will boastfully take care of himself, then he may sever the bonds which bind him to the highest worlds; but if he will put himself under God's care, the angels will encamp round about him, and bear him up in their hands, lest at any time he dash his foot against a stone.

11. *For the Son of man is come to save that which was lost.*

There is something remarkable about the utterance of this declaration in such a connection. What has "saving the lost" to do with settling the question of gradation in the kingdom of heaven,—the question which immediately occasioned the discourse? The declaration had reference rather to the method of illustrating the subject than to the question itself. The "little child" was still in "the midst;" the discourse had been founded on that living text; and the meaning of these words must be sought in that circumstance. What had been *lost?* Evidently, *the child-like spirit!* Modesty, self-repression, every graceful attribute of created and dependent life had been *lost*, and the Son of man came to save it. His was a meek and lowly heart, and by so much He was qualified to recover the humility which man had cast off. If it be asked, had not these words reference to Christ's sacrificial work? there need not be any hesitation about the answer, for of course *they had*. That work, however, was a means to an end: the end was the re-creation, the new birth of men, the recovery and preservation of *the child-like spirit*. We know that men have passed from death unto life, when they love the brethren with child-like love; in the absence of this love, all faith is void and worthless. That we are not exaggerating the importance of the child-like spirit may be proved by a collation of many texts. A few will show the drift of the evidence. " Put on therefore as the elect of God . . . kindness, humbleness of mind, meekness, longsuffering" (Col. iii. 12). "Walk worthy of the vocation wherewith ye are called, with all lowliness and meekness " (Eph. iv. 1. 2). " Be clothed with humility" (1 Pet. v. 5). "If I then, your Lord and Master, have washed your feet, ye ought to wash one another's feet " (John xiii. 14). Christ's whole ministerial course may be summed up in the great purpose of recovering and honouring the *child-like spirit*.

He appends an illustration :—

12. How think ye? If a man have an hundred sheep, and one of them be gone astray, doth he not leave the ninety and nine, and goeth into the mountains, and seeketh that which is gone astray?

13. And if so be that he find it, verily I say unto you, He rejoiceth more of that sheep, than of the ninety and nine which went not astray.

14. Even so it is not the will of your Father which is in heaven that one of these little ones should perish.

All that we know of the Divine government goes to show *God's minute and all-including care of the universe*. Nothing escapes Him. Though He has so many stars, He would not lose one! Is the good Father indifferent about any of His children? Does He not attend most to the sick one, and brood most over the prodigal? God could not be content with anything *incomplete*. His eye would be on the vacancy. His thought would go after that which is *lost*.

The cross of Jesus Christ is God's great protest against *loss*.

The word rendered "be gone astray" ($\pi\lambda\alpha\nu\eta\theta\hat{\eta}$) is very suggestive; $\pi\lambda\alpha\nu\hat{a}\sigma\theta\alpha\iota$, to wander,—hence, to wander from the truth, to stray from the right line or the appointed place. The word occurs thirty-eight times in the New Testament, and is variously rendered: for example, "ye do *err*" (Matt. xxii. 29); "are gone *astray*" (2 Pet. ii. 15); "to *seduce* my servants" (Rev. ii. 20). So much did God feel the wandering of the world from the right way, that He left the ninety-nine—the unfallen angels—on the hills ($\dot{\epsilon}\pi\grave{\iota}\ \tau\grave{a}\ \ddot{o}\rho\eta$) and came to save the child, the little one, the child-like spirit, all that was modest, meek, and trustful; for it is not the Father's will that the least of the little ones should perish.

There is undoubtedly here a spring of the richest comfort to parents, whose children have been removed by death. No little child is lost. No bud has been thrown away by the heavenly husbandman.

Looked at homiletically, the paragraph shows:—1. That *God* is the shepherd of the flock; 2. That His love is *impartially* shown to all who are in His fold; 3. That the salvation of the *least* is worth all the efforts of the *Highest*. Imagination will instantly suggest the method of the shepherd who has left his fold on a mission of recovery.

The subsequent paragraph is in exact accord with the discourse now concluded:—

15. Moreover if thy brother shall trespass against thee, go and tell him his fault between thee and him alone: if he shall hear thee, thou hast gained thy brother.
16. But if he will not hear thee, then take with thee one or two more, that in the mouth of two or three witnesses every word may be established.
17. And if he shall neglect to hear them, tell it unto the church: but if he neglect to hear the church, let him be unto thee as an heathen man and a publican.

18. Verily I say unto you, Whatsoever ye shall bind on earth shall be bound in heaven : and whatsoever ye shall loose on earth shall be loosed in heaven.

The treatment of erring brothers is one which makes a heavy demand on the child-like spirit. It is possible for any man to be amiable under amiable circumstances; what if the circumstances be *not* amiable? Looked at from what may be called the primeval point, nothing could well be more monstrous than the conception that brothers could possibly "sin" against one another. How did the antagonism *begin?* Not between brother and brother, but between *man and God.* The primary relation was disturbed, and as a necessary consequence all the subordinate relations were disorganised. The beginning of evil was between man and God,—a most startling and most impressive fact. There is not a man in heaven who has not offended God. From Adam unto the last regenerated sinner who entered heaven, every man has been at war with *God !* Why point this out ? To show that *the cure must begin where the disease began.* The disease is fundamental, the cure must be fundamental. Man cannot treat his "brother" properly until he has been put into a right relation with God. It was man's *religious* nature that fell, and in its fall it brought down the whole manhood; and the only hope for a thorough and durable restoration of a right understanding between man and man is in a right understanding between man and his Maker.

In this method of attempting to "gain a brother," we find—1. Privacy; 2. Witness; 3. Discipline. Human influence is, of course, greatly affected by circumstances. An offender may be subdued when confronted alone; he may be irritable and defiant in the presence of a third party. Jesus Christ says,—Give the erring man every advantage; don't goad or exasperate him; don't expose him to needless humiliation. Besides the deeply *religious* tone of this method, there is, what might have been expected from the Son of man, a perfect adaptation to the peculiarities of human nature. "He knew what was in man." How much of the child-like spirit is required, to go to a man who has injured, insulted, defied his brother!

The subsequent directions as to the treatment of an offending brother show most impressively Christ's recognition of *the judicial and penal authority of His Church*. All matters are not to stand over until the last assize. Certain things are to be dealt with finally here and now. What a chasm Christ allows,—"an heathen man and a publican." But even then the man will not be hated or injured by the child-like spirit; we are to love our enemies, and pray for them that despitefully use us. What a strain upon the child-like spirit! No offending man is to be cast off while any effort can be made to save him;—go to him alone, take witnesses, consult the Church, and if the obstinacy continue, let him be given up. A faint emblem of declining God's own last offer of gracious treaty!

Christ says (verse 18) that the deed of alienation shall be ratified in heaven; or if the event should turn otherwise, if the offender be forgiven, that also shall be ratified in heaven. There is one common law throughout Jesus Christ's dominions,—right never changes, wrong is wrong everywhere. Whither, then, can man flee from Christ's spirit? In heaven, in earth, in hell, the law is the same.

Christ now takes a step farther in showing the union of the worlds. He says:—

19. Again I say unto you, That if two of you shall agree on earth as touching any thing that they shall ask, it shall be done for them of my Father which is in heaven.
20. For where two or three are gathered together in my name, there am I in the midst of them.

That is the true binding or the true absolving,—acting in harmony with the Divine will as revealed in answer to prayer. Not acting on the strength of mere natural sagacity. "*To bind* is to declare a thing forbidden, *i.e.*, not to be done under pain of the Divine displeasure" (VALPY); but the Divine mind can be ascertained only by prayer, The expression "shall agree"—(συμφωνησωσιν=*consenserint*)—is emphatic; the two who pray must be of one heart, and must speak with one voice, if they would prevail with the Father who is in the heavens. The prayer must be a *symphony*,— the voices going together without discord. We find a form of the same word in 2 Cor. vi. 15, where the Apostle asks, "What συμφώνης (concord) hath Christ with Belial?"— there is no symphony, the chord is broken, they cannot be harmonised.

What is the reason of this prevalence in prayer? The answer is—*Christ is in the midst of them.* This affirmation proves:—1. That Christ is identified *mediatorially* with all effectual prayer; 2. That Christ is interested in the *deepest experiences* of the human heart; and 3. That Christ is *omnipresent.* As if Peter could not forget what had been said respecting the treatment of an erring brother, he put a question which was intended to draw out further information upon the point :—

21. Then came Peter to him, and said, Lord, how oft shall my brother sin against me, and I forgive him? till seven times?

22. Jesus saith unto him, I say not unto thee, Until seven times : but. Until seventy times seven.

This answer shows :—1. The *temper* of Christianity,—forgiving; 2. The *incomparable beneficence* of Christianity,—not seven times, but seventy times seven; 3. The *human* sympathy of Christianity,—all this to gain an erring man! As if too much could not be done! And how this doctrine was seconded by Christ's own deeds!

23. Therefore is the kingdom of heaven likened unto a certain king, which would take account of his servants.

24. And when he had begun to reckon, one was brought unto him, which owed him ten thousand talents.

25. But forasmuch as he had not to pay, his lord commanded him to be sold, and his wife, and children, and all that he had, and payment to be made.

26. The servant therefore fell down, and worshipped him, saying, Lord, have patience with me, and I will pay thee all.

27. Then the lord of that servant was moved with compassion, and loosed him, and forgave him the debt.

28. But the same servant went out, and found one of his fellowservants, which owed him an hundred pence: and he laid hands on him, and took him by the throat, saying, Pay me that thou owest.

29. And his fellowservant fell down at his feet, and besought him, saying, Have patience with me, and I will pay thee all.

30. And he would not: but went and cast him into prison, till he should pay the debt.

31. So when his fellowservants saw what was done, they were very sorry, and came and told unto their lord all that was done.

32. Then his lord, after that he had called him, said unto him, O thou wicked servant, I forgave thee all that debt, because thou desiredst me:

33. Shouldest not thou also have had compassion on thy fellowservant, even as I had pity on thee?

34. And his lord was wroth, and delivered him to the tormentors, till he should pay all that was due unto him.

The principal ideas suggested by this parable are:—1. The kingdom of heaven recognises individual *responsibility*,—a king would take account of his servants; 2. The kingdom of heaven is a kingdom of *justice*,—" his lord commanded him to be sold," &c. (verse 25); 3. The kingdom of heaven is a kingdom of *mercy*,—" the lord of that servant was moved with compassion; " 4. The kingdom of heaven teaches that *personal obligation* should become a *social benefit*,—he who has been forgiven should forgive; 5. The kingdom of heaven having failed in mercy will have recourse to absolute justice, —" his lord was wroth, and delivered him to the tormentors, till he should pay all that was due unto him."

35. So likewise shall my heavenly Father do also unto you, if ye from your hearts forgive not every one his brother their trespasses.

We have seen the parabolic illustration: now we see the practical result. Taking the parable as our guide, we may affirm this principle of the Divine government to be:—1. So *simple* that all may understand it; 2. So *just* that none need complain of it; 3. So *merciful* that all may hope from it; 4. So *watchful* that none can elude it.

### GENERAL NOTE ON THE CHAPTER.

Christian life, subjective and objective, is entirely a question of the *spirit*. It is not a question of mere identification with manners and forms which have a place before men; it is the bowing down of the heart in perfect lowliness before God, a thing which cannot be done but through the mediation of Jesus Christ. The influence of Christian men will be in exact proportion to the intensity of their Christian spirit. Their dogmas may be correct; but if they manifest a haughty and self-seeking spirit, their theology will be rendered powerless by their lives. In all other departments of human inquiry or human education, the quality of the spirit is of inferior consideration. In mathematics, in natural science, in philology, there is nothing to prevent an immoral spirit making the highest attainments and exercising the widest influence: but no man can so much as enter the kingdom of heaven if he approach otherwise than in a lowly spirit. The right spirit will be anxious to discover the right doctrine; and the right spirit will defend the right doctrine by right methods. The right spirit will neither seek controversy nor shun it; but being called to it, will conduct it with a gentleness and charity, magnanimity and trustfulness which will add the beauty of grace to the strength of argument. It would be a profound mistake to imagine that a child-like and a childish spirit are synonymous. There is nothing puerile, vapid, or amiably weak about Christianity. It has been too commonly supposed that any imposition might be attempted upon a Christian; he has been thought deficient, if not in sagacity yet in spirit and force of character. It is a popular error respecting true power; it is forgotten that self-repression is more forceful than the most boisterous demonstration of anger; that the silence which comes of high discipline is more impressive than the storm of lawless passion. Not only is the child-like spirit compatible with the highest quality of character, but the highest quality of character is unattainable except through the child-like spirit. "He *humbled* himself . . . wherefore God hath *highly exalted* him."

## CHAPTER XIX.

1. And it came to pass, that when Jesus had finished these sayings, he departed from Galilee, and came into the coasts of Judæa beyond Jordan ;
2. And great multitudes followed him ; and he healed them there.

When Jesus departed from Galilee and came into the coasts of Judæa, He was about to proceed to Jerusalem, the passover at which He was crucified being in view. The point of special interest is that great multitudes followed Christ to be healed of Him. Men were constantly needing, and Christ was constantly giving; not giving in small donations, not putting people off with trifles, as if He had limited resources and was anxious to husband them; but giving most lavishly,—healing and blessing "great multitudes." This is a hint of His world-wide mission; He came to give Himself, to give *all*.

3. The Pharisees also came unto him, tempting him, and saying unto him, Is it lawful for a man to put away his wife for every cause?
4. And he answered and said unto them, Have ye not read, that he which made them at the beginning made them male and female,
5. And said, For this cause shall a man leave father and mother, and shall cleave to his wife : and they twain shall be one flesh?
6. Wherefore they are no more twain, but one flesh. What therefore God hath joined together, let not man put asunder.
7. They say unto him, Why did Moses then command to give a writing of divorcement, and to put her away?

8. He saith unto them, Moses because of the hardness of your hearts suffered you to put away your wives: but from the beginning it was not so.

9. And I say unto you, Whosoever shall put away his wife, except it be for fornication, and shall marry another, committeth adultery : and whoso marrieth her which is put away doth commit adultery.

10. His disciples say unto him, If the case of the man be so with his wife, it is not good to marry.

11. But he said unto them, All men cannot receive this saying, save they to whom it is given.

12. For there are some eunuchs, which were so born from their mother's womb : and there are some eunuchs, which were made eunuchs of men : and there be eunuchs, which have made themselves eunuchs for the kingdom of heaven's sake. He that is able ro receive it, let him receive it.

This is a portion which will very rarely, if ever, be required for homiletic purposes; hence it hardly falls within the scope of this analysis. It is not, however, devoid of practical interest. From Jesus Christ's side of the argument we learn: —1. That Christianity holds the marriage bond as most sacred; 2. Jesus Christ recognises the validity of the great primeval transactions as recorded in the Old Testament; 3. That the rupture of the nuptial bond is permissible only under the most extreme conditions of wickedness.

On the other, DR. CLARKE remarks: "It is dangerous to tolerate the least evil, though prudence itself may require it: because toleration, in this case, raises itself insensibly into permission, and permisson soon sets up for command." LANGE says that the question which elicited this answer was founded upon "a misapplication of the passage (Deut. xxiv. 1), which the Lord exposes and answers. The object of Moses in laying down the rules about giving a writing of divorcement was not to countenance or promote divorces; but to diminish their number by subjecting them to certain rules and limitations, with the view of again elevating the marriage relationship, and realising its idea." On the eighth verse, THEOPHYLACT paraphrases Christ's words thus:

"Moses wisely restrained, by civil regulations, your licentiousness, and permitted divorce only under certain conditions, because of your brutality; but you perpetrate something worse, namely, make away with them by sword or poison." GROTIUS makes a similar comment: "Moses is named as the promulgator, not of a common, primeval, and perpetual law, but of one only Jewish, and given in reference to the times."—*(See Blomfield's Greek Testament.)*

It is important to remember that the words "because of the hardness of your hearts" inadequately represent the force of the word which Christ employed. That word ($\sigma\kappa\lambda\eta\rho o\kappa\alpha\rho\delta\iota\alpha\nu = duritiem\ cordis$) means properly an unforgiving temper, amounting to brutality. The root of the word is $\sigma\kappa\lambda\eta\rho\acute{o}s$; in this form it occurs six times in the New Testament, and is generally rendered "*hard;*" for example, "Thou art an hard man" (Matt. xxv. 24); and "It is hard for thee to kick against the pricks" (Acts ix. 5). In calling to their mind that the regulation in question was made under special circumstances, Jesus Christ draws a wide distinction between that which was "from the beginning," and that which was exceptional; in other words, between the fundamental and accidental, or between laws and bye-laws. This distinction should guide all historical and critical inquiry which relates to the Scriptures. We are not at liberty to call exceptional or temporary regulations into antagonism with principles which are moral, and consequently of perpetual and universal force. The author of "Ecce Homo" says,—" On the question of divorce, He (Christ) declared the Mosaic arrangement to have been well suited for the 'hard-heartedness, of a semi-barbarous age, but to be no longer justifiable in the advanced condition of morals." This is not an adequate exposition of the case. It is forgotten, or at least overlooked, that Jesus Christ expressly said that "from the beginning it was not so;" hence "the advanced condition of morals" was but a return, in this particular, to that which was "from the beginning."

13. Then were there brought unto him little children, that he should put his hands on them, and pray: and the disciples rebuked them.

14. But Jesus said, Suffer little children, and forbid them not, to come unto me; for of such is the kingdom of heaven.

15. And he laid his hands on them, and departed thence.

This scene presents three impressive aspects of Jesus Christ:—1. As the centre of a *necessitous* world; 2. As surrounded by men who did not understand the *universality* of His mission—(*a*) men may have mistaken notions respecting the *dignity* of Jesus Christ; (*b*) some men have presumed to define the *classes* that shall approach Christ; (*c*) even well-meaning men may be, unintentionally, *obstacles* in the way of Christianity; 3. As asserting the *sovereignty and fulness* of His grace.

16. And, behold, one came and said unto him, Good Master, what good thing shall I do, that I may have eternal life?

17. And he said unto him, Why callest thou me good? there is none good but one, that is, God: but if thou wilt enter into life, keep the commandments.

18. He saith unto him, Which? Jesus said, Thou shalt do no murder, Thou shalt not commit adultery, Thou shalt not steal, Thou shalt not bear false witness,

19. Honour thy father and thy mother: and, Thou shalt love thy neighbour as thyself.

20. The young man saith unto him, All these things have I kept from my youth up: what lack I yet?

21. Jesus said unto him, If thou wilt be perfect, go and sell that thou hast, and give to the poor, and thou shalt have treasure in heaven: and come and follow me.

22. But when the young man heard that saying, he went away sorrowful: for he had great possessions.

[For a full discourse on this passage, see the end of this volume.]

23. Then said Jesus unto his disciples, Verily I say unto you, That a rich man shall hardly enter into the kingdom of heaven.

24. And again I say unto you, It is easier for a camel to go through the eye of a needle, than for a rich man to enter into the kingdom of God.

25. When his disciples heard it, they were exceedingly amazed, saying, Who then can be saved?

26. But Jesus beheld them, and said unto them, With men this is impossible; but with God all things are possible.

There are three things which operate against the rich man in relation to a new spiritual life:—1. He has property which is of *present* value; 2. The spirit of Christianity would fundamentally *change his view* of that property; 3. There is a natural disposition towards *combining the advantages* of the material and the spiritual. How are these disadvantages to be overcome? *By Divine power,*—" with God all things are possible." At this point man must have recourse to the supernatural. Here is a problem which man cannot solve. The *disciples* gave it up; are *we* able to answer it? Jesus Christ gives not only the problem but the solution—*God!*

27. Then answered Peter and said unto him, Behold, we have forsaken all, and followed thee; what shall we have therefore?

28. And Jesus said unto them, Verily I say unto you, That ye which have followed me, in the regeneration when the Son of man shall sit in the throne of his glory, ye also shall sit upon twelve thrones, judging the twelve tribes of Israel.

29. And every one that hath forsaken houses, or brethren, or sisters, or father, or mother, or wife, or children, or lands, for my name's sake, shall receive an hundredfold, and shall inherit everlasting life.

30. But many that are first shall be last; and the last shall be first.

How far Peter is now below the point at which he received the keys! He wishes to know something about compensation; as he then stood, the prospect was not very bright; he knew what he had given up, and wished to see the other side of the account. The answer is singularly characteristic of the *invariable generosity* of Jesus Christ. We *never* see any contractedness about Him; the times of His forgiveness are not seven, but seventy times seven; His reward is not double; it is an hundred-fold, and everlasting upon that! How could *such* a man have given any other answer? We might have known, had the statement been anonymous, that Jesus Christ conceived this magnificent idea; it is *like* Him; it is *part* of Him; it is in perfect keeping with all His other far-reaching thoughts of love towards those who trust Him. " The promise of the Lord implies the full establishment of His spiritual kingdom, which consists not merely in the restoration of the original state of things in Paradise, but also in the full development of the first into the second life. In other words, the complete redemption of the world will at the same time be its transformation, when regenerated humanity shall dwell in a completely regenerated world. The centre of this completion of all things shall be the manifestation of Christ in His glory, when He shall appear in all His heavenly brightness. Then all relationships shall partake of and reflect the splendour of His manifestation. This will also apply to the administration of His apostles, as the representatives of His rule over the twelve tribes—a symbolical term, intended to indicate the whole variety of spiritual stages and experiences in the kingdom of heaven."—(LANGE.)

The 30th verse strikingly reproves the carnal miscalculations of men as to rank or precedence in the time of reward. The little child will be first; the modest man will take the highest seat! There had been a discussion as to gradation in the heavenly kingdom; here is a rule which shows that we know not what order or arrangement may be made by the sovereign Disposer. There will be nothing disorderly in the settlement of rank; the great law of affinities will make all easy: he who has most of Christ will be nearest Christ. Meantime let men be on their guard against judging by appearances, by technical classifications, or even by personal claims. They are not called to judgment except in cases of necessity; and where the subtlest modifications may change the value of human character, it is not only presumptuous but futile for any man to say who will be either first or last.

The only thing of which we are certain is, that *character* is the basis of the Divine adjudication; great character means great exaltation; littleness, and poverty of character, means abasement and inferiority of influence. The man who is least in his own eyes, who forgives most, who forsakes most for Jesus Christ, shall be highly exalted in the kingdom of heaven.

### CHAPTER XX.

1. For the kingdom of heaven is like unto a man that is an householder, which went out early in the morning to hire labourers into his vineyard.

2. And when he had agreed with the labourers for a penny a day, he sent them into his vineyard.

3. And he went out about the third hour, and saw others standing idle in the market-place,

4. And he said unto them; Go ye also into the vineyard, and whatsoever is right I will give you. And they went their way.

5. Again he went out about the sixth and ninth hour, and did likewise.

6. And about the eleventh hour he went out, and found others standing idle, and saith unto them, Why stand ye here all the day idle?

7. They say unto him, Because no man hath hired us. He saith unto them, Go ye also into the vineyard; and whatsoever is right, that shall ye receive.

8. So when even was come, the lord of the vineyard saith unto his steward, Call the labourers, and give them their hire, beginning from the last unto the first.

9. And when they came that were hired about the eleventh hour, they received every man a penny.

10. But when the first came, they supposed that they should have received more; and they likewise received every man a penny.

11. And when they had received it, they murmured against the goodman of the house,

12. Saying, These last have wrought but one hour, and thou hast made them equal unto us, which have borne the burden and heat of the day.

13. But he answered one of them, and said, Friend, I do thee no wrong: didst not thou agree with me for a penny?

14. Take that thine is, and go thy way: I will give unto this last, even as unto thee.

15. Is it not lawful for me to do what I will with mine own? Is thine eye evil, because I am good?

16. So the last shall be first, and the first last: for many be called, but few chosen.

There is undoubtedly great reason on the part of the men who complained of their treatment, if we view the subject within the narrow limits of a secular compact. It seems inequitable that those who have worked but one hour should receive as much as those who have worked all day. This is the view of the case which many of us would take if we occupied the position of the men who complained. The parable, if read literally and taken as a guide in arranging affairs between masters and workmen, certainly affords scope for most irreligious inferences. It might be inferred, for example, that *they who do least in life will be equally rewarded with those who do most.* This is written upon the very surface of the parable; they who began at five o'clock in the evening received as much as they who began at six o'clock in the morning, *cum prima luce!* Is not this offering a bounty to indolence? In the next place it might be inferred that *the affairs of the kingdom of heaven are conducted in a bargaining spirit.* Nothing can be more off-hand than the manner in which the householder (οἰκοδεσπότη=*patrifamilias*) addressed the complainants; he referred to the agreement, took his stand upon the letter of the bond, and yielded nothing to the protest. Does not this favour the doctrine that the religious life is entirely without grace? It is simply an affair of doing so much work for so much reward, and those who don't like it may complain without redress. Kindred inferences, equally dishonouring to the spirit of the Gospel, may be drawn from this extraordinary parable. The whole parable may be pronounced narrow, ungenerous, very sharp in worldly prudence, but quite destitute of the grace and charm of a Divine Gospel. How is this conclusion to be escaped?

First of all, it must be borne in mind that *a parabolic representation of truth is not to be forced into literal evidence.* The main line is to be discovered, and the great *purpose* of

that main line is to be kept steadily in view. There may
be a good deal that is floral, poetic, or tributary, which must
be set aside in prosecuting an analysis of the doctrine. It
is enough to hint at this as a general principle in her-
meneutics; it will save the reader the pains of finding far-
fetched meanings in all the details of a parable.

Secondly, *the exact circumstances of the case must be apprehended.* What are those circumstances? A householder
goes out early in the morning (ἅμα πρωΐ, with the first light,
showing earnestness and determination on his part) and
engages all who are willing to work. A vineyard has to be
cultivated, a recompense will be given, men accept the
terms; so far, there is no ground of complaint. About the
third hour he goes into the market-place and finds others
(ἄλλους) and engages them; the same thing is done at the
sixth hour, the ninth hour, and the eleventh hour; the point
to be remembered is that the householder called all the men
who were accessible at the first hour, the third, the sixth,
the ninth, and the eleventh. The men who were hired at
the third hour were not within reach at the first; the men
hired at the sixth hour were not within reach at the third;
the men who were hired at the ninth hour were not within
reach at the sixth; and the men hired at the eleventh hour
were not within reach at the ninth. The labourers were
not all present at the first hour. They came into the market-place at different times; and as soon as the proposition
was made to them by the householder "they went their
way." This circumstance entirely relieves the parable of
all difficulty, so far as the engagement of the men is concerned. The householder could not have gone out earlier;
could not have shown greater interest in the work; could
not have called more; could not have worked later: while,
on the other hand, the labourers could not complain of the
householder for not having called them when they were not

present to be called. The next difficulty relates to the reward; they who worked least got a penny as well as they who worked most. Taking a merely secular view of the case, this was inequitable; but the parable is not designed to illustrate the principles of trade, its object is purely spiritual. Looked at spiritually, does the Christian worker get nothing but the outward recompense, say the penny? Is there nothing *in the work itself* to enrich the spirit of the worker? Is the matured Christian on a level with the man who came but yesterday into the vineyard? The "penny," even though it stand for heaven itself, is only the outward final recognition of service—but *the service itself* is recompense! In the right disposing of the heart; in the constant aspiration of the affections; in the deepening knowledge of God and the spiritual universe; and the extending mastery of the worker over himself—the Christian servant is enjoying a perpetual and growing recompense. The merely secular interpretation of the parable is, of course, inadmissible; and the moment we view it in a spiritual light it is fruitful of recompense long before we reach the hour of reckoning.

Recall the point of engaging the labourers at various hours, and give it a spiritual significance. It is clear that God has at various times called the various nations of the earth to His service. Some He called at the first hour, some at the third, others at the sixth and ninth, and some have not even yet heard the call. We have to do with the *fact;* the *sovereignty* which lies behind it we cannot interpret. The apostasy of the world was the case which Divine wisdom had to meet; where and how it was to be first touched were God's questions; what nations were accessible early in the morning, He knew and He alone. He has continued the call; every hour has heard His voice; how far we are yet from the eleventh hour it would be as presumptuous to conjecture as it is impossible to determine. The one practical point with which we have to do is that *we ourselves have been distinctly called to go into the vineyard.* However difficult may be the speculative part of the passage, the practical aspect is entirely clear.

Recall the point of recompense, and say whether those nations which have obeyed the call have not already received an incalculably precious reward. The "penny" has yet to come; heaven is yet in the future; but everywhere the recompense has already come. In science, in art, in commerce, in literature, in refinement of manners, in benevolence of sentiment, in elevation of spiritual life, we are every moment feeling how many are the indirect, as well as how rich are the immediate, results of Christian service. All this before we receive the "penny," the world that is to be given to us at the evening hour! Take two workmen of opposite types. The one does his work simply because without it he could not live, the other does his work because he takes a pleasure in it; even if at the end of the day they received the very same amount of *money,* the latter would have an incalculable advantage over the former. The simple reason is, that the drudge never can be as well compensated as the artist; the drudge works to live, the artist lives to work. They calculate results by different arithmetical standards; the drudge thinks of the "penny," the artist thinks of all the gladness of his work.

What will be the result of this spiritual discipline in relation to the reward which other nations shall receive? *The utter annihilation of all discontent and reproachfulness of spirit on our part* will be one conspicuous result. England will not complain that Africa accompanies her into heaven. The nation which has been longest at work will not envy the crown of the nation which was born yesterday. Nations, like individuals, never can be equalised. Capacity, sensibility, will always separate the degrees of enjoyment or suffering allotted to men. The morning comes alike to the clown and to the poet; the one sees it with the eye of an animal, the other sees many an omen and many a prophecy in the variations of that great fire.

Is there not something dispiriting in the words, "So the last shall be first, and the first last: for many be called, but few chosen"? Not at all. The meaning is to be found in the different *spirit* in which men accept God's call to work in the vineyard. The first men referred to in the parable stood upon what they regarded as their rights; they did not care for the work for the work's sake; they worked merely for what they could get. Those who went later in the day set up no argument founded upon the proportion between time and wages; they accepted what the steward gave without remark, though no fixed terms had been agreed upon. Giving a spiritual application to the case, Jesus Christ showed, as He had repeatedly showed before, that a man's *spirit* determines his grade in the kingdom of heaven; not technical services, not casting out devils and doing many wonderful works, but modest and thankful acquiescence in the Divine will. All men are *called* to the vineyard, but all men do not accept the call; even of the many who do respond to the call, comparatively *few* work in the right spirit, and those alone who work in the right spirit are *chosen;* many who do mighty works will not be known by Jesus Christ; He determines everything by the *spirit;* many who are working in secret, doing nothing to attract the eye of man, will be called to high places. The householder *called* the first men, but *chose* the latter; when he saw the spirit in which the first men worked he was not drawn towards them; but when he saw that the last accepted his terms without murmuring, he chose them as a man would choose friends; many are called, but few are chosen; the many are mere bargain makers and time servers; the few receive what is given, without murmuring, and they alone are chosen of God. There is nothing in the declaration which limits God's love; He calls all men; whom He calls He is willing to choose; the call comes freely as the expression of God's boundless and priceless love, but the choice is determined entirely by the *spirit* in which man accepts the call: to murmur is to go last or to be rejected; to acquiesce is to have eminence and safety in the kingdom of God.

Looking at the parable in the light of these suggestions, it is evident:—1. That the kingdom of heaven is associated with *work*. 2. That work in the kingdom of heaven is associated with *reward*. 3. That the reward for heavenly work will be distributed on *right principles*. 4. That those right principles cannot be understood by a *technical spirit*, but by a *grateful and loyal heart*.

The calling and choosing of men are equally founded upon love. Love prompts the call; where it is responded to in a spirit kindred to its own, the choice follows as a matter of moral necessity; where it is examined in a cold, technical, and bargaining spirit, no choice can take place. The rain falls upon all the globe; the sands and rocks drink it up and yield no return, the garden and the field yield in answer many a fruit and flower. It is so with hearts; men may turn God's call away, or they may hail it in a spirit of confidence and thankfulness; they are only elected by God because they themselves elect to serve God in all the pleasure of His loving and sovereign will.

17. And Jesus going up to Jerusalem took the twelve disciples apart in the way, and said unto them,
18. Behold, we go up to Jerusalem; and the Son of man shall be betrayed unto the chief priests and unto the scribes, and they shall condemn him to death,
19. And shall deliver him to the Gentiles to mock, and to scourge, and to crucify him: and the third day he shall rise again.

The third announcement of the sufferings and death of

Jesus Christ, made by Himself to His disciples. Common men go forward unconsciously to their destiny; they are ignorant of it; if they forecast it at all it is generally with hopefulness. Jesus Christ, in this as in everything else separate from sinners, knew His destiny in all its tragic details, and spoke of it with reverent and tender familiarity. In what repulsive terms does He give an outline of His course,—betrayed, condemned, mocked, scourged, crucified! Yet in the face of all He went forward with more than human resolution. The above passage shows:—1. *That the life of Jesus Christ was founded upon a plan.* There was no uncertainty or experiment about that life; every detail was foreseen from the beginning. Every man's life may be planned by Divine wisdom, but the man himself is ignorant of his own course, unable to foresee the next hour! 2. *That Jesus Christ knew all the developments of His plan of life.* The sorrow of the first day, the sleep of the second, the triumph of the third, were all before Him, as conditions and factors in His daily labour. 3. *That though He knew the result He patiently fulfilled the whole process.* There was no precipitancy; there was no fretfulness; every case of need was attended to as though it were the only case in the world. The Christian knows that heaven will be his portion at last; let him be stimulated to constant activity, as though human want demanded his whole attention. 4. *That Jews and Gentiles were alike engaged in carrying out a work which was for the highest benefit of the whole world.* How unconsciously we work! We may be pulling down in the very act of setting up! The condemnation came from the Jew, the cross was the device of the Roman. The infinite wisdom of permitting both the great divisions of the world to partake in the crucifixion, will be increasingly seen as the results of that crucifixion are felt by the population of all lands. The crucifixion of Jesus Christ by the Jews and

Romans, is the most impressive illustration of God's power to turn the purposes of the wicked upside down. " The stone which the builders rejected," &c. 5. *That the assured triumph of the right is a source of strength to the good man.* Jesus Christ spoke not only of the crucifixion but of " the third day." The picture was not all gloomy. Light broke through the very centre of the darkness. How hopeless, but for " the third day," is the lot of suffering men! The third day may suggest :—1. The brevity of bad influence; 2. The impossibility of destroying that which is good; 3. The transference of power from a temporary despotism to an eternal and beneficent sovereignty. Brief and frail is the tenure of all malign powers!

TISCHENDORF reads ἐγερθήσεται *shall be awakened,* instead of ἀναστήσεται *shall rise again.*

<small>20. Then came to him the mother of Zebedee's children with her sons, worshipping him, and desiring a certain thing of him.
21. And he said unto her, What wilt thou? She saith unto him, Grant that these my two sons may sit, the one on thy right hand, and the other on the left, in thy kingdom.</small>

1. The natural result of extreme ambition is *selfishness.* 2. Parental feeling may degenerate into *misanthropy.* What did this woman care for other people? 3. Ambition may not be the less criminal for being associated with *religious* position and influence. The feeling shown by this woman should always be discouraged. There is an earnestness that is fanaticism. The ambition that is unholy is always also *unreasonable.*

"That the sons of Zebedee wished for ecclesiastical, rather than secular honours, may be thought probable from the allusion that is made here to the supreme dignities in the great Sanhedrin. The *prince* of the Sanhedrin (HA-NASI) sat in the midst of two rows of senators or elders; on his right hand sat the person termed AB (*the father* of the

Sanhedrin); and on the left the CHACHAM or *sage*. These persons transacted all business in the absence of the *president*."—*(Adam Clarke.)*

The mother of Zebedee's children asked for honour in *the kingdom*, she did not ask for fellowship in the preliminary *suffering*. BENGEL well remarks: "Very different were those whom our Lord was first to have on His right hand and on His left."

> 22. But Jesus answered and said, Ye know not what ye ask. Are ye able to drink of the cup that I shall drink of, and to be baptized with the baptism that I am baptized with? They say unto him, We are able.
> 23. And he saith unto them, Ye shall drink indeed of my cup, and be baptized with the baptism that I am baptized with: but to sit on my right hand, and on my left, is not mine to give, but it shall be given to them for whom it is prepared of my Father.

LANGE says: "Different views are entertained of this reply. DE WETTE explains it: Your request arises from an incorrect view of the character of my kingdom, which is spiritual. MEYER paraphrases: Ye know not that the highest posts in my kingdom cannot be obtained without sufferings such as I have to endure." LUTHER says: "The flesh ever seeks to be glorified before it is crucified, exalted before it is abased." Referring to the latter part of the 23rd verse, ADAM CLARKE says: "The true construction of the words is this: To sit on my right hand and on my left, is not mine to give, except to them for whom it is prepared of my Father;" DR. CLARKE argues that the words "it shall be given to them," "are interpolated by our translators." BISHOP HORSLEY says the meaning is, "I cannot arbitrarily give happiness, but must bestow it on those alone for whom, in reward of holiness and obedience, it is prepared, according to God's just decrees." BURKITT says: "When Christ therefore saith, He could only give this to them for whom it was appointed of His Father, this doth not signify any defect in His power, but a perfect conformity to His Father's will, and that He could not do this unless the Divine essence and nature abided in Him."

The practical ideas of the passage might be homiletically expressed thus:—1. Human ignorance should restrain human ambition,—"ye know not what ye ask;" 2. Human weakness should modify the expression of human confidence,—"are ye able? they say we are able;" 3. Human history should be left to the development which God has purposed for it,—"ye shall drink; ye shall be baptised; but ——;" 4. Human position will be determined by human character.

24. And when the ten heard it, they were moved with indignation against the two brethren.

The primary conditions of brotherhood had been violated by the two brethren and their mother, and the ten had a right to be angry. All men who wish to outreach their brethren deserve indignation. Religion does not annihilate anger, it regulates its expressions and penalties. The incident may be homiletically used, as—1. A warning against an unbrotherly disposition; and 2. An example of Christ's method of treating unbrotherly men. Jesus Christ does not expel them; He declares their ignorance, He points out their weakness, He shows that suffering is the portion of those who follow Him, and that such suffering is to be endured, apart from promised official position in His kingdom.

25. But Jesus called them unto him, and said, Ye know that the princes of the Gentiles exercise dominion over them, and they that are great exercise authority upon them.

26. But it shall not be so among you : but whosoever will be great among you, let him be your minister ;

27. And whosoever will be chief among you, let him be your servant :

28. Even as the Son of man came not to be ministered unto, but to minister, and to give his life a ransom for many.

29. And as they departed from Jericho, a great multitude followed him.

This exhortation shows that the spirit of self-abasement is to distinguish the entire course of the Christian life.

The Church is not to look to secular governments for precedents or patterns, but to the Son of man alone. The ἄρχοντες were proud, domineering, fond of power, and self-sufficient; nothing could be more foreign to the spirit of Christianity, and this was emphatically the time to say so. Jesus Christ adapted His teaching to the varying phases of human nature; at this time the phase of ambition was uppermost, and the exhortation took its course and tone accordingly. Adaptation is the secret of successful teaching. The teacher who speaks to the line of actual experience will never want a theme, and if his teaching be wise he will never speak without profit to his hearers. 1. Christian influence is not *official;* 2. Christian influence is *spiritual;* 3. Christian influence can be legitimately attained only by the Christian *spirit,*—"whosoever will be great among you let him be your minister (διάκονος), and whosoever will be chief among you let him be your servant (δοῦλος)." It has often been explained that διάκονος means a servant of a superior order, always near his master's person and admitted to a certain degree of his confidence, whereas δοῦλος means a *slave,* one who may be employed in the most menial service. The distinction, however, is not always maintained in the Christian writings. For example, in chapter xviii. and 23rd verse, we have a king "which would take an account of his servants (δούλων);" all the officers of oriental courts were regarded as slaves, but the servants here referred to are the provincial officers employed to collect the revenue for government; in the Persian court they were called *satraps.* In Matthew xxv. 21, the word is used, "Well done, good and faithful servant (δοῦλε)." Without insisting upon any fanciful or even real distinctions between these words, the spirit of the exhortation is perfectly intelligible; abasement is the condition of true and permanent eminence. The simplicity of the condition is not without its dangers, for is it not possible to *simulate* humility? Is there not a stooping to conquer, which is merely an attitude of the *body*, not a gesture of the soul? There is an amiability which covers a hard and relentless heart; there is an outward austerity which may conceal the tenderest geniality of spirit.

The expression, "to give his life a ransom for many," is not to be taken as limiting Jesus Christ's atonement. The atonement is not the subject of discourse; Jesus Christ is speaking of Himself simply as an example *of service*,—a service so profound and so pure as to include even the surrender of life itself.

The whole address bears upon Christian position, the spirit by which it is to be attained, and in which it is to be held. Jesus Christ is not speaking against secular authority, civil magistracy, and the like; His remarks are exclusively confined to the affairs of His own kingdom. There must be rulership in civil society, and in religious society as well. Rulership is by no means arbitrary; it is founded upon the instincts and necessities of human nature. In civil society sovereignty may descend from generation to generation without regard to the fitness of the sovereign; in Christian society true rulership is a question of character and capacity. The modest, cultivated, intellectual Christian will, in time, attain his proper position. Zealous and foolish mothers may secure for their children an external position of authority, but the real authority will always be held by men who have drunk most deeply into the spirit of Jesus Christ. Such men care nothing for authority for its own sake; they are not the slaves of officialism; yet even in the absence of nominal status they wield the profoundest and most durable influence over the thought and sentiment of the Church.

30. And, behold, two blind men sitting by the way side, when they heard that Jesus passed by, cried out, saying, Have mercy on us, O Lord. thou Son of David.

31. And the multitude rebuked them, because they should hold their peace: but they cried the more, saying, Have mercy on us, O Lord, thou Son of David.

32. And Jesus stood still, and called them, and said, What will ye that I shall do unto you?

33. They say unto him, Lord, that our eyes may be opened.

34. So Jesus had compassion on them, and touched their eyes: and immediately their eyes received sight, and they followed him,

Here we have several homiletic lines:—1. Necessitous men making the best of their *opportunities*,—"when they heard that Jesus passed by;" 2. The possibility of one class of necessitous persons failing to sympathise with another,—"the multitude rebuked them:" had the multitude no wants? 3. Necessitous men founding their appeal upon the *right ground*,—" have mercy on us:" sin is the cause of all affliction, and sin can appeal to *mercy* alone of all the Divine attributes. 4. Necessitous men presenting a right condition of *will*,—"what will ye?" as if all things were placed at the disposal of the right *will*. Man must co-operate with God, or salvation will be impossible. 5. Necessitous men securing *a physical result* through *a moral process*.

### GENERAL NOTE ON THE CHAPTER.

In this chapter we find three classes of men in connection with the kingdom of heaven:—1. Discontented men (ver. 11); 2. Disappointed men (ver. 21); 3. Rejoicing and grateful men (ver. 34). Throughout the whole of these classes it is remarkable how much stress Jesus Christ lays upon the *spirit of men;* the first men were rebuked for *murmuring*, which is a bad spirit; the second were rebuked for *selfish ambition*, which is also a bad spirit; the third were healed and blessed, because their spirit was contrite, reverent, and trustful. Jesus Christ never rebukes men for asking *much*, if they ask in the right *spirit*. The method in which those three classes were treated shows that neither murmuring nor selfish men can enter the Christian kingdom, but that all may enter it who are consciously necessitous, who rely entirely on Divine mercy, and whose will is in harmony with the redemptive purposes of Jesus Christ. The chapter shows that Jesus Christ refuses some petitions and grants others; a circumstance on which may be founded a discourse upon *Zebedee's sons and the blind men, or Christ's different method of replying to men's requests.*

### CHAPTER XXI.

1. And when they drew nigh unto Jerusalem, and were come to Bethphage, unto the Mount of Olives, then sent Jesus two disciples,
2. Saying unto them, Go into the village over against you, and straightway ye shall find an ass tied, and a colt with her: loose them, and bring them unto me.
3. And if any man say ought unto you, ye shall say, The Lord hath need of them; and straightway he will send them.
4. All this was done, that it might be fulfilled which was spoken by the prophet, saying,
5. Tell ye the daughter of Sion, Behold, thy King cometh unto thee, meek, and sitting upon an ass, and a colt the foal of an ass.
6. And the disciples went, and did as Jesus commanded them,
7. And brought the ass, and the colt, and put on them their clothes, and they set him thereon.
8. And a very great multitude spread their garments in the way; others cut down branches from the trees, and strawed them in the way.
9. And the multitudes that went before, and that followed, cried, saying, Hosanna to the son of David: Blessed is he that cometh in the name of the Lord; Hosanna in the highest.

In analysing this passage in the life of Jesus Christ, we shall, in a few points, take the account as given by the other evangelists. The simplicity of the circumstance should not conceal from us its great significance, viz., that Christ's Divinity was illustrated by the manner in which He pointed out the place where the ass and the colt were, and the circumstances under which the disciples would find them.

" By the ass is to be understood the synagogue of the

Jews, and by the colt the Gentiles; for according to God Judæa is the mother of the Gentiles; the ass had gone under the yoke before, for the Jews went under the yoke of the law, but the colt was free, and hitherto living in pleasure, never yet bearing any burthen or under any yoke, and so were the Gentiles."—(JEROME.) "By the ass understand the Samaritans, by the colt the rest of the Gentiles: so that here is a double calling of the Gentiles set forth,—the first of the Samaritans living according to some observances of the Jews before, the other of the rest of the Gentiles who were altogether untamed and wild; for, accordingly, two are sent to loose them being bound with the bonds of error; Philip to loose Samaria, and Peter to Cornelius."—(HILARY.) The remark of AUGUSTINE upon this passage may be accepted as an excellent canon in biblical criticism; it is this:— "There is some difference betwixt Matthew and John in this relation, for Matthew speaketh both of an ass and the colt, but John of a young ass only. But the difference ariseth from the interpretation of the Seventy: Matthew, as is likely, writing in Hebrew, and so following the ancient Hebrew copies. For the interpretation of the Seventy hath doubtless many things in it different from the Hebrew, the reason whereof, as I take it, is, that they being guided by the same Spirit with the prophets, as appeareth by their admirable consent in every word, and differing in sundry things from them, we might not any whit the more doubt of the writings of the evangelists, though they differ much the one from the other, seeing they differ not from His will to which we must all agree. For we must not think that the truth is so fenced with consecrated sounds of words, as that God doth commend unto us the words even as the matter; but there were no need at all to respect the words, if we could know the matter without them, as God knoweth it and His holy angels in Him. If Matthew speaketh of the ass and the

colt, and the rest of the colt only, there is no cause why any man should be moved at it, seeing here is no contradiction, notwithstanding John's speaking of the one; there being liberty to Matthew to speak of the one and the other also."
—(*De Consensu Evangeliorum, lib.* ii., *cap.* 66.)

For homiletic purposes the narrative may be used to show *the features which will characterise the day of Christ's recognised royalty.* When Christ's royalty is fully recognised—

I. ALL POSSESSIONS WILL BE CONSECRATED TO HIS SERVICE. Jesus Christ gave His disciples a word whose power was to overcome all hesitation on the part of the owners of the ass and the colt; that word was—" The Lord hath need of them." The expression itself is peculiar. Why should the *Lord* have *need?* Strange combination of ideas—lordship and necessity! Yet, on the other hand, what necessity can He have who has but to express it in order to have it satisfied? By a legitimate exercise of fancy, we may amplify the idea and include all orders of men, all degrees of talent, all capacities of endurance and activity. Say to the poet, the painter, the musician, the orator, the rich man, the man of influence, "the Lord hath need of thee," and there will be instantaneous and grateful response!

When Christ's royalty is fully recognised—

II. ALL THE SERVICES OF CHRIST WILL BECOME THE SUBJECTS OF ARDENT AND UNIVERSAL PRAISE. According to Luke, "the whole multitude began to rejoice and praise God with a loud voice for all the mighty works that they had seen." 1. The true worker will eventually be recognised; 2. *Works* will be the basis of just and permanent elevation; 3. *God* will be praised as the fontal source of all true benefaction,—the multitude praised God.

When Christ's royalty is fully recognised—

III. HIS ESSENTIAL GREATNESS WILL OVERCOME HIS MOMENTARY HUMILIATION. "Behold thy King;" "Blessed be the King that cometh." (Trace Jesus Christ's life, and show how much there was in it to depress and crush; yet, through all, there is a shining of His Divine lustre.) In addition to doing this *a contrast may be drawn between what is transient and what is permanent in the Messianic life:* poverty, sorrow, humiliation, all kinds of social and temporal disadvantage, on the one hand; on the other, riches, rapture, exaltation above every created height, and all the honour and homage of the universe.

When Christ's royalty is fully recognised—

IV. RELIGIOUS ENTHUSIASM WILL OVERWHELM OR ABSORB ALL PHARISAIC FORMALITY. According to Luke, "some of the Pharisees from among the multitude said unto him, Master, rebuke thy disciples; and he answered and said unto them, I tell you that, if these should hold their peace, the stones would immediately cry out." Enthusiasm is natural; stoicism is unnatural. When the soul is inspired, the lips must speak. About enthusiasm three things should be remarked:—1. That it is essential to success in *all* pursuits; 2. That it reaches its highest intensity in the development of the *religious* life; 3. That its suppression would excite *the reproaches of nature.*

The whole scene shows the effect of a true view of Jesus Christ upon the heart of man. Such a view transports the soul with the holiest delight, and draws the worshipper, even while in the poverty and feebleness of the body, nearly into the ecstasy of the heavenly worshippers. The scene gives a hint of the joy which shall one day fill the hearts of all men.

10. And when he was come into Jerusalem, all the city was moved, saying, Who is this?
11. And the multitude said, This is Jesus the prophet of Nazareth of Galilee.

The movement of a whole city! There are many ways

in which a whole city may be moved; (*a*) News of *war;* (*b*) News of a *great loss*, as of a monarch or other illustrious person; (*c*) News of *great joy*, arising from success in war, or in peaceful counsels, which will bring joy to those who have had much sorrow; (*d*) But the most profound and beneficent agitation of any city must be occasioned *by the presence of Jesus Christ.* Show how this must be so:—1. Christ meets the *great necessities* of human life; 2. Christ shows the *great possibilities* of human life; 3. Christ is gentle towards the *great sorrows* of human life. With regard to the intense excitement which was generally associated with Christ's presence, it is to be noted:—1. That some men raise great expectations without being able to satisfy them; 2. Some men create great excitement without be able to control it; 3. Some men arouse popular tumult that they may profit by it; 4. Jesus Christ was able to satisfy, control, liberalise, and sanctify all the excitement of which He was the occasion.

12. And Jesus went into the temple of God, and cast out all them that sold and bought in the temple, and overthrew the tables of the money-changers, and the seats of them that sold doves,

13. And said unto them, It is written, My house shall be called the house of prayer; but ye have made it a den of thieves.

14. And the blind and the lame came to him in the temple; and he healed them.

These verses, taken in combination, present a vivid view of Christ's twofold method of conducting His ministry: that method was first destructive, then constructive. About the cleansing of the temple four things are noticeable:—1. Jesus Christ did not connive at abuses for the sake of securing *popular favour;* 2. Jesus Christ did not allow abuses to be continued on the ground that the circumstances were *temporary,*—He knew that the temple was soon to be destroyed; 3. Jesus Christ showed that man's convenience was to be subordinated to God's right,—"my house is the house of prayer" (Luke xix. 46); 4. Jesus Christ showed in this, as in all other cases, that the right *one* is morally stronger than the wicked *many*. The incident of healing "the blind and the lame" occurs most impressively in this connection; after anger came peace; after an assault upon strength came a gentle ministry upon weakness. The incident may be separately treated, as showing :—1. That the temple is spiritual not in an *exclusive* but in an *inclusive* sense,—the wants of the spirit include the necessities of the body; praying included healing, but money-changing did not include praying; and—2. That society should be taught to connect the temple with the most benevolent, practical, and spiritual ideas. It is a great error in any community to shut up the house of God six days out of seven. When society is penetrated with true Christianity, the house of God will be a library, a hospital, a school, and a prayer-house, all in one.

15. And when the chief priests and scribes saw the wonderful things that he did, and the children crying in the temple, and saying, Hosanna to the son of David ; they were sore displeased,

16. And said unto him, Hearest thou what these say? And Jesus saith unto them, Yea ; have ye never read, Out of the mouth of babes and sucklings thou hast perfected praise?

Official men take official views; and mere officialism can never be raised to the point of enthusiasm. Officialism has never led the world. All historic crises have been associated with intense enthusiasm in the lower and younger orders, for enthusiasm is the unwritten but irresistible law of the popular heart. The verses may be used as showing :—1. That Jesus Christ's presence and benefactions are not to be coldly received; 2. That the reception of homage produces no bad effect upon Jesus Christ ; a man cannot be injured by applause so long as he is *worthy* of it; the moment that applause gets beyond the point of *worth*, danger sets in; "*worthy* is the Lamb that was slain to receive power, and riches, and wisdom, and strength, and honour, and glory, and blessing;" 3. That all young religious life is viewed by Jesus Christ with special complacency: this is natural for obvious reasons,—(*a*) He Himself was "the child Jesus," (*b*) young life offers all its unwasted strength, (*c*) young life enters into service with enthusiasm, (*d*) young life can give the most continuous illustration of the manifold influence of Christian truth in human discipline and human development.

Christ's reference to the prophetic word, "Out of the mouth of babes and sucklings thou has perfected praise," was not expected by the displeased and reproachful oligarchy. Some men are not content unless prophecy be fulfilled exactly according to their own notions. They are not infidel enough to doubt the prophecy, and not Christian enough to accept unexpected fulfilments. Looking over the field of prophecy, one cannot but feel that unexpected fulfilments will often come up in history. Such unexpected fulfilments are entirely consistent with the genius of God's method of governing and educating the world. A discourse might be delivered on *unexpected developments of Divine purposes as seen in the life of Jesus Christ*. Nowhere do we find Jesus Christ and the theological parties of His day *concurring in the interpretation of prophecy,*—a most remarkable and even startling fact. Jesus Christ *read* the prophecies as if He had *written* them. He always presents new views, or aspects which had been overlooked, and even at the time that men were complaining of His course He showed that the very thing they were complaining of was actually a fulfilment of prophecy! From this point the most interesting and useful excursions into prophecy and history, as connected with Jesus Christ, might be made. After a collation of illustrative examples we should find ourselves in possession of *a great hope*, viz., that in a manner quite impossible for us to foresee, the nations of the world will be led into the most intelligent, rapturous, and reverent worship of Jesus Christ.

248    HOMILETIC ANALYSIS.

Putting the two incidents together, we have for a subject —*What may be, and what may not be, done in the temple;* 1. (*a*) prayer, (*b*) healing, (*c*) praise, are allowed; 2. Buying and selling, self-enriching, and secularisation are disallowed.

17. And he left them, and went out of the city into Bethany ; and he lodged there.
18. Now in the morning as he returned into the city, he hungered.
19. And when he saw a fig tree in the way, he came to it, and found nothing thereon, but leaves only, and said unto it, Let no fruit grow on thee henceforward for ever. And presently the fig tree withered away.
20. And when the disciples saw it, they marvelled, saying, How soon is the fig tree withered away !
21. Jesus answered and said unto them, Verily I say unto you, If ye have faith, and doubt not, ye shall not only do this which is done to the fig tree, but also if ye shall say unto this mountain, Be thou removed, and be thou cast into the sea ; it shall be done.
22. And all things, whatsoever ye shall ask in prayer, believing, ye shall receive.

This incident may be homiletically used to show:—1. *The doom of those things which do not meet the wants of the time;* 2. *The terrific prospect of meeting a disappointed Christ;* 3. *The perfect dominion of the spiritual over the material;* 4. *The vast possibilities of undoubting prayer.*

OLSHAUSEN has some striking observations as to the cursing of the fig-tree : " The difficulty is diminished here, if we understand by it that kind of figs which remain hanging on the branches all winter, and are gathered in early spring. In that case, the sense of the words would be this—while the common kind of figs were not yet ripe, and the time for gathering them in had not come, Jesus yet perceived that this tree on which He sought for figs belonged to that other kind, which bore at that time ripe and refreshing fruit, and thus He could rightly expect figs on the tree."

Upon this passage several of the ancient comments should be considered, though some of them are obviously fanciful. " Here is nothing else set forth but that Christ hath power to punish, as well as to help and save; He had divers times showed His power in helping, but never yet in punishing; therefore, for His disciples' sake who should see Him apprehended and crucified, He doth this miracle upon a tree full of sap, that they might understand that He could as easily destroy the Jews His enemies."—(CHRYSOSTOM.) "The fig-tree setteth forth the synagogue of the Jews, which is unfruitful to the end of the world, when, as the fulness of the Gentiles should come in, it withered whilst Christ was living upon earth, the sap and virtue thereof being translated to the Gentiles. The mountain which they should remove is Satan, who is cast by every faithful one into the sea, that is, into the bottomless pit."—(ORIGEN.) "Here arise two questions, First, How could Christ be deceived in the fig-tree? Secondly, How happened it, that He cursed the tree, seeing no impatience could be incident to Him? For the first, as He was man He might go unto it, not perceiving at the first what tree it was; and for the second, it is to be thought, that finding no bodily food He took occasion to do this miracle, thus feeding Himself, as His manner was, by doing the will of His Father. And by this figure He figureth out the state of hypocrites, all whose ostentation is vain and nothing worth."—(CALVIN.) This opinion is controverted by MAYER, who says, "I hold with CHRYSOSTOM that this (coming to seek fruit when there was none) is spoken according to the suspicion of the disciples, who thought He went to seek fruit there when as He had another end."

23. And when he was come into the temple, the chief priests and the elders of the people came unto him as he was teaching, and said, By what authority doest thou these things? and who gave thee this authority?
24. And Jesus answered and said unto them, I also will ask you one thing, which if ye tell me, I in like wise will tell you by what authority I do these things.
25. The baptism of John, whence was it? from heaven, or of men?

And they reasoned with themselves, saying, If we shall say, From heaven; he will say unto us, Why did ye not then believe him?

26. But if we shall say, Of men; we fear the people; for all hold John as a prophet:

27. And they answered Jesus, and said, We cannot tell. And he said unto them, Neither tell I you by what authority I do these things.

28. But what think ye? A certain man had two sons; and he came to the first, and said, Son, Go work to-day in my vineyard.

29. He answered and said, I will not: but afterward he repented, and went.

30. And he came to the second, and said likewise. And he answered and said, I go, sir: and went not.

31. Whether of them twain did the will of his father? They say unto him, The first. Jesus saith unto them, Verily I say unto you, That the publicans and the harlots go into the kingdom of God before you.

32. For John came unto you in the way of righteousness, and ye believed him not: but the publicans and the harlots believed him: and ye, when ye had seen it, repented not afterward, that ye might believe him.

The question related to Jesus Christ's authority. What the chief priests and elders of the people had seen produced a deep impression upon them, and naturally excited wonder as to the source of so great a power. The spectators often asked, "Whence hath this man this wisdom?" or questions of similar import. Jesus Christ declined to give a direct answer to the inquiry as to His authority, yet He threw the responsibility of decision upon the inquirers themselves by setting forth two parables. This method of dealing with the case may be used to show that *the truly authorised worker leaves his service to be its own exponent and defence.* Viewing the subject of Christ's authority from this point, we have to inquire, *What are the uses to which Christ puts His authority?* If the *uses* be Divine we shall have a strongly presumptive argument that the *authority* itself is Divine.

I. CHRIST USES HIS AUTHORITY IN ASSERTING GOD'S PATERNAL RELATIONSHIP TO MAN.

The parable is constructed in the fullest recognition of this fact; for example, "A certain man had *two sons*,"— "whether of them twain did the will of *his father?*" By teaching the fatherhood of God, Christ incidentally, but most convincingly, asserts the Divinity of His authority. Jesus does not so represent the Unseen One as to repel men from His service, but on the contrary continually sets Him forth as the Father of men. Whenever Christ reverts to the *power* of God, it is to show how it is exercised in *love*.

II. CHRIST USES HIS AUTHORITY IN CALLING ALL MEN TO SPIRITUAL SERVICE.

"Son, go work to-day in my vineyard." A call to *work* for God must be Divine. Any religion which bids man desist from work cannot be heavenly in authority. There are two noticeable things about God's call to work :—1. God fixes the *time*,—"to-day;" 2. God fixes the sphere,—"my vineyard."

III. CHRIST USES HIS AUTHORITY IN DECLARING THE WILL OF GOD TO BE THE FINAL STANDARD OF RIGHTEOUSNESS.

"Whether of them twain did the will of his father?" Christ makes the heart its own judge. The reference must always be to "the will of the Father,"—not to superficial *success;* not to the promptings of natural *instinct;* not to the decisions of human *corporations;*—but to *God,* God the *Father!*

IV. CHRIST USES HIS AUTHORITY IN MARKING MORAL DISTINCTIONS (ver. 31, 32).

These verses show:—1. That responsibility is measured by opportunity; 2. That opportunity is given to all classes; 3. That only the obedient can enter the kingdom.

We are thus brought again to the question, "By what authority doest thou these things?" Jesus answers—Let my works testify; if you believe not my labours you will not believe my credentials; judge me by the uses I make of my power; I tell you God is man's Father, man's mission is to *work* in the Father's vineyard, man's work is to be determined by God's will, and that your relation to that will determines all the *distinctions* which the Father will recognise in the great judgment.

The argument of the answer may be applied to two classes of hearers.

First, *Those who have unfulfilled vows resting upon them,*—"I go: but went not."

Second, *Those who have openly refused to serve God,*—"I will not." This said to a *father*, and that Father *God !*

33. Hear another parable : There was a certain householder, which planted a vineyard, and hedged it round about, and digged a winepress in it, and built a tower, and let it out to husbandmen, and went into a far country :

34. And when the time of the fruit drew near, he sent his servants to the husbandmen, that they might receive the fruits of it.

35. And the husbandmen took his servants, and beat one, and killed another, and stoned another.

36. Again, he sent other servants more than the first : and they did unto them likewise.

37. But last of all he sent unto them his son, saying, They will reverence my son.

38. But when the husbandmen saw the son, they said among themselves, This is the heir ; come, let us kill him, and let us seize on his inheritance.

39. And they caught him, and cast him out of the vineyard, and slew him.

40. When the lord therefore of the vineyard cometh, what will he do unto those husbandmen ?

41. They say unto him, He will miserably destroy those wicked men, and will let out his vineyard unto other husbandmen, which shall render him the fruits in their seasons.

1. *Here are men called to the highest service,*—to work in God's vineyard ; 2. Here are men called to the highest service *under the most favourable conditions,*—" hedged it round about, and digged a winepress in it, and built a tower ; " 3. *Here are men abusing the first principles of individual and social justice,*—the husbandmen took the servants, and beat one, and killed another, and stoned another. It is important to remember that irreligion is an outrage of *first principles ;* not a breach of recondite and subtle relations, but of the

most obvious claims of intelligence, gratitude, and filial instincts; 4. Here are men whose course *illustrates the tremendous speed by which sin attains its climax.* They who kill a servant to-day will kill a son to-morrow! The education of depravity is soon perfected; 5. *Here are men exposed to a doom which the common conscience of the universe will approve,*—" They say unto him, he will miserably destroy those wicked men." "He will bring these wretches to a wretched death."—(CAMPBELL.) It is important to point out that the hearers themselves gave the verdict; God's judgment will but express the moral convictions of all who know the cases which are judged.

LANGE has some excellent hints on the parable of the husbandmen; for example:—1. The fearful wickedness of God's labourers, who would turn His vineyard into a private possession; 2. Misunderstanding of the Lord's external absence; 3. The ruinous delusion of the servants of Christ, who turn an office of labour into an office of rule. This is not the order in which they are given.

42. Jesus saith unto them, Did ye never read in the scriptures, The stone which the builders rejected, the same is become the head of the corner : this is the Lord's doing, and it is marvellous in our eyes?
43. Therefore say I unto you, The kingdom of God shall be taken from you, and given to a nation bringing forth the fruits thereof.
44. And whosoever shall fall on this stone shall be broken : but on whomsoever it shall fall, it will grind him to powder.
45. And when the chief priests and Pharisees had heard his parables, they perceived that he spake of them.
46. But when they sought to lay hands on him, they feared the multitude, because they took him for a prophet.

This was the application of the parable, an application which was not general but personal, exposing the Speaker to all the consequences of having made an attack upon individual hearers. The doctrines of this application are:—
1. That unexpected persons are called to the highest places;
2. That persons who have abused their election will be dis-

inherited and degraded; 3. That all men have a choice of treatment so far as this stone is concerned; 4. That men whose moral intentions are right, may demoralise themselves by the most unnatural and contradictory resentments; 5. That the most violent resentments are sometimes held in check even by secondary causes.

STIER becomes almost angry with a certain school of commentators. He says: "Must we, in opposition to the perverted and obstinate exegesis even of believing commentators, begin to prove that the 118th Psalm is Messianic—that the corner-stone of which it speaks is a real prophecy of the Spirit respecting Christ? We frankly confess ourselves to be so often vexed by such contentions with brethren who do not understand the *Scripture*, that we lose patience; and, however unscientifically, are inclined rather to rebuke them with Christ (Luke xxiv. 25), until their hearts burn, and their burning *hearts* begin to read in the light of the Pentecostal fire what is written."

Referring to the falling of the stone, BLOMFIELD says: "Here WETSTEIN and others suppose an allusion to the different ways of stoning among the Jews, whereby, a scaffold being erected twice the height of the person to suffer the punishment, the criminal was violently pushed from it. If then he died by coming in contact with some stone, nothing further was done; if not, a heavy stone was hurled upon him, which despatched him at once. But the real allusion, I should rather say, is to that stone spoken of by the prophet Daniel (ii. 34)."

### CHAPTER XXII.

1. And Jesus answered and spake unto them again by parables, and said,
2. The kingdom of heaven is like unto a certain king, which made a marriage for his son,

3. And he sent forth his servants to call them that were bidden to the wedding : and they would not come.

4. Again, he sent forth other servants, saying, Tell them which are bidden, Behold, I have prepared my dinner: my oxen and my fatlings are killed, and all things are ready: come unto the marriage.

5. But they made light of it, and went their ways, one to his farm, another to his merchandise :

6. And the remnant took his servants, and entreated them spitefully, and slew them.

7. But when the king heard thereof, he was wroth : and he sent forth his armies, and destroyed those murderers, and burned up their city.

8. Then saith he to his servants, The wedding is ready, but they which were bidden were not worthy.

9. Go ye therefore into the highways, and as many as ye shall find, bid to the marriage.

10. So those servants went out into the highways, and gathered together all as many as they found, both bad and good : and the wedding was furnished with guests.

If there is a reverent sense in which the terms may be employed, the text would warrant a discourse upon *the revenge of Divine disappointment.* The term revenge would be used not as implying a bad passion, but a righteous principle of retribution. The parable sets forth :—I. *The King of heaven inviting men to an occasion of great joy;* He made a marriage for His Son, and provided a feast of oxen and fatlings. The figure is fully realised in the Gospel of Jesus Christ. God always calls men to joy. Whenever men are travelling upon a path which is not fraught with gladness, they are travelling upon a path which God did not appoint for their feet. Of Wisdom it is said, " Her ways are ways of pleasantness, and all her paths are peace : " to such ways and paths alone does the King of heaven call. Not only is the call to an occasion of great joy, but *the joy itself is associated with the choicest gifts of the King.* All that the King could do was done. A most important reflection ! When *God* exhausts Himself, who can add to the bounty ? The Gospel shows the fullest reach of Divine love. God Himself has nothing more to offer to hungering men. What a spectacle, then, does this parabolic table present! The parable sets forth :—II. *The possibility of treating the highest gifts with indifference and contempt;* " They made light of it, and went their ways, one to his farm, another to his merchandise." The argument on this point may be made cumulative: for example, there are laws of courtesy among men ; how is the man regarded who wantonly tramples upon the first principles of civilised society ? Let each man put himself in the position of the King in this parable. Ascending from the common walks of life, try the case as one between the subject and the sovereign ; not only is courtesy (which is due to the humblest man) set at nought, but loyalty is ignored, and high office treated with contempt. How may a *king* be supposed to feel under such circumstances ? Carry the case forward until *God* Himself is reached, and then say how *He* must feel when His love, His kingship, His fatherhood, His majesty, are treated as if they were empty names ? Multiply your human suffering by infinitude, and then say what must be God's feeling. The parable sets forth :—III. *The operation of the retributive functions of Divine providence;* the king was wroth, and sent forth his armies, and destroyed those murderers, and burned up their city. He who breaks the law will be broken by the law. Life is continually showing that it carries a principle of self-vindication. It is always " hard to kick against the pricks." Retribution is not confined to spheres which are technically known as religious. No man can injure his fellow-creature without suffering loss in his own soul; no man can help his fellow-creature without receiving strength into his own spirit. The great law of recompense is inexorable in its operation, being terrible or benignant according to the moral course of man. We are in danger of looking only on the penal side of retribution, and forgetting its compensative aspect. Confining our view to the former, as that is the phase more particularly presented in the text, how terrible is the prospect of the man who rejects the invitations of God! The parable sets forth:—IV. *The Divine method of turning human wrath into an occasion of human blessing.* "Go ye therefore into the highways, and as many as ye shall find bid to the marriage." There is undoubtedly considerable difficulty in making all the possible views of this portion of the parable consist with the universal benevolence of God; at the same time there are two obvious considerations which should arrest a false judgment:—1. Sometimes results are hastened by violence which would have been reached by ordinary operations. 2. Any parable, however liberal its tone, must fall infinitely short of the reality of God's love. Only in its most expansive features can any parable give the remotest hint of infinite bounty.

ADAM CLARKE says: "Among the Mohammedans, refusal to come to a marriage feast, when invited, is considered a breach of the law of God. Any one that shall be invited to a dinner, and does not accept the invitation, disobeys God and His messenger: and any one who comes uninvited, you may say is a thief and returns a plunderer."

"By the oxen understand the fathers of the Old Testament, by the fatlings understand the fathers of the New Testament; for they did smite with the horn their enemies, and these mounted up aloft by the wings of heavenly contemplation."—(GREGORY.) "Oxen are strong, and fatlings are sweet and pleasant; hereby are set forth the oracles of God, which do both strengthen and delight those that feed upon them."—(ORIGEN.) "They that excuse themselves by the occupying of a farm are the common people of the Jews, the other the priests and ministers about the temple."—(CHRYSOSTOM.)

11. And when the king came in to see the guests, he saw there a man which had not on a wedding garment :

12. And he saith unto him, Friend, how camest thou in hither not having a wedding garment? And he was speechless.
13. Then said the king to the servants, Bind him hand and foot, and take him away, and cast him into outer darkness; there shall be weeping and gnashing of teeth.
14. For many are called, but few are chosen.

These verses supply three homiletic points:—1. The principle of *discrimination* is ever operative in the Divine economy,—"the king came in to see the guests." 2. Escape from this principle is utterly impossible. The King of heaven is omniscient. 3. Those who have complied with the King's conditions have nothing to fear from the King's scrutiny. The man *might* have had a wedding garment. Only those who *choose* are chosen. A man must accept the *King's* conditions and not his own, if he would be an accepted guest at the Gospel feast.

"For the wedding garment it is vain to contend whether it be faith or a godly life, for neither is faith without a godly life, neither can a godly life proceed but from faith."—(CALVIN.) "The man without a wedding garment was one that had not amended his manners."—(ORIGEN.) "All the fathers have ever expounded it of an unreformed life, or, with GREGORY, of the want of love, which is in effect the same. It is not, then, to be understood of faith, for to believe, that is to come in to this wedding; but of that effect which a saving faith always worketh, that is, purity of heart and life, so that in whom this is wanting he shall be cast into outer darkness, notwithstanding his embracing of the faith of Christ."—(MAYER.)

15. Then went the Pharisees, and took counsel how they might entangle him in his talk.
16. And they sent out unto him their disciples with the Herodians, saying, Master, we know that thou art true, and teachest the way of God in truth, neither carest thou for any man: for thou regardest not the person of men.

MATTHEW XXII. 259

17. Tell us therefore, What thinkest thou? Is it lawful to give tribute unto Cæsar, or not?
18. But Jesus perceived their wickedness, and said, Why tempt ye me, ye hypocrites?
19. Show me the tribute money. And they brought unto him a penny.
20. And he saith unto them, Whose is this image and superscription?
21. They say unto him, Cæsar's. Then saith he unto them, Render therefore unto Cæsar the things which are Cæsar's; and unto God the things that are God's.
22. When they had heard these words, they marvelled, and left him, and went their way.

From this point to the end of the chapter we have striking illustrations of the readiness and precision of Jesus Christ as an extemporaneous speaker. In the first instance we have:—1. A *prepared* assault upon Jesus Christ. 2. An appeal to His supposed *vanity* (verse 16). 3. An answer which recognises the *moral validity* of political as well as religious relations.

23. The same day came to him the Sadducees, which say that there is no resurrection, and asked him,
24. Saying, Master, Moses said, If a man die, having no children, his brother shall marry his wife, and raise up seed unto his brother.
25. Now there were with us seven brethren: and the first, when he had married a wife, deceased, and, having no issue, left his wife unto his brother:
26. Likewise the second also, and the third, unto the seventh.
27. And last of all the woman died also.
28. Therefore in the resurrection whose wife shall she be of the seven? for they all had her.
29. Jesus answered and said unto them, Ye do err, not knowing the scriptures, nor the power of God.
30. For in the resurrection they neither marry, nor are given in marriage, but are as the angels of God in heaven.
31. But as touching the resurrection of the dead, have ye not read that which was spoken unto you by God, saying,
32. I am the God of Abraham, and the God of Isaac, and the God of Jacob? God is not the God of the dead, but of the living.
33. And when the multitude heard this, they were astonished at his doctrine.

An instance which shows how a little puzzle may be

exaggerated into a great problem, and how one ray of light may disperse the darkness which hangs over futurity. For homiletic purposes, the following points may be dwelt upon :—1. The impossibility of educing ultimate doctrine from a limited number of facts.  2. The temptation to exaggerate extraordinary circumstances into inexplicable mysteries.  3. The danger of setting up human wisdom as the test of Divine revelation.  4. The importance of ascertaining Christ's opinion before affirming our own conclusions.  How He dispels the mystery with a word!  He shows them, too, how superficial must have been their reading of the Holy Scriptures,—" Have ye not read ? " He inquires, in a tone which meant that if they *had* read they would not have been troubled with this phantom difficulty.

34. But when the Pharisees had heard that he had put the Sadducees to silence, they were gathered together.
35. Then one of them, which was a lawyer, asked him a question, tempting him, and saying,
36. Master, which is the great commandment in the law?
37. Jesus saith unto him, Thou shalt love the Lord thy God with all thy heart, and with all thy soul, and with all thy mind.
38. This is the first and great commandment.
39. And the second is like unto it, Thou shalt love thy neighbour as thyself.
40. On these two commandments hang all the law and the prophets.

1. The possibility of asking a right question in a wrong spirit.  2. The impossibility of asking Christ a question which He cannot answer.  3. The exceeding breadth of the Divine commandment,—love of God and love of man.

" It had become a question long amongst the expounders of the law, but could not be decided, and therefore they consent it should be moved unto Christ."—(ORIGEN.)  " Forasmuch as every one of God's commandments is great, whatsoever He should answer in affirming one above the rest to be great, He might be entrapped."—(JEROME.)  " The meaning of this question was, whether anything were more perfect than the law, because He taught a new kind of doctrine, whereby the expounders of the law held themselves to be disgraced."—(CALVIN.)

Putting the three cases together, they afford a most impressive illustration of the "fulness" of Jesus Christ. His mind overreached every difficulty, and was at home in the midst of the darkest mystery. Now He changes sides; instead of being the respondent, He becomes the inquirer, and yet in a most striking manner confounds His superficial though most boastful and obstinate interlocutors. We have seen Jesus Christ under the shock of three subtle and resolute attacks: now we see how He occupies the position of interrogator :—

41. While the Pharisees were gathered together, Jesus asked them,
42. Saying, What think ye of Christ? whose son is he? They say unto him, The son of David.
43. He saith unto them, How then doth David in spirit call him Lord, saying,
44. The Lord said unto my Lord, Sit thou on my right hand, till I make thine enemies thy footstool?
45. If David then call him Lord, how is he his son?
46. And no man was able to answer him a word, neither durst any man from that day forth ask him any more questions.

The question, it must be observed, did not relate to Himself personally, but to Christ generally; He did not say, "What do you think of *me* as Christ?" but, "What do you think of the man who is promised to the world under the name of Christ?" Like all readers of the mere letter, they answered by a technical quotation. Then came the difficulty which has been perplexing various schools of theology ever since; viz., How a man can be both son and lord. This is the difficulty which pursues certain readers throughout the whole history of Jesus Christ; this duality; this being servant of all, yet chief of all; this unparalleled humiliation, yet this enthronement over all empire. We are distinctly asked to accept this mystery, for apart from it there is no progress in Christian theology. "His meaning is not to prove that He is not David's Son, but to confute their error, who, by saying that He was David's Son, meant that He was man only; wherefore He bringeth David in, saying, *The Lord said unto my Lord*, which He doth in much humility, not applying it to Himself, to avoid contempt."—(CHRYSOSTOM.)

GENERAL NOTE ON THE CHAPTER.

In a discourse upon the 40th verse, Dr. SHERLOCK (1754), Bishop of London, says:—1. These two principles, from which our Lord tells us all religion flows, must be consistent with one another; otherwise they could not both be principles of the same religion. 2. Nothing is or ought to be esteemed religion that is not reducible to one or other of these principles.

*CHAPTER XXIII.*

From the nature of the conversations which had just been concluded, it might have been inferred by the disciples that Christ's relation to the law was in some respects latitudinarian, or that at least He had a summary method of characterising and interpreting it; the opening of this chapter forms an admirable supplemement to His teachings on the spirit and meaning of the law :—

1. Then spake Jesus to the multitude, and to his disciples,
2. Saying, The scribes and the Pharisees sit in Moses' seat :
3. All therefore whatsoever they bid you observe, that observe and do ; but do not ye after their works : for they say, and do not.

From these words we infer:—1. Generally, the possibility

of *knowing* the law without obeying it. 2. Particularly, the possibility of actually *teaching* the law without obeying it ; and 3. That duty is to be determined by the law, and not by the example of its teachers. In Jesus Christ alone we find perfect consistency between the teacher and the teaching.

"When Christ had put all His enemies to silence, lest He should be thought an enemy to the law, He commandeth here all reverence to be given unto it."—(CHRYSOSTOM.) "They which cleave to the letter of the law are the scribes ; they which take upon them more profession, being, as it were, divided from others, are the Pharisees. But there be some which interpret Moses in a spiritual sense, the beloved disciples of Christ, and no scribes or Pharisees, yet sitting in Moses' chair, or rather upon the chair of Christ, which is His Church."—(ORIGEN.) "I know not whence this phrase (Moses' chair) is taken, unless the pulpit be meant, out of which the priests are said to have spoken in Ezra."— (CALVIN.)

4. For they bind heavy burdens and grievous to be borne, and lay them on men's shoulders ; but they themselves will not move them with one of their fingers.

A fine indirect illustration of the spirit of the Gospel, which is one of the utmost human consideration and gentleness. The spirit of the Gospel is not one which demands the performance of cumbrous duties; it touches the heart, and brings the whole life under the omnipotent rule of love. How Jesus Christ separated Himself from the teachers of His day! The gentle Teacher thus un-gently bade other teachers stand off! Jesus seems to harden Himself, and to rise in obstinate antagonism when He turns towards the incapable and selfish men who had set themselves as the leaders of religious thought; He never speaks kindly of them for the sake of their office, but on the contrary omits no opportunity of bringing them into discredit.

> 5. But all their works they do for to be seen of men : they make broad their phylacteries, and enlarge the borders of their garments,
> 6. And love the uppermost rooms at feasts, and the chief seats in the synagogues,
> 7. And greetings in the markets, and to be called of men, Rabbi, Rabbi.

A minute and faithful delineation of selfish teachers,—men-pleasers, hypocrites, gourmands, aspirants. All their life is public; they have no hidden intercourse with God; so the life be seen and applauded, they have all the reward they seek. From this portraiture of the false teacher we may infer the characteristics of the true,—gentleness, human sympathy, consciousness of the Divine presence, independence of human applause, modesty; whoever is deficient of these marks is not a teacher sent of Christ.

The phylacteries ($\phi v \lambda a \tau \tau \epsilon \iota v$, *to guard*) were bands of parchment, on which were written certain portions of the law. "Because the Lord would not have His benefits forgotten, He appointed little books to be written, and fastened to their hands; the strings fastening them were called phylacteries, that is *keepers*, keeping them before their eyes continually, as some women do now-a-days, hanging some piece of the Gospel, for memory's sake, about their necks, and as forgetful persons are wont to tie a thread about their finger. The fringe was a blue silk ribbon, sewed upon the nether part of their garment, hanging down to the ankle, for a remembrance of the commandments."—(CHRYSOSTOM.)

> 8. But be not ye called Rabbi : for one is your Master, even Christ ; and all ye are brethren.
> 9. And call no man your father upon the earth : for one is your Father, which is in heaven.
> 10. Neither be ye called masters : for one is your Master, even Christ.

11. But he that is greatest among you, shall be your servant.
12. And whosoever shall exalt himself shall be abased; and he that shall humble himself shall be exalted.

Jesus Christ now passes from the negative to the affirmative. The picture of the Teacher thus instructing teachers is most impressive. 1. No unworthy ambition is to be cherished. 2. No merely nominal superiority is to be coveted. 3. The most entirely fraternal spirit is to be cultivated. 4. This spirit can be cultivated most effectually by a constant recognition of Christ's Headship.

"Be not called Doctor: how doth Paul agree to this, when he calleth himself the doctor of the Gentiles. It is one thing to be a father or doctor by nature, and another by indulgence; God only is by nature, man by consorting with the true Father and Master; even as one God and one Son of God doth not prejudice others, but that they may be called gods and sons of God by adoption, so is it with one Father and Master."—(JEROME.) "Christ doth not mean to deny altogether the title of master and father unto men, for that were absurd, seeing He hath committed unto men the office of teaching in His own place; but He only is Master, because of all men to be heard and obeyed; men that teach are masters, as they sustain His person, and He speaketh in them."—(CALVIN.)

"One is your Leader,"—$\kappa\alpha\theta\eta\gamma\eta\tau\eta s$=*ductor*. GRIESBACH prefers $\kappa\alpha\theta\eta\gamma\eta\tau\eta s$ to $\delta\iota\delta\acute{a}\sigma\kappa\alpha\lambda os$, which is found in many MSS. The highest of titles is "*Servus Servorum Dei.*" As Diogenes in rags was prouder than Plato in his robes, so many an untitled man is more masterful than some who are laden with all the poor honours which the world can give. The whole meaning turns entirely upon the *spirit*.

In the 12th verse, Jesus Christ lays down one of those apparent paradoxes which so startle men who have been walking in the light of half-truths or of positive sophisms.

To go up is to go down, to go down is to go up! The meaning is to be found in the word *himself.* Individuality should not occupy the first place. Selfish aspirants do succeed for a time, under some circumstances; but viewing their case in its completeness it will be found that their exaltation, lacking the element of virtue which is always associated with sound merit, is temporary, and entails upon its holder endless fencing with men who suffer from their usurpation, but who must eventually depose them from their ill-gotten eminence. God always works for the meritorious man. Instead of accepting a policy marked by a bold or dazzling ambition, young men should reflect that the universe, with God at its head, is on the side of him who has the requisite faculty and the true spirit. His patron is God,—his hope is Time!

13. But woe unto you, scribes and Pharisees, hypocrites! for ye shut up the kingdom of heaven against men: for ye neither go in yourselves, neither suffer ye them that are entering to go in.

14. Woe unto you, scribes and Pharisees, hypocrites! for ye devour widows' houses, and for a pretence make long prayer: therefore ye shall receive the greater damnation.

15. Woe unto you, scribes and Pharisees, hypocrites! for ye compass sea and land to make one proselyte, and when he is made, ye make him twofold more the child of hell than yourselves.

16. Woe unto you, ye blind guides, which say, Whosoever shall swear by the temple, it is nothing; but whosoever shall swear by the gold of the temple, he is a debtor!

17. Ye fools and blind: for whether is greater, the gold, or the temple that sanctifieth the gold?

18. And, Whosoever shall swear by the altar, it is nothing; but whosoever sweareth by the gift that is upon it, he is guilty.

19. Ye fools and blind: for whether is greater, the gift, or the altar that sanctifieth the gift?

20. Whoso therefore shall swear by the altar, sweareth by it, and by all things thereon.

21. And whoso shall swear by the temple, sweareth by it, and by him that dwelleth therein.

22. And he that shall swear by heaven, sweareth by the throne of God, and by him that sitteth thereon.

23. Woe unto you, scribes and Pharisees, hypocrites! for ye pay tithe of mint and anise and cummin, and have omitted the weightier matters of the law, judgment, mercy, and faith : these ought ye to have done, and not to leave the other undone.

24. Ye blind guides, which strain at a gnat, and swallow a camel.

25. Woe unto you, scribes and Pharisees, hypocrites! for ye make clean the outside of the cup and of the platter, but within they are full of extortion and excess.

26. Thou blind Pharisee, cleanse first that which is within the cup and platter, that the outside of them may be clean also.

27. Woe unto you, scribes and Pharisees, hypocrites! for ye are like unto whited sepulchres, which indeed appear beautiful outward, but are within full of dead men's bones, and of all uncleanness.

28. Even so ye also outwardly appear righteous unto men, but within ye are full of hypocrisy and iniquity.

29. Woe unto you, scribes and Pharisees, hypocrites! because ye build the tombs of the prophets, and garnish the sepulchres of the righteous,

30. And say, If we had been in the days of our fathers, we would not have been partakers with them in the blood of the prophets.

31. Wherefore ye be witnesses unto yourselves, that ye are the children of them which killed the prophets.

32. Fill ye up then the measure of your fathers.

33. Ye serpents, ye generation of vipers, how can ye escape the damnation of hell?

This speech, so impetuous, so overwhelming, is like the bursting forth of a long-pent flood; in point of style it presents a strong contrast to the general character of Jesus Christ's speech. Look at the epithets: hypocrites, devourers, blind guides, fools and blind, whited sepulchres, serpents, generation of vipers! This maledictory outburst shows:—1. That faithful teachers are bound to give faithful delineations of their times; 2. That faithful delineations of the most corrupt men can only be effectual for good, when given by those who are meek and lowly in heart; 3. That those who address themselves to the exposure and redress of current evils should be unimpeachable in their own lives; 4. That the denunciation of bad men is only one side of the Christian mission, and should be regarded strictly as a preliminary work.

The passage may be broken up, and dealt with, homiletically, in sections; still it is one, as a flood is one, and should receive attention as a unity. No doubt the Flood might have been divided into streamlets, but such a division would have deprived it of its peculiar character. Treatment of the several parts of this tremendous indictment might take some such turn as the following :—

Verse 13. *The double mischief of moral obstinacy,*—" ye neither go in yourselves," &c.

Verse 14. *The immorality of combining prayer with self-aggrandisement,*—" ye devour, ye make long prayer."

Verse 15. *The debasing effect of bad teaching,*—" ye make him twofold more the child of hell than yourselves." " Christ doth here condemn them for two things:—1. Because they were so unprofitable to the salvation of others, that they could scarce, though they laboured much, draw any; 2. Having drawn them, they were so vile that they did not keep, but as betrayers brought them by their evil example into greater danger."—(CHRYSOSTOM.)

Verses 16–22. *The false relations into which corrupt men throw all things;*—temple and gold; altar and gift; temple and Him that dwelleth therein. The corrupt man reverses all natural and spiritual gradations. " If any man, in chiding with another, had broken out into swearing, and were convicted to have sworn falsely, if it were by the temple, as one not guilty he was dismissed without mulct; but if it were by the gold or money which in the temple was offered, that come to the priests, he was presently compelled to pay so much as he swore by; likewise by the altar there was no guilt, but if by the offerings, whether beast, fowl, flour, or any other thing, which used to be offered upon the altar, they compelled him to pay it ; now the Lord overthroweth this as a foolish colour, showing that the temple was greater than the gold, and again that in swearing by the

temple they did swear by the gold and all things therein."
—(JEROME.)

A very clear and well-sustained antithesis between the benedictions and the maledictions is drawn by LANGE. A specimen is subjoined:—

1. Poverty in spirit,=Devouring widows' houses, &c.
2. The mourners,=The kingdom of heaven shut, &c.
3. The meek,=Zeal of proselytism.

On building the tombs of the prophets, LANGE says: "The antithesis is delicate: *And garnish the sepulchres of the righteous* (canonised good men). The latter are acknowledged at once, and received their monuments; the prophets, on the other hand, often lay long in their uncelebrated or even dishonoured graves. Later generations then began to become enthusiastic about them, and make their common graves elaborate monuments." The comment of CHRYSOSTOM is good: "The Lord doth not reprove them for building sepulchres; but because doing thus, and condemning their fathers, they themselves did worse. This Luke openeth—*ye take pleasure in the works of your fathers*; He speaketh not against their building, but against their mind. He taxeth them not for being sons of murderers, but foretelling His own death by their murderous hands, and therefore daring to do this to the Master, they would much more have done it to His servants the prophets, if they had lived in their days."

34. Wherefore, behold, I send unto you prophets, and wise men, and scribes: and some of them ye shall kill and crucify; and some of them shall ye scourge in your synagogues, and persecute them from city to city:

35. That upon you may come all the righteous blood shed upon the earth, from the blood of righteous Abel unto the blood of Zacharias son of Barachias, whom ye slew between the temple and the altar.

36. Verily I say unto you, All these things shall come upon this generation.

1. Jesus Christ thus represents Himself as the Sender of

the great men who are able to lead the religious thought of the ages,—"I send prophets and wise men and scribes." This is a prerogative too high for any mere man; and, as it was assumed prior to His resurrection, it is to be inferred that it was personal, not official. 2. Jesus Christ shows how the accumulated guilt of ages is charged upon the wicked men of the current day,—"that upon you may come all the righteous blood shed upon the earth, from the blood of righteous Abel," &c. Think of the wicked man's bad lineage! By historic references give him a view of his kindred. "All these things shall come upon this generation,"—every sinner contributes to darken the doom of every other sinner. 3. Jesus Christ shows how He notes the treatment of all His servants, Abel, Zacharias, all the righteous blood! "Zacharias is held by some to be the father of John the Baptist, by others a certain priest of two names." — (CHRYSOSTOM.) "Some think that he was Zachary, the eleventh of the small prophets; but this cannot be, because that in his days there were scarce any ruins of the temple remaining, betwixt which and the altar he is said to be slain."—(JEROME.) "We have a certain tradition that there was a certain place for virgins to pray in, near unto which no man might come; into this place the Virgin Mary entered after that she had brought forth Christ, whereupon a contention arose, they saying that she ought not to come in; but Zachary stood against them, affirming that she was still a virgin; for this cause being accounted a manifest transgressor of the law, he was slain there."—(ORIGEN.) "Here we must first consider that Jesus speaks of a *specific* bloodguiltiness,—that with which mankind, in its malignity, has burdened itself in its hatred against holiness, namely, the guilt of shedding the blood of martyrs. Hence the line of martyrs very rightly commences with Abel; he was put to death directly on account of his piety. Secondly, it must be considered that Jesus speaks of *ancient* bloodguiltiness of this kind *incurred in times long past;* and concerning this He declares that they have not yet been expiated, and hence that they would be increased, and in due time their measure filled up, by heavier bloodguiltiness of a like kind. On this ground it is surely clear, that in the person of Zacharias we must recognise that martyr Zechariah, who is spoken of in 2 Chronicles xxiv. 20. The juxtaposition of these two names is then explained by the fact, that the death of Abel is the first case, the murder of Zechariah the last 'prophet-murder of which mention is made in Holy Scripture.' But there is still this difficulty, that 'that Zacharias was not a son of Barachias, as the Zacharias in Matthew is called, but the son of Jehoiada.' This difficulty has been explained in different ways. 1. That Zechariah had two fathers, a natural and a foster-father. But this is a mere hypothesis. 2. That the prophet Zechariah is meant, since his father was called Barachiah. Only 'nothing is known concerning his murder.' . . . OLSHAUSEN explains the difficulty thus: 'Now there is nothing offensive in the supposition, that Matthew might have confused the name of the murdered man's father with the father of the Zacharias whose book we have in the canon of Scripture.' "—(LANGE.)

37. O Jerusalem, Jerusalem, thou that killest the prophets, and stonest them which are sent unto thee, how often would I have gathered thy children together, even as an hen gathereth her chickens under her wings, and ye would not?

38. Behold, your house is left unto you desolate.

39. For I say unto you, Ye shall not see me henceforth, till ye shall say, Blessed is he that cometh in the name of the Lord.

Words of wrath, turned to exclamations of pity! The Man who uttered those words did not pour out vengeance as the expression of any low passion. He felt every blow Himself! This was the justice that was merciful, and the mercy that was just. 1. Jesus Christ's willingness to gather to Himself the most depraved of men and the most corrupt of cities,—"Thou that killest the prophets, and stonest them which are sent unto thee!" 2. The most gracious offers of Jesus Christ declined,—"ye would not." "He was despised and rejected of men." 3. The terrible crisis which supervenes in cases of moral obstinacy,—"your house is left unto you desolate." Desolate! What is the meaning of such word? "The word here translated 'desolate' is sometimes used in a peculiar sense, as, for instance, a forum where no judicial proceedings were carried on was said to be desolate."—(BENGEL.)

*As a hen gathereth her chickens.* "The hen expresseth such affection to her young as is seldom seen in other creatures, being affected with infirmity through their infirmities, and protecting them under her wing from kites; so our mother, the Wisdom of God, becoming weak after a sort by taking flesh, doth protect our infirmity, resisting the devil that would snatch us away."—(AUGUSTINE.)

*How often would I have gathered thee.* "Some do cunningly seek by these words to establish free will, because He would and they would not; but the will of God here spoken of is to be considered by the effect. When He sendeth forth preachers to move all to turn to Him, it is rightly said that He would gather them, not by that will which is His secret counsel, for this standeth firm, but by that will which we call so by reason of the word preached, offering grace unto all men."—(CALVIN.)

*Blessed is He that cometh in the name of the Lord.* "Some understand this as spoken of the last judgment; some of the event which followed long after, when some of the Jews did humbly adore Christ. But it seemeth to me to have none other meaning, but as that saying of Joseph touching Mary, 'he knew her not till she had brought forth her first-born,' whence it is not to be inferred that they did afterwards accompany together like man and wife. It is much as if He should have said,—I have hitherto been amongst you as a minister, but My course being finished, I will go away and ye shall not see Me any more as a minister, but feel Me as a judge. And He doth secretly nip them, for that they were wont daily to pronounce out of the Psalm, *Blessed is He that cometh in the name of the Lord*, but when this blessed One was offered them they made a mock of Him."—(CALVIN.) "They were soon to say this, but without referring to Christ, in reciting the Paschal Hallel, or hymn of praise (of which the 118th Psalm formed part). The prediction here given shall be fulfilled in its appointed time. . . . And when shall they say this? Willingly never; but unwillingly at His second coming, in power and great glory, when the confession can avail them nothing."—(*Critical English Testament.*)

### CHAPTER XXIV.

1. And Jesus went out, and departed from the temple: and his disciples came to him for to show him the buildings of the temple.
2. And Jesus said unto them, See ye not all these things? verily I say unto you, There shall not be left here one stone upon another, that shall not be thrown down.

The disciples showed the present; Jesus showed the future; this difference will perpetually distinguish the teacher from the taught. The minute manner in which Christ foretells the destruction of Jerusalem would seem to be foreign to the gentleness of His nature: this is the impression conveyed by a superficial idea of gentleness; a profounder conception recognises gentleness as an aspect of justice, and justice as a necessity wrought out by an attempt to adjust the balance which the moral universe has lost.

From the third verse we have a detailed statement of the signs of Christ's coming and of the end of the world; and as the statement is one of extraordinary interest, whose inter-

T

pretation has elicited the most conflicting opinions, we shall cite the testimony of a learned council, so that preachers may have material for homiletic outlines. The various expositors have not kept strictly to Christ's own order of prediction, so that we must suffer the inconvenience of a little transposition.

*This Gospel shall be preached for a witness to all nations, and then shall the end be.* " That is the end of Jerusalem, before the destruction whereof the Gospel was preached throughout the world. Witness Paul, saying, *Their sound hath gone out into all the earth;* and again, *The Gospel is preached to every creature under heaven, so that ye may see it running from Jerusalem into Spain.* And if one only apostle, Paul, spread the Gospel so far, what shall we think did all the rest? And this was a great miracle for the convincing of the unbelieving Jews before their destruction, for the Gospel to be preached in all parts of the world, in twenty or thirty years at the most; if this would not move them to believe, nothing could."—(CHRYSOSTOM.) " This must not be understood as done by the apostles, for there are many barbarous nations of Africa amongst whom the Gospel was never yet preached, as we may gather by such as have been captives there. This therefore remaineth yet to be accomplished; and because it is a secret when the world shall be filled with the Gospel, it is a secret likewise when shall be the day of judgment, before which this must be."—(AUGUSTINE.) " That is before the end of the world, which hath not yet been; for many, not only barbarous nations, but even of our own, have not yet heard the Gospel."—(ORIGEN.) " Notwithstanding these persecutions, there should be a universal publication of the glad tidings of the kingdom, for a testimony to all nations. God would have the iniquity of the Jews published everywhere, before the heavy stroke of His judgments should fall upon them; that all mankind, as it were, might be brought as witnesses against their cruelty and obstinacy in crucifying and rejecting the Lord Jesus."—(ADAM CLARKE.) "The Gospel had been preached through the whole *orbis terrarum*, and every nation had received its testimony, before the destruction of Jerusalem; see Col. i. 6, 23; 2 Tim. iv. 17. This was necessary, not only as regarded the Gentiles, but to give to God's people the Jews, who were scattered among all these nations, *the opportunity of receiving or rejecting the preaching of Christ*. But in the wider sense, the words imply that the Gospel shall be preached in *all the world, literally taken*, before the great and final end come. *The apostasy of the latter days*, and the *universal dispersion of missions*, are the two great signs of the end drawing near."—(ALFORD.) " The Gospel is not merely to be preached to the nations, but to be preached faithfully, even unto martyrdom; it will be a witness unto them, and then it will be a witness concerning them and against them."—(LANGE.)

*When ye see the abomination of desolation.* " This was the state of him that should destroy the city, which he after the destruction placed there within. O new thing and unheard of! The Romans, with an innumerable army, overcame the infinite multitude of the Jews, but are themselves overcome by twelve poor men!"—(CHRYSOSTOM.) " Some do not amiss understand hereby the evils themselves, for we read of evil days in the Scriptures, not because the days are evil, but the accidents of those days; which are said to be shortened, either because God giveth strength to bear them, or because they are lessened. Some again understand that those days should be shortened by the sun going his compass more speedily in a shorter time."—(AUGUSTINE.) "The prophet spake this of Anti-Christ's time; it is called abomination because he should take unto him the honour of God, and the abomination of desolation because he should waste the country with destruction and slaughters; *standing where it should not*, that is, in the place where God was wont to be worshipped, and to have prayers offered unto Him, for there shall Anti-Christ be worshipped of infidels."—(HILARY.) "Most interpreters refer this to Daniel xi.; but they are deceived, for neither is the same word precisely used, nor was any other thing there foretold but the profanation of the temple by Antiochus. Wherefore this hath relation to Daniel xii., where an utter cessation of Divine worship and sacrificing in that temple is foretold after a certain term of days. It is called abomination of desolation, because a general ruin of the whole commonwealth and kingdom shall come therewith."—(CALVIN.)

*For as the lightning cometh out of the east and shineth even unto the west.* "By the lightning, understand the truth, which is said to pass from east to west, because it is apparent from all parts of the Scriptures, from the beginning of Christ even to His passion, which is His west, or from the beginning of the world to the last writings of the apostles; or else the east is the law, the west is the end of the law, John's prophecy."—(ORIGEN.) "Hereby is set forth a distinction between the Church of Christ and assemblies of heretics: the Church is spread all over the whole world, like the lightning, clearly to be seen; the assemblies of heretics are but in some corners and private conventicles." —(AUGUSTINE.) "The coming of the Lord in the end, even as that in the type was, shall be *a plain unmistakable fact*, understood of all;—and like that also, *sudden* and *all-pervading*. But here again the full meaning of the words is only to be found in the *final fulfilment* of them. The lightning, lighting both ends of heaven at once, seen of all beneath it, can only find its full similitude in HIS personal coming, whom every eye shall see."—(ALFORD.)

## CHAPTER XXV.

1. Then shall the kingdom of heaven be likened unto ten virgins, which took their lamps, and went forth to meet the bridegroom.
2. And five of them were wise, and five were foolish.
3. They that were foolish took their lamps, and took no oil with them:
4. But the wise took oil in their vessels with their lamps.
5. While the bridegroom tarried, they all slumbered and slept.
6. And at midnight there was a cry made, Behold, the bridegroom cometh; go ye out to meet him.
7. Then all those virgins arose, and trimmed their lamps.
8. And the foolish said unto the wise, Give us of your oil; for our lamps are gone out.
9. But the wise answered, saying, Not so; lest there be not enough for us and you: but go ye rather to them that sell, and buy for yourselves.
10. And while they went to buy, the bridegroom came; and they that were ready went in with him to the marriage: and the door was shut.
11. Afterward came also the other virgins, saying, Lord, Lord, open to us.
12. But he answered and said, Verily I say unto you, I know you not.
13. Watch therefore, for ye know neither the day nor the hour wherein the Son of man cometh.

The common interpretation of this parable may be set aside for a few moments, that less known renderings of its meaning may have greater prominence. CHRYSOSTOM says that the whole of the parables contained in this chapter are designed to stir up to almsgiving, and to live to the benefit of one another. With regard to this particular parable, he says the Bridegroom is Christ, the sleep of the virgins is death, Christ comes at midnight to show that He will appear when He is least expected, and that the cry heard is the sound of the last trumpet. His interpretation of the passage is novel: the foolish, he says, want oil, for nothing is so foolish as to gather money here and to depart naked; the wise deny them oil, not through inhumanity, but to show that if we lose the time of doing good works it will never return; "them that sell" are the needy, but when Christ comes it will be too late to procure oil by giving the poor alms which they no longer need.

JEROME is more fanciful in his interpretation. He says that the five senses in the wise hasten towards the heavenly kingdom, especially the sight, the hearing, and the touch; they who have oil are those who join good works to faith, and they who have no oil are those which seem to have faith but have no good works.

AUGUSTINE is still more fanciful. The virgins, he says, are such as are called by the name of Christ, for how can infidels be said to prepare to go out to meet Him? They are all virgins because they are called to continency, and they are five because of the five senses whose desires are to be controlled. There are two sorts of continency: the wise keeping continency before God, and the foolish only before men. On the expression, "lest there be not enough for us and you," AUGUSTINE well says: "The testimony of one man will not then profit another, and the best shall find testimony little enough from his own conscience for his comfort."

ORIGEN says that the virgins are the senses of all those who have received the word, because they have departed from the worship of idols to the worship of God. He further says that the lamps are the organs of the body, together with the mind; the oil is the word of God, feeding the mind and cherishing it: the wise receive enough of the doctrine of this word, so that, though the Bridegroom tarries, there is no want of oil; but the foolish, being negligent in receiving it, are altogether without oil at His coming.

HILARY says the lamps are bright souls, the oil is the fruit of good works, the five wise and five foolish are the faithful and the unfaithful, the marriage is the assumption of immortality.

So much for the testimony of learned ancients. As the parable relates to a marriage, it should be borne in mind that the marriages of the Jews were celebrated in the evening, when the bridegroom led his new bride to his home in procession; and that she might be received in a suitable manner, his female friends of the younger sort were invited to come and wait with lamps the arrival of the bridegroom. When they arrived they conducted them into the house, and were themselves afterwards invited to join in the bridal festivity.—(VALPY.)

Looked at in relation to the whole life of humanity, the parable appears to proceed upon a recognition of four facts:—

I. THAT HUMAN LIFE IS MARKED BY THE MOST SOLEMN DISTINCTIONS. Of these virgins it is said "five of them were wise, and five were foolish;" a terrible difference when viewed morally! To be *morally* "foolish" is to stand towards God in the relation of an alien. An uneducated *brain* is constantly feeling its disadvantage; it cannot cope with the trained mind, it is ignominiously worsted by the disciplined powers of men who from childhood have been drilled in intellectual exercises; its processes are slow, involved, cumbrous; it drags in the far rear, while the agile mind of the trained athlete is on the foremost lines of progress. But what shall be said of a foolish *heart?* A temple defiled by unclean beasts,—an altar darkened, and strewn with cold white ashes! A foolish heart has thrown away God's statute-book, and dismissed God Himself from its counsels. The fool hath said in his heart there is no God. To narrow the universe until it is measurable by our own span; to exalt ourselves until we overshadow all rivals; to silence all voices with the thunder of our self-congratulations, is to show how far we can get from God, how foolish, how mad is moral apostasy.

The presence of this word "foolish" in the story of

human life is a witness against man. How did the word force itself into existence? It was not born of music, for it is most harsh and dissonant; it did not come of beauty, for every line is a hideous deformity. How came it? We are thrown back upon our own consciousness, and back upon the gloomy record of human life; and there we find how we have rebelled against God, and gone from Him as if He had wronged our souls. We have heard that five were *wise*, but where are they? Will any man say that his moral course has been one of wisdom? Is not our very wisdom but a flattering phase of our folly? Comparing ourselves with ourselves, we may claim wisdom; but, looking at the Divine standard, we may truly say with the Psalmist, " So foolish am I and ignorant, I am as a beast before thee."

"The kingdom of heaven" is the great dividing force, according to which men stand or fall. There are innumerable subjects upon which they may differ with impunity; but upon this subject they must be agreed, or the stone will fall upon them and grind them to powder.

II. THAT THOSE DISTINCTIONS WILL BE MADE MANIFEST AT THE COMING OF JESUS CHRIST. When the bridegroom came "the foolish said unto the wise, Give us of your oil; for our lamps are gone out." As they went out to meet the bridegroom in the first instance, who could have told which of them were wise and which foolish? As they all slumbered and slept, who could have judged them accurately? Then comes the revealing hour! The light will strike every man, and show exactly what he is! (Sincere: hypocritical: misunderstood: diligent: slothful: all!) 1. Think of every man getting his due reward! Who is prepared to be pronounced *a fool*, and to be carried away by the whirlwind from the presence of God? 2. What changes will take place in human relations, what depositions, what elevations! The first last, &c.

III. THAT AT THE COMING OF JESUS CHRIST NO MAN WILL FIND HIMSELF IN POSSESSION OF SUPERFLUOUS GRACE. The righteous may *scarcely* be saved ! If this be so, then :— 1. *Personal* growth is the law of the Christian life. 2. *Continuous* personal growth is the privilege of the Christian spirit. 3. The *realisation* of continuous personal growth is the chief joy of the Christian heart.

IV. THAT WHILE NO MAN WILL FIND HIMSELF IN POSSESSION OF SUPERFLUOUS GRACE, THE ILL-PROVIDED WILL BE COMPELLED TO CONFESS THEIR DESTITUTION. Job said, " How oft is the candle of the wicked put out ! " and now the virgins say, " Our lamps are gone out. 1. A result which might have been *avoided*. 2. A humiliation the most ignominious. 3. A destitution which cannot be repaired. Men (who might have been living in the heavenly light) standing, groping, falling, in the final darkness ! 1. Darkness a *prison*. 2. Darkness a *terror*.

Whatever difficulty may attend an exposition of some of the phrases in this parable, four things are clear :—1. That the coming of the Bridegroom will be sudden and unexpected. 2. That the wise will enjoy His fellowship for ever. 3. That the foolish will be doomed to utter desolation. 4. That vigilance is the duty of all.

The ancient expositions given at the beginning find a counterpart in modern suggestions. EUSTACE CONDER says : " The great lesson of the parable is faithfulness with our own hearts, lest we deceive ourselves." Referring to the lamps, he says : " The lamps are that light of holy character, example, truth, and usefulness, which we are to let shine before men ; or, if we distinguish between the *lamp* and the *light*, the lamp (and the carrying of it) corresponds to the knowledge, capacities, and outward privileges, by means of which, if rightly used, our light may be caused to shine in deeds of love and duty. The oil is the well-known emblem in Scripture of the grace of the Holy Spirit. . . . The wise virgins are the true members of Christ's Church; the foolish are those who are members by outward standing and profession, *i.e.*, the avowed belief of Christian truth and outward practice of Christian duty—who are foolishly content with that which is external in religion," &c. In BENGEL's Gnomon (English adaptation) we find the following opinion: "*Ten*—There is mystery in this number (comp. Luke xix. 13), which is divided into two equal parts. [Either because the number on each side will be equal, or because their inequality will not appear.—V. GER.] It was thought fitting that a bride should have at least ten bridesmaids." [And generally, at all events among the Jews, ten was looked on as the number necessary for a congregation.—V. GER.] NEANDER says: "The parable of the virgins was designed to set vividly before the disciples the necessity of constant preparation for the uncertain time of Christ's second advent, without at all clearing up the uncertainty of the time itself; thus harmonising exactly with all His teachings on the subject. It is certainly, also, the representation (so often made by Christ) of the idea of Christian virtue under the form of prudence; and illustrates the connection between Christian prudence and that ever-vigilant presence of mind which springs from one constant and predominant aim of life. But we must distinguish between the fundamental thought of the parable and its supplementary features. It may be that one of these latter is the fruitless application of the foolish virgins to the wise for a supply which they might have secured for themselves by adequate care and forethought; yet perhaps Christ, piercing the recesses of the human heart, and seeing its tendency to trust in the vicarious services and merits of others, may have intended, by this feature of the parable, to warn His disciples against such a fatal error." BURKITT says: "By *the kingdom of heaven* is meant the state of the visible Church on earth; it cannot be understood of the kingdom of glory, for there are no foolish virgins in that kingdom; nor yet of the invisible kingdom of grace, for therein are no foolish virgins neither. But in the visible Church there ever has been a mixture of wise and unwise, of saints and hypocrites."

14. For the kingdom of heaven is as a man travelling into a far country, who called his own servants, and delivered unto them his goods.

15. And unto one he gave five talents, to another two, and to another one; to every man according to his several ability; and straightway took his journey.

16. Then he that had received the five talents went and traded with the same, and made them other five talents.

17. And likewise he that had received two, he also gained other two.

18. But he that had received one went and digged in the earth, and hid his lord's money.

/ 19. After a long time the lord of those servants cometh, and reckoneth with them.

20. And so he that had received five talents came and brought other five talents, saying, Lord, thou deliveredst unto me five talents: behold, I have gained beside them five talents more.

21. His lord said unto him, Well done, thou good and faithful servant; thou hast been faithful over a few things, I will make thee ruler over many things: enter thou into the joy of thy lord.

22. He also that had received two talents came and said, Lord, thou deliveredst unto me two talents: behold, I have gained two other talents beside them.

23. His lord said unto him, Well done, good and faithful servant; thou hast been faithful over a few things, I will make thee ruler over many things: enter thou into the joy of thy lord.

24. Then he which had received the one talent came and said, Lord, I knew thee that thou art an hard man, reaping where thou hast not sown, and gathering where thou hast not strawed:

25. And I was afraid, and went and hid thy talent in the earth: lo, there thou hast that is thine.

26. His lord answered and said unto him, Thou wicked and slothful servant, thou knewest that I reap where I sowed not, and gather where I have not strawed:

27. Thou oughtest therefore to have put my money to the exchangers, and then at my coming I should have received mine own with usury.

28. Take therefore the talent from him, and give it unto him which hath ten talents.

29. For unto every one that hath shall be given, and he shall have abundance : but from him that hath not shall be taken away even that which he hath.
30. And cast ye the unprofitable servant into outer darkness : there shall be weeping and gnashing of teeth.

Most of the practical truths taught by this parable may be classified under two heads:—1. *Distribution,*—gave to every man according to his several ability. 2. *Examination,* —the lord of those servants cometh and reckoneth with them. Take the point of DISTRIBUTION, as indicating some of the principles of the Divine government of human society.

I. *The great principle of sovereignty is affirmed.* The king called his own servants and delivered unto them his goods. There was no consultation, the act was personal and sovereign ; the king called whom he would, and distributed as he pleased. This is a hint of God's position, and if we overlook it we shall leave behind a light which would relieve the darkness of many a mystery. There can be but one Sovereign : to attempt a division of His sovereignty is to repeat the first crime in human history. An acceptance of the doctrine of Divine sovereignty gives the heart very deep repose. Certainly at the centre gives steadiness to all the lines which radiate from it. " The Lord reigneth, he is clothed with majesty ; the Lord is clothed with strength wherewith he hath girded himself: the world also is stablished that it cannot be moved." (Ps. xciii. 1.) This is a great rock on which men may build securely ;—whatever is doubtful, this at least is certain ; wherever there may be darkness, here is a full and constant light.

II. *The true relation of men to God is defined.* They are servants. Ambition for mastery was, as just said, the first crime in human history. The man who devoutly accepts this relation, and works according to its claims, falls into God's order, and fulfils his calling with confidence, simplicity, and success. He is not the law-maker; he is not the source of the counsels by which he walks; he looks to the Strong for strength, and to the Wise for wisdom. How this simplifies human life! A servant may be happy; but a servant striving to be king must always be miserable; he overstrains himself, he is without legitimate sympathy, and all the laws of the universe are fighting against him. Order is a prime condition of peace. A man's capacity is the limit of his power; when he seeks to transcend it he practically disputes God's wisdom, and challenges God's power.

III. *The fact of individual endowment is asserted.* The king did not give to one or two only, he gave "to every man according to his several ability." The question is not, How many talents *ought* He to have given me? but, How many talents *has* He given me? God has set the members of the body every one of them as it hath pleased Him, and so He has distributed human talents. Every responsible man has *something* to begin with, some gift that is *his own*, an endowment which he may double if he will. This is a peculiarity of Divine gifts,—they are seeds, or germs; they will grow and bear fruit. To what perfection have some men trained their muscular power! To what splendour have others brought their imagination! To what magnificence have others educated their moral nature! They did not create, they developed their powers; and for the development alone they are held responsible.

A man may find fault with his endowment; but he does so at the expense of God's sovereignty: he may say, I shall not work, because I have not this gift or that; but he thereby impugns the wisdom of the relation which God has established. See the apostle's rebuke of the schismatic spirit in 1 Cor. xii. 14-27.

II. EXAMINATION. "After a long time the lord of those servants cometh and reckoneth with them." The judicial principle has the fullest sanction even of human reason. It is operative in all the arrangements of associated life. Society itself is founded upon a judicial basis. We need not, therefore, pause to argue the reasonableness of this examination. The parable justifies four conclusions respecting the final " reckoning."

I. *That every man will have to render his own personal account.* " He that had received the five talents came;" "he that had received the two talents came;" "he which had received the one talent came." Every man has his turn! Though the king be a long time away, yet the writing does not fade, all the original entries are perfect in clearness and legibility,—*you* had five,—*you* had two,—and even *you* had one! "We shall all stand before the judgment-seat of Christ;" "every one of us shall give account of himself to God;" "we must all appear before the judgment-seat of Christ, that every one may receive the things done in his body, according to that he hath done, whether it be good or bad." As there was something to begin with, so there is something to look forward to.

II. *That those who have worked in their Lord's interest will meet Him with joy.* This they will do for three reasons: —1. They have worked with *His* gifts; 2. They have enjoyed the satisfaction which always attends fidelity; 3. They have not only done their duty, but they have secured substantial results.

III. *That those who have not worked with their Lord shall be dispossessed and cast out of His presence.* About "the unprofitable servant" three things are remarkable:—1. Though he had little, he was expected to employ it; 2. Though he had an excuse, he had no reason; 3. Though he had not done anything, he was a wicked and slothful servant,—the negative becomes the positive. *Not* to work with God, *is* to serve the devil.

IV. *That the profitable servants will be enriched with the forfeited talents of the unprofitable*—ver. 28, 29.  1. A redistribution will take place;  2. Nothing will be lost;  3. Every one of God's talents is valuable;  4. The one despised talent is worthy to be numbered with the talents which have been doubled. The difference is not in quality, only in number.

The whole spirit of the parable is intensely practical, yet one or two points of special application may be urged. 1. The man with many talents should never undervalue the man with few,—what hast thou that thou hast not received? 2. Every man should study his own gifts, and work according to the Divine appointment,—"whether prophecy, let us prophesy according to the proportion of faith; or ministry, let us wait on our ministering: or he that teacheth, on teaching; or he that exhorteth, on exhortation." (Rom. xii. 6-8.)  3. Men should consider the reasonableness of God's judgment of the unprofitable servant; it is precisely what we do ourselves in business, in public appointments, in domestic service,—the unprofitable servant is always "cast out."

"The man travelling afar off is Christ going up into heaven; the five talents are the five senses; the two talents are the intellectual and operative faculties; the one talent the intellectual faculty only."—(GREGORY.) "The five talents are the gift of understanding the Scriptures so as to bring all sensible things of the Scriptures to more Divine senses; the two talents, the gift of understanding the Scriptures in the two Testaments according to the literal sense; the one talent is not to be able to understand so much, yet a talent not contemptible, coming from so great a Lord."—(ORIGEN.) "The servant receiving five talents sets forth the believing Jew, whose gift is doubled when to the obedience of the law he adds the faith of the Gospel. The servant with two talents is the believing Gentile. The evil servant with one talent is the Jew persisting in the law, hiding his talent by detracting from the Gospel, in regard of the Lord's suffering."—(HILARY.) In his *Harmony of the Evangelists,* CALVIN says : "The number of the servants and talents is not so much to be stumbled at: Luke says that he delivered to every one a talent, that is a gift according to the which he would have him exercise; and Matthew sets forth somewhat more, that there are diversities of gifts given unto men, according to which it is required that they should do ; where God delivers more talents He gives a faculty of using them. The occupying is communicating one with another to the glory of God ; the talent taken away from the unprofitable servant, and given to him with ten talents, shows that the sloth and negligence of the evil shall redound to the greater praise and glory of the faithful."

31. When the Son of man shall come in his glory, and all the holy angels with him, then shall he sit upon the throne of his glory:

32. And before him shall be gathered all nations : and he shall separate them one from another, as a shepherd divideth his sheep from the goats :

33. And he shall set the sheep on his right hand, but the goats on the left.

34. Then shall the King say unto them on his right hand, Come, ye blessed of my Father, inherit the kingdom prepared for you from the foundation of the world :

35. For I was an hungred, and ye gave me meat : I was thirsty, and ye gave me drink : I was a stranger, and ye took me in :

36. Naked, and ye clothed me : I was sick, and ye visited me : I was in prison, and ye came unto me.

37. Then shall the righteous answer him, saying, Lord, when saw we thee an hungred, and fed thee ? or thirsty, and gave thee drink?

38. When saw we thee a stranger, and took thee in? or naked, and clothed thee?

39. Or when saw we thee sick, or in prison, and came unto thee?

40. And the King shall answer and say unto them, Verily I say unto you, Inasmuch as ye have done it unto one of the least of these my brethren, ye have done it unto me.

41. Then shall he say also unto them on the left hand, Depart from me, ye cursed, into everlasting fire, prepared for the devil and his angels :

42. For I was an hungred, and ye gave me no meat : I was thirsty, and ye gave me no drink :

43. I was a stranger, and ye took me not in : naked, and ye clothed me not : sick, and in prison, and ye visited me not.

44. Then shall they also answer him, saying, Lord, when saw we thee an hungred, or athirst, or a stranger, or naked, or sick, or in prison, and did not minister unto thee ?

45. Then shall he answer them, saying, Verily I say unto you, Inasmuch as ye did it not to one of the least of these, ye did it not to me.

46. And these shall go away into everlasting punishment : but the righteous into life eternal.

This paragraph presents a series of contrasts :—

1. The grandeur of the scene, and the apparent insignificance of the proceedings : on the one hand there is the Son of man in His glory, sitting upon the throne of His glory, and all the holy angels with Him ; on the other hand there is a dialogue about acts of kindness. An apparent disproportion ! Incidentally we thus see that the simplest *goodness* transcends in value the most splendid *glory*. 2. A magnificent aggregation, and a final dispersion ; — "all nations," yet " separated one from another." Proximity is not unity. The breaking up of a world ! This breaking up is (*a*) heart-rending, (*b*) final, (*c*) but not inevitable,—there is a way of mercy. 3. Physical service directed by spiritual considerations,—bread was given, but it was given out of regard for Jesus Christ ; the motive is the measure of the deed. 4. A private act, and a public recognition,—done to "one of the least of these," and acknowledged before "all nations." 5. An election and a reprobation,—Come, Depart. Nothing can so effectually separate men as *moral* considerations.

The paragraph may be taken as expressing the *philanthropic side* of Christian truth. 1. This is not a merely impulsive generosity; 2. It is generosity to man, arising out of love to Jesus Christ; 3. It is generosity displayed under circumstances unfavourable to personal vanity,—done to "one of the least of these my brethren." On the dark aspect of the parable it may be remarked:—1. That merely external service to Jesus Christ is not valued;—those on the left hand *would* have been givers had they only *known!* 2. Giving that is regulated by selfish calculation is lost. 3. Those who are doing most to *keep* their lives are most effectually *losing* them,—everlasting punishment is the natural consummation of everlasting selfishness.

The paragraph may be discussed as showing the relation of Jesus Christ to the human family:—1. Jesus Christ represents Himself as the *Brother* of redeemed men; 2. Jesus Christ represents Himself as in necessitous circumstances; 3. Jesus Christ represents Himself as the *Observer* of all human actions; 4. Jesus Christ represents Himself as the *Judge* of human life.

"*Ye blessed of my Father.*" "It is not said of the other sort, Ye cursed of my Father, because though God be the Author of blessing, yet men are the authors of cursing unto themselves."—(ORIGEN.) "Herein is set forth the fountain of our happiness, the free favour of God. . . . Christ being about to set forth the salvation of the faithful, begins with the free love of God, out of which they were predestinated to life which, by the Spirit guiding, aspire unto righteousness."—(CALVIN.) "A prince deals one way in punishing a citizen offending, and another way against an enemy rebelling: against the one he proceeds according to law; against the other by war, not respecting any proceedings appointed by law. Some men say that a fault having end ought not to be punished world without end; I answer, this were true, if God looked only to the fact, not to the heart: but it is just that they should never be without punishment whose minds are never without a will to sin."— (GREGORY.)

## CHAPTER XXVI.

1. And it came to pass, when Jesus had finished all these sayings, he said unto his disciples,
2. Ye know that after two days is the feast of the passover, and the Son of man is betrayed to be crucified.
3. Then assembled together the chief priests, and the scribes, and the elders of the people, unto the palace of the high priest, who was called Caiaphas,
4. And consulted that they might take Jesus by subtilty, and kill him.
5. But they said, Not on the feast day, lest there be an uproar among the people.

The rapid movement from "sayings" to "crucified." Christ's perfect idea of *time* in relation to His mediatorial development. His last sayings had related to His "glory," and now He turns to His crucifixion,—the climax of speech was to be succeeded by the climax of suffering. 1. We have the PREPARED Christ,—He knew His work, He proclaimed it, He was ready for it. 2. We have the HESITATING murderers,—they consulted that they might take Jesus by subtilty and kill Him, but they said, Not on the feast day, lest there be an uproar among the people: (*a*) subtilty, a sign of *cowardice*; (*b*) the moral guarantee of popular instincts. LANGE says: "What is it that the Lord lays most stress upon when He announces His passion? 1. Not that He should be hung upon the cross; but 2. That He should be betrayed—perfect truth mourning over perfect falseness in the deepest grief—the sufferings of Christ, the consummation of all Joseph's sufferings: to be *betrayed* and *sold* by His brethren;" and again: "The greatest of all insurrections (against the Lord's Anointed) must always be in dread of the phantom of insurrection:—1. They lift themselves up against the Lord; and 2. Brand the possible uprising for His defence as rebellion." LANGE'S last reflection is excellent: "God can make sacrifices of His own, but He does not give them up to secret murder. They might crucify Him openly before the world; but secretly do away with Him they could not. The blood of the saints does not sink silently into the ground; it publicly flows, and preaches aloud." The perfect consistency between Christ's manner of life and Christ's preparation for death should not be overlooked; in both cases there is:—1. Entire self-possession. 2. Co-operation with the Father. 3. Universal benevolence. 4. Perfect adaptation to the necessities of the case,—human ignorance (doctrine), human guilt (atonement).

6. Now when Jesus was in Bethany, in the house of Simon the leper,
7. There came unto him a woman having an alabaster box of very precious ointment, and poured it on his head, as he sat at meat.
8. But when his disciples saw it, they had indignation, saying, To what purpose is this waste?
9. For this ointment might have been sold for much, and given to the poor.
10. When Jesus understood it, he said unto them, Why trouble ye the woman? for she hath wrought a good work upon me.
11. For ye have the poor always with you; but me ye have not always.
12. For in that she hath poured this ointment on my body, she did it for my burial.
13. Verily I say unto you, Wheresoever this gospel shall be preached in the whole world, there shall also this, that this woman hath done, be told for a memorial of her.

1. *The all-surrendering generosity of love.* Only *one* box, and it was given,—*given*, not demanded. The heart may be wealthy, though the hand be poor. If this woman had laid away her one box of ointment, how much could she have afforded for Jesus Christ? 2. *The moral depravity of selfish calculation in the Christian life.* "To what purpose is this waste" (*wasting*, literally)? The astounding anomaly of arithmetical love! The same word is used in the original to denote *waste* and *perdition;* it was the son of perdition who called this service waste! What is the

lesson? *The men who denominate other people's service "waste" are themselves the most likely to be cast away as the refuse of the universe.* What became of Judas? He had an ethical system of his own,—he carried the bag. 3. *The all-comprehending wisdom and benevolence of Jesus Christ's judgment* (ver. 10-12),—"She hath wrought a good work," literally, a beautiful work. 1. Christ is anxious for the peace of all who serve Him,—" Why trouble ye the woman?" Questions of casuistry; questions of frivolous distinction. 2. Christ shows that every age brings its own opportunities for doing good,—"Ye have the poor *always*." 4. *The assured immortality of goodness* (ver. 13). 1. Only a Divine being can guarantee immortality to any action. 2. In immortalising goodness Christ gives assurance of a happy future. 3. The nature of a being is known by the nature of the actions which he would immortalise.

The whole subject gives a word:—1. To those who have few resources. 2. To those who form a superficial estimate of the services of their brethren. 3. To those who are waiting for opportunities of doing good. 4. To those who would leave a memory to be praised. There is one mournful reflection occasioned by the circumstance, viz., the rarity of *the truly heroic element in human history*,—the deed is spoken of as standing by itself, a solitary but magnificent heroism. "Many women had come unto Him before, but none without some bodily disease impelling; this woman comes last, and is impelled only by the disease of her sins." —(CHRYSOSTOM.) " John says that she anointed His feet, and other two His head; but this is reconciled if we say that she anointed both head and feet."—(AUGUSTINE.) " I think that the women spoken of by the four evangelists are three. One by Matthew and Mark in the house of Simon the leper, at whom the disciples murmured; another by Luke, when there was no murmuring; and a third by

John, not in the presence of Simon, but of Lazarus, not two days, but six days before the Passover, Judas only murmuring."—(ORIGEN.) "Mary Magdalene, or Mary of Magdala, the name of her city, was probably a very respectable woman, out of whom our Lord had cast seven devils : but this was no stain upon her moral conduct. It is therefore from a baseless tradition that the Italian painters have painted exquisite pictures of penitent dishonoured women, and called them Magdalenes ; and somewhat of injury is done to her memory, by applying her name to this class of females."—(RICHARD WATSON.)

14. Then one of the twelve, called Judas Iscariot, went unto the chief priests,
15. And said unto them, What will ye give me, and I will deliver him unto you? And they covenanted with him for thirty pieces of silver.
16. And from that time he sought opportunity to betray him.

This action on the part of Judas shows :—1. *The power of man to resist the most convincing evidence of a Divine mission ;* the evidence was twofold—(*a*) the magnificence of power ; (*b*) the persuasiveness of love. 2. *The tremendous despotism of avarice,*—"*What will ye give me ?*" The avaricious man (*a*) makes life a mere question of calculation; (*b*) all the calculation is limited to self-aggrandisement. 3. *The influence of present gain as blinding man to consequences.* Judas sold Christ for what would be about four pounds ten shillings of English money ; he knew not that he " would pierce himself through with many sorrows." 4. *The connection which subsists between moral actions,*—"From that time he sought opportunity to betray him ; " whether the actions be bad or good, the actors should jealously watch the *beginning.*

17. Now the first day of the feast of unleavened bread the disciples came to Jesus, saying unto him, Where wilt thou that we prepare for thee to eat the passover?

18. And he said, Go into the city to such a man, and say unto him, The Master saith, My time is at hand; I will keep the passover at thy house with my disciples.

19. And the disciples did as Jesus had appointed them; and they made ready the passover.

20. Now when the even was come, he sat down with the twelve.

21. And as they did eat, he said, Verily I say unto you, that one of you shall betray me.

22. And they were exceeding sorrowful, and began every one of them to say unto him, Lord, is it I?

23. And he answered and said, He that dippeth his hand with me in the dish, the same shall betray me.

24. The Son of man goeth as it is written of him: but woe unto that man by whom the Son of man is betrayed! it had been good for that man if he had not been born.

25. Then Judas, which betrayed him, answered and said, Master, is it I? He said unto him, Thou hast said.

1. An incidental illustration of the poverty of Jesus Christ,—He had no house of His own, in which to eat the passover. 2. A positive declaration of the method of His end. It was *betrayal*. This method in harmony with the whole development of the diabolic element in human history; from the very beginning it has been a system of *treachery*. 3. An acknowledgment of the power of one individual to do mischief,—" One of you shall betray me." The power of the *individual* has again and again been acknowledged in the Bible: for example, the Devil; Cain; Achan; Jonah; Judas; &c. 4. A distinction between mere association and vital fellowship,—" He that dippeth his hand with me in the dish, the same shall betray me." The very climax of treachery, and so much the more in keeping with the tragic scene. There is a marvellous consistency throughout the whole development, —the consistency of diabolism! 5. The sorrow of the Church preliminary to its joy. The growth of the Church starts from an opposite point to that of the world; the world began with joy, the Church with sorrow. 6. The difference between betrayal and atonement: the betrayal

gives the diabolic side; the atonement the Divine side. Men are not saved by the betrayal, but by the atonement.

"Our Lord not only ate the paschal, and not a common supper, but He did so at the same time in which it was eaten by at least the generality of the Jews."—(RICHARD WATSON.) The same writer says, on the 24th verse : " It had been BETTER for him (the positive being used for the comparative) never to have had any existence, than to be doomed to eternal shame and punishment. This passage is conclusive against Judas's repentance and forgiveness in this life, and equally cogent to prove the doctrine of the eternity of future punishment. For if all lapsed intelligences are to be restored to happiness, then Judas must be amongst the number ; and if so, since, however long the punishment may be, it is but temporary and the ultimate felicity eternal, it could not be said that it had been better for him not to have existed."

26. And as they were eating, Jesus took bread, and blessed it, and brake it, and gave it to the disciples, and said, Take, eat; this is my body.
27. And he took the cup, and gave thanks, and gave it to them, saying, Drink ye all of it ;
28. For this is my blood of the new testament, which is shed for many for the remission of sins.
29. But I say unto you, I will not drink henceforth of this fruit of the vine, until that day when I drink it new with you in my Father's kingdom.
30. And when they had sung an hymn, they went out into the mount of Olives.

Lord's Supper :—1. *Sacrifice.* 2. *Fellowship* with Jesus Christ and with one another. 3. *Simplicity* of observance.

Or, 1. Time of recollection of sin. 2. Time of triumph over the torrent of memory.

Or, 1. Common observances elevated into Christian sacraments. 2. Common objects made into Divine symbols.

Or, 1. Out of the deepest sorrows may come the richest joys. 2. This can only be the case when we suffer *with*

Christ or *for* Christ. 3. Then the most solemn and saddening revelations may be succeeded by the singing of a hymn,—a hymn shall conclude all God's ministry amongst men.

Or, 1. The division yet the unity of human life,—*as they were eating*, JESUS TOOK BREAD, &c., the lower life and the highest, &c. 2. The *great meanings* which are possible to the realising power of faith and love,—*common bread* became as the *body of the Lord*.

31. Then saith Jesus unto them, All ye shall be offended because of me this night : for it is written, I will smite the shepherd, and the sheep of the flock shall be scattered abroad.
32. But after I am risen again, I will go before you into Galilee.

1. The great events of time developed according to Divine prediction. 2. The loneliness of Jesus Christ in the final scene an incidental proof of His Divine mediation. 3. Christ's Divine power of looking beyond the process to the great result. 4. Though Jesus Christ was deserted by His disciples, yet the disciples were not deserted by Jesus Christ,—"I will go before you into Galilee." Abandonment of Jesus Christ, up to the degree of absolute loneliness, seems to have been necessary to the full realisation of His mission. Who could have been His companion? The loneliness of Jesus Christ is a circumstance not to be lightly passed over; it was a *necessity;* His work was fundamental, relating not to men but to man—to every man, though those men who stood near Him and bore the name of His disciples might not seem to require to be included in the final service. At the point where Jesus Christ's absolute loneliness became a necessity, the great mystery of the atonement begins.

33. Peter answered and said unto him, Though all men shall be offended because of thee, yet will I never be offended.

34. Jesus said unto him, Verily I say unto thee, That this night, before the cock crow, thou shalt deny me thrice.
35. Peter said unto him, Though I should die with thee, yet will I not deny thee. Likewise also said all the disciples.

The announcement shocked the natural feelings of the heart, so little does the heart know itself! The announcement, however, showed, in a most unexpected manner, the minuteness and accuracy of Jesus Christ's knowledge, though it did shock the strongest instincts of the disciples. Jesus Christ "knew what was in man," and yet, knowing it, He loved man even unto death. The incident may be homiletically used as showing:—1. That the most unlikely men may fail in the great crises of life. 2. That the Saviour's resources were equal to the most terrible strain of sorrow. 3. That all vows made in unaided human strength are unreliable. 4. That even now, when pain is threatened, men are in danger of repeating the first apostasy of the disciples. The last reflection might form the basis of a discourse upon *Methods of deserting Jesus Christ:* some of the methods are obvious, some are subtle, all are bad. Special attention should be given to *unintended* desertions; the disciples did not *plan* the apostasy. Men may wound Christ without *intending* it.

A discourse might be prepared upon the three characteristics of the individuals who took a prominent part in the final scene:—1. Mary; or, all-surrendering love. 2. Judas; or, all-grasping avarice. 3. Peter; or, all-promising impulsiveness.

36. Then cometh Jesus with them unto a place called Gethsemane, and saith unto the disciples, Sit ye here, while I go and pray yonder.

Gethsemane (*gath*=a press; *shemen*=oil), the garden of the oil press, or olive-press. "I have trodden the winepress alone." Jesus separates Himself from His disciples, but it is that He may *pray!* Even in Gethsemane He is

Lord and the disciples are servants. Man cannot always pray, even in the presence of his most cherished friends. There are sobs of the breaking heart, which friendship may not hear,—God alone is fit auditor! Jesus says, "*While* I go and pray yonder;" "while" (ἕως) sometimes signifies continuous, indeterminate duration; how *long* the prayer of His great sorrow might continue was not foretold; who can tell when sorrow will utter its last pleading word to God?

37. And he took with him Peter and the two sons of Zebedee, and began to be sorrowful and very heavy.

Peter, James, and John, the same who had beheld the glory of the Transfiguration. Special persons are often elected for special revelations. Why may not this principle of election be in operation now? Has God no further disclosures of truth to make? Is the Infinite exhausted? It often happens, in common as well as in sacred history, that the persons who see most of light are led into the deepest darkness, as if it were only by the violence of extremes that men could be balanced in mind.

Jesus Christ "began to be sorrowful and very heavy:" ἀδημονεῖν=*gravissimè-angi*, to be oppressed with grief; λυπεῖσθαι, to be sad, from λύω, to dissolve, a very expressive word; His vigour was dissolved, His strength became as water, it was as though body and soul would be separated.

38. Then saith he unto them, My soul is exceeding sorrowful, even unto death: tarry ye here, and watch with me.

"Exceeding sorrowful," περίλυπος; περι is used intensively, as in περίεργος, exceedingly diligent, περιχαρης very much delighted. The sorrow was extreme, the very next point was death! It was emphatically a sorrow of the soul; no mere dread of physical suffering, but a pain as it were at the very centre of the moral nature; a sorrow that was occasioned by such a view of sin as the Divine eye alone can take. According to the capacity and culture of the moral nature is the measure of any man's sorrow.

39. And he went a little farther, and fell on his face, and prayed, saying, O my Father, if it be possible, let this cup pass from me : nevertheless not as I will, but as thou wilt.

"Fell on his face," the ordinary posture of the suppliant, when a great favour was asked or great humiliation required.

"'Let this cup pass from me;' perhaps there is an allusion here to several criminals standing in a row, who are all to drink of the same cup; but the judge extending favour to a certain one, the cup *passes by him* to the next."— (ADAM CLARKE.) "Παρελθέτω, *let pass*, as we should say of a threatening cloud, 'It has *gone over*.' But what shall we say of the ποτήριον or ὥρα, of which our Lord here prays that it may *pass by?* Certainly not the mere present feebleness and prostration of the bodily frame, not any mere section of His sufferings; but *the whole*, the betrayal, the trial, the mocking, the scourging, the cross, the grave, and all besides which our thoughts cannot reach. Of this all, His soul, in humble subjection to the higher Will which was absolutely united and harmonious with the Will of the Father, prays that if possible it may pass over. And this prayer *was heard* . . . on account of His pious resignation to His Father's will, or *on the ground* of it, so that it prevailed,—He was strengthened from heaven."— (ALFORD.)

40. And he cometh unto the disciples, and findeth them asleep, and saith unto Peter, What, could ye not watch with me one hour?

A reproof of the presumptuous impulsiveness which had promised to go with Him even unto death. There is peculiar significance in the fact that the inquiry was addressed to Peter, who had promised so much. If a man cannot watch, how can he die ? A very proper accommodation of the words would give us the principle that indifference is the first step towards denial : *when the bodily is in excess of the spiritual influence, the man must apostatise.* In the case, however, of the disciples, Jesus Christ makes every allowance, knowing as He did the strain which had distressed the physical faculties of His disciples; hence He says :—

41. Watch and pray, that ye enter not into temptation : the spirit indeed is willing, but the flesh is weak.

The only method of sustaining all the energies is by holding vigilant and continuous communion with God—watch and pray; the very exercise that would seem to weaken the powers strengthens them. No man ever wastes the energy he spends in prayer. Better to have a willing spirit and a feeble body, than a strong body and an unwilling spirit. We shall not have both in perfection until resurrection has done for the flesh what regeneration has done for the soul.

42. He went away again the second time, and prayed, saying, O my Father, if this cup may not pass away from me, except I drink it, thy will be done.

We may obtain by a second prayer what was not obtained by a first. In the case of Jesus Christ the second prayer was a continuation of the first, and an enlargement of it in the direction of self-surrender. Even in Jesus Christ's humanity there was a point to be conquered. "None of the damned had ever so large a capacity to take in a full sense of the wrath of God as Christ had. The larger any one's capacity is to understand and weigh his troubles fully, the more grievous and heavy is his burden. If a man cast vessels of greater and lesser quantity into the sea, though all will be full, yet the greater the vessel is, the more water it contains. Now Christ had a capacity beyond all mere creatures to take in the wrath of His Father; and what deep and large apprehensions He had of it may be judged by His bloody sweat in the garden, which was the effect of His mere apprehensions of the wrath of God. Christ was a large vessel indeed; as He is capable of more glory, so of more sense and misery than any other person in the world."—(FLAVEL.)

43. And he came and found them asleep again : for their eyes were heavy.
44. And he left them, and went away again, and prayed the third time, saying the same words.
45. Then cometh he to his disciples, and saith unto them, Sleep on now, and take your rest : behold, the hour is at hand, and the Son of man is betrayed into the hands of sinners.
46. Rise, let us be going : behold, he is at hand that doth betray me.

"Here, then, we have two subjects of contemplation distinctly marked out for us. 1. The irreparable Past. 2. The available Future. The words of Christ are not like the words of other men : His sentences do not end with the occasion which called them forth ; every sentence of Christ's is a deep principle of human life, and it is so with these sentences: 'Sleep on now'—that is a principle ; 'Rise up, and let us be going'—that is another principle. The principle contained in 'Sleep on now' is this, that the past is irreparable, and after a certain moment waking will do no good. You may improve the future, the past is gone beyond recovery. As to all that is gone by, so far as the hope of altering it goes, you may sleep on and take your rest; there is no power in earth or heaven that can undo what has once been done."—(ROBERTSON.) "Here seems to be a contradiction : He bids them rest, and yet by-and-bye He says, 'Arise, let us go hence.' Some answer that He speaks by way of upbraiding and not of permitting; but Mark makes it plain, that after this speech, staying awhile, He stirred them up again, saying, 'Let us go hence.' For having bidden them sleep, He says, as after some interim granted, It sufficeth, and then the hour cometh, &c."—(AUGUSTINE.) "Even as water may be pierced with a weapon, and so likewise the fire and the air, yet they cannot be said to be wounded; so the body of Christ might be beaten, hanged up, and crucified, yet these passions in His body did lose the nature of passions, and the virtue of His body, without the sense of pain, received the violence of pain raging against Him. The Lord's body indeed had been sensible of pain, if our body had been of the same nature to go upon the water, and not to make impression with our footsteps, and to go through doors that were shut. But seeing this nature is proper only to the Lord's body, why is the flesh conceived by the Holy Ghost judged by the nature of a common body? He had a body indeed to suffer, but He had no nature to grieve."—(HILARY.)

The paragraph included between the 36th and 46th verses may be thrown into homiletic form as a whole. Let the subject have some such designation as *The Decisive Struggle of Life*; then, as strictly limited to human experience (most carefully distinguishing between that and the sacrificial element that marked our Lord's suffering), we shall find:— 1. That the decisive struggle of life is associated with the intensest agitation of the soul; man cannot give up the past without sorrow. 2. That the decisive struggle of life develops the religious capacities and sensibilities of men; Jesus prayed, prayed alone, prayed repeatedly. 3. That the decisive struggle of life can be triumphantly conducted only as the true character of God is apprehended. In what terms does Christ address God? As the Omnipotent, the Eternal, the Sovereign? He addresses Him as *Father*, and as *My* Father. An inferior conception of God would have meant hesitancy, partial trust, defeat! In the decisive struggle, the struggle which determines a man's future for ever, the heart cannot rest upon an inanimate immensity, a lifeless infinitude; it must touch the life of life, the love of love, the very essence of the highest Being, which is *fatherliness*. 4. That the decisive struggle of life ends well only in proportion to the subordination of the human will to the Divine. " God's pleasure is the wind our actions ought to sail by: man's will is the stream that tides them up and down. It is safer to strive against the stream, than to sail against the wind."—(QUARLES.)

47. And while he yet spake, lo, Judas, one of the twelve, came, and with him a great multitude with swords and staves, from the chief priests and elders of the people.

"*One of the twelve*,"—a good name heading a bad cause. The fact shows the possibility of using Christian advantages for unchristian purposes,—the consummation of treachery, the very extremity of diabolism!

"*And with him a great multitude*,"—the power of one man to do mischief! Could Judas ever have prevailed upon a great multitude to follow him in a *good* work? We see how easy it is to go down, and how in the descent men gather appropriate increments until they become very powerful for mischief. As a supposed Christian, Judas was only one of twelve; but as an opponent of Jesus Christ he was the chief of a great multitude. If moral force is to be measured by numerical majorities, the cause of Christianity was evidently doomed to make an impotent struggle and find its way to an early and dishonoured grave. As the numbers stand in the text, we have twelve men, counting the Saviour Himself, confronted by "a great multitude:" who or what can withstand the stormy anger of an incensed host?

"*With swords and staves*,"—the radical error of superficial controversialists! Can truth be put down by a staff? Can any man cleave a sunbeam with a sword? We may conceive of insane men attempting to pluck the sun from the heavens, or to blow back the billows of the sea, or to derange the order of nature, and, having conceived the monstrous idea, can treat it with the contemptuous pity which it deserves; but there is a gloomier madness than this, and it reached its extremity in the attempt to destroy the kingdom of truth by sword and staff.  The man who speaks truth may be put down, may not only be silenced but killed; yet his doctrine will subdue the obstinacy and compel the homage of the world.  If truth could be endangered, God Himself might be put in jeopardy!

"*From the chief priests and elders of the people:*" the great multitude was not a mere rabble; the authority, the culture, the influence of the time, was with them.  Whatever there was of saintliness in the word *priest*, or of venerableness in the word *elder*, was on the side of the multitude.

The great lesson taught by this verse is that *principles should not be judged by circumstances*.  It would be as reasonable to say that there cannot be a summer because December has been darkened by a snowstorm, as to say that Christianity can never be predominant because all social, political, and ecclesiastical forces were opposed to Jesus Christ.  Confine the attention to the scene depicted in the text; regard the contest as simply between one degree of physical force and another; and who would hesitate to pronounce against the little band headed by Jesus Christ?  So much for the impression produced by outward circumstances!  This will be instantly acknowledged as a historic certainty; yet there is the greatest difficulty in applying its practical lesson to contemporaneous life: some good men are as easily swayed by disastrous circumstances of to-day, as if history had given no illustration of their evanescence.  Let it be remembered that while Judas, with his great multitude with their swords and staves and their authority from the chief priests and elders of the people, are execrated by the civilised world, Jesus Christ is worshipped and loved by unnumbered millions of redeemed men in heaven and on earth. The history of darkness is the history of a declension; the history of light is an expanding and brightening climax, satisfying and gladdening an amazed and thankful world.

48. Now he that betrayed him gave them a sign, saying, Whomsoever I shall kiss, the same is he: hold him fast.

49. And forthwith he came to Jesus, and said, Hail, master; and kissed him.

As in the 47th verse we saw a high name debased to a vicious design, so now we see a token of love perverted into a signal of treachery,—" Whomsoever I shall kiss, that same is he." Is there anything sacred to the bad man? Is there anything in the simplicity of childhood or in the purity of love, in the dignity of honour or in the holiness of religion, which he would scruple to press into his infernal service? When veneration decays, a man loses vitality and responsiveness to all good influences: he has, if the expression be not irreverent, lost so much of God; and by so much as the Divine element has been impaired or abated, all earthly sources of pathos or chivalrous unselfishness, of ennobling inspiration or subduing charity, have been impoverished or exhausted.

There is enough in the picture of Judas kissing Christ, to enkindle at once the anger and the imagination of the world. Did ever such extremes meet? The son of perdition kissing the Son of God! The devil entered into a serpent that he might tempt Eve; but he entered into a *man* that he might betray her Son. The higher the work, the higher the instrument required. Why did not Jesus Christ smite the deceiver, and beat back the multitude as if with a blast of fire? Because He had a work of salvation to carry forward to a sublime and permanent completeness, and to His omniscience suffering and death were but steps in His way to the supremacy of the universe. *Justice* has a line that can neither be extended nor curtailed; *honour* stands upon the same pedestal from age to age; *ethical righteousness* never changes her tests and standards; but *Love* dies to live, suffers that she may increase her power, and for a moment hides her head in the tomb that she may lift it up for ever above the thrones and powers of heaven.

Judas kissing Jesus! After such a kiss, what nail or spear could hurt the body of Christ? The iron pierced the flesh, but the traitorous kiss wounded the soul. To-day the Church has more to fear from hypocrisy than open hostility. Who can protect himself against treachery? If the sign of love may itself be used as a sign of enmity, how great is that enmity!

50. And Jesus said unto him, Friend, wherefore art thou come? Then came they, and laid hands on Jesus, and took him.

Why use the term *friend*? Was it to touch the conscience of the traitor? Was it to throw into bolder relief the perfidy of the deceiver? Was it to give the traitor a final opportunity of breaking down in his purpose?

51. And, behold, one of them which were with Jesus stretched out his hand, and drew his sword, and struck a servant of the high priest's, and smote off his ear.

An illustration of the power of the times over human actions. Viewed from any point short of the very highest altitude, the action of Peter was most natural and most proper. Regarded as a combination of force against force, of the many against the few, this organisation (whilst involving an incidental tribute to the power of Jesus Christ) betrayed the most abject and contemptible cowardice. There is a touch of the heroic about this action of Peter,—animal heroism, which is the lowest form of courage. Peter instinctively proceeded upon the principle that certain people must be fought with their own weapons, that men who trust in staves should feel the weight of their own instruments. The great battles of the world are not between staff and staff, but, as we shall see in another stage of this tragedy, between heart and heart.

52. Then said Jesus unto him, Put up again thy sword into his place : for all they that take the sword shall perish with the sword.

A personal reproof, and an universal doctrine. It is a poor cause that requires the assistance of the sword. To fight even for truth is to put truth in a false position. Neither truth nor error can be deposed by the sword; but while error can use the sword without lowering its own nature, truth cannot touch it without distrusting the omnipotence and love of God. It is laid down as an universal doctrine that they who use the sword shall perish by the sword; they shall conduct a small war to a small issue; they shall never know aught of the inspiration and magnificence of real battle. Steel can beat steel. The supremacy of one sword over another is merely a question of time and training. It will be found as civilisation develops that war will be destroyed by the mere competition of martial genius in the formation of new engines of death. Already the stoutest iron is shattered by tremendous projectiles; and, by the multiplication and improvement of all kinds of arms, war is wearing itself out, and the day cannot be far off when the red and reeking monster shall fall by its own hand as an exploded barbarism, an exhausted device of the devil.

Whatever opinion may be held of war generally, it is distinctly taught that Jesus Christ is never to be laid under obligation to the use of carnal weapons. Even when His cause is in the utmost extremity, they are not to be employed. His kingdom is not of this world. It is a spiritual, ideal, heavenly kingdom, of which the sword is not only a palpable but a demoralising contradiction.

53. Thinkest thou that I cannot now pray to my Father, and he shall presently give me more than twelve legions of angels?
54. But how then shall the scriptures be fulfilled, that thus it must be?

A most pathetic yet noble declaration! It is as though He had said: "My Father is looking on: a word from Me, and all His angels will come as a host of defence; the Lord God of Elisha, who filled the mountain with horses and chariots of fire, and smote the Syrians with blindness, is My Father: His ear is open to My cry, but there is something higher and better than mere personal self-protection." A great purpose was to be realised; a word upon which the Church had lived for many an age was to become a great wonder and a melancholy joy to all nations; the Seed of the woman was to bruise the head of the serpent! Jesus was not the victim of His own weakness; He was not overmatched by numbers; all heaven was within reach of His prayer; the whirlwind and the earthquake, the darkening storm and the shattering thunderbolt, the floods of great waters and the plague of darkness, —each was within the hearing of His voice, so that at His bidding His assailants might have been swallowed up as those that go down to the pit. The Son of man came not to destroy men's lives, but to save them; and even in the hour of His humiliation He was constant to His gracious purpose to redeem and save the world. Captured as an enemy of Cæsar, despised and rejected by the people of Israel, forsaken by the very persons who had sunned themselves in the light of His love, He is still faithful to the all-gracious and all-comprehending purpose of His incarnation: the ancient word must be to the uttermost fulfilled!

The admonition which was addressed to Peter may serve to show the true character of Jesus Christ's sacrifice. He *gave* Himself; the entire service was voluntary; no outward force could have touched the Son of God; He had power to lay down His life, and He had power to take it again; in the exercise of that power lay the whole quality and virtue of the atonement for the sins of the world.

55. In that same hour said Jesus to the multitudes, Are ye come out as against a thief with swords and staves for to take me? I sat daily with you teaching in the temple, and ye laid no hold on me.

56. But all this was done, that the scriptures of the prophets might be fulfilled. Then all the disciples forsook him, and fled.

Jesus Christ treated as a "thief," and forsaken by His chosen friends,—this was the hour and the power of darkness! Was He then alone? Yes; yet not alone, for the Father was with Him! A saddening spectacle, yet a necessary element in the process of redemption, was this being left alone with the Father. The work must lie between the Father and the forsaken Man, the *one* Man: in His sacrifice He goes alone; in His victory He takes with Him a multitude not to be numbered. There is a loneliness which means preparation for sovereignty: there is also a loneliness which precedes insanity and suicide. Jesus was alone; Judas, too, was alone at a later stage in the same proceedings: what was the difference? The Father was with the one; the other had made himself an orphan. Jesus died; Judas died: what was the difference? Jesus offered Himself as the sacrifice for sins: Judas was the victim of his own transgression; and as we look upon him—a mangled and revolting spectacle—we see how true it is that they who use the sword shall perish by the sword.

57. And they that had laid hold on Jesus led him away to Caiaphas the high priest, where the scribes and the elders were assembled.

58. But Peter followed him afar off unto the high priest's palace, and went in, and sat with the servants, to see the end.

59. Now the chief priests, and elders, and all the council, sought false witness against Jesus, to put him to death ;

60. But found none : yea, though many false witnesses came, yet found they none. At the last came two false witnesses,

61. And said, This fellow said, I am able to destroy the temple of God, and to build it in three days.

62. And the high priest arose, and said unto him, Answerest thou nothing? what is it which these witness against thee?

63. But Jesus held his peace. And the high priest answered and said unto him, I adjure thee by the living God, that thou tell us whether thou be the Christ, the Son of God.

64. Jesus saith unto him, Thou hast said : nevertheless I say unto you, Hereafter shall ye see the Son of man sitting on the right hand of power, and coming in the clouds of heaven.

65. Then the high priest rent his clothes, saying, He hath spoken blasphemy ; what further need have we of witnesses? behold, now ye have heard his blasphemy.

66. What think ye? They answered and said, He is guilty of death.

67. Then did they spit in his face, and buffeted him ; and others smote him with the palms of their hands,

68. Saying, Prophesy unto us, thou Christ, Who is he that smote thee?

69. Now Peter sat without in the palace : and a damsel came unto him, saying, Thou also wast with Jesus of Galilee.

70. But he denied before them all, saying, I know not what thou sayest.

71. And when he was gone out into the porch, another maid saw him, and said unto them that were there, This fellow was also with Jesus of Nazareth.

72. And again he denied with an oath, I do not know the man.

73. And after a while came unto him they that stood by, and said to Peter, Surely thou also art one of them ; for thy speech bewrayeth thee.

74. Then began he to curse and to swear, saying, I know not the man. And immediately the cock crew.

75. And Peter remembered the word of Jesus, which said unto him, Before the cock crow, thou shalt deny me thrice. And he went out, and wept bitterly.

Is it no trial even now to be identified as a disciple of Jesus Christ? There are easily conceivable circumstances under which any man might feel honoured in having his name associated with Jesus Christ, but such circumstances do not test the sincerity of faith. We must put ourselves in Peter's position, before presuming to reproach him. The Master was in the hands of His enemies; all the brightness of Peter's dream had faded away; he was alone, surrounded by taunting observers, charged with being the ally of a blasphemer; the day was dark; the storm was breaking upon the lonely man with great fury; the star in whose light he had trusted had been extinguished,—how then could he be strong enough to withstand so great a pressure? Is there not a point in every man's life when his strength is exhausted,—when his love lies, so to speak, bleeding on the wreck of his will? There is, too, a point in human life when a man cannot bear one word from without, so pressed is he by secret and most painful emotion; we have seen a child with a heart so full, that even an enquiring look from the most friendly eye would cause the tears to overflow. Under such circumstances parents have preserved silence, and thus the fortitude of the child has remained unbroken. We are not entitled to say that at heart Peter was an apostate; in his innermost spirit there might have been a loving and reverent trust; but the man was in heavy trouble, the day had gone against him: there was a great wonder rousing and tempting his spirit,—and at that moment there was but a taunting word required to urge him to extremity. The subtlety of the tempter is seen in the adaptation of suggestion to circumstances. It is when a man is "an hungered" that the devil tempts him to make bread; when he is lonely and powerless, that he offers terms of worldly luxury and dominion. Peter was in that mental condition in which a man's future may be decided by a word; his power of self-control is exhausted; every faculty is strained to the utmost, and one cruel touch alone is needed to produce reaction sudden and complete,—often, indeed, fatal.

This reaction will, of course, be in proportion to the

capacity and quality of the sufferer. The self-possessed and carefully-trained nature will, even in extremity, seek to shelter itself from open scandal; but the sanguine and fervid nature will express itself with all eruptiveness and desperation. All we have ever known of Peter is realised in this scene; his boldness in being near the palace; his cowardice in falling before the first charge; the vehemence of his language, the bitterness of his tears,—all are characteristic. The other disciples might have denied Jesus Christ as utterly, yet not one of them would have displayed the same violence,—they might have subsided as a river, but he heaved and trembled like a volcano.

The practical point to be noted is that every disciple, at some time or under some circumstances, will have to endure *the trial of being identified as a follower of Jesus Christ;* to each will be said: " Thou also wast with Jesus of Galilee." The strength of the trial depends mainly upon the circumstances under which it is sustained. Take illustrative instances. *Young man*, among worldly campanions; *poor man*, seeking aid from the openly wicked; *rich man*, surrounded by the thoughtless and gay.

In connection with the fall of Peter there are four circumstances specially monitory:—

I. *He was the oldest of the disciples.* We are accustomed to regard age as a guarantee of character, and our judgment is founded upon a sound principle. The man who has sustained the trials of a life-time without dishonouring the Christian name, is entitled to the confidence and love of the whole Church. He is an "epistle of commendation." He is a monument of Divine mercy. Travel-worn, and even travel-stained, with staff and sandals which have never been laid aside, he is deserving of all honour for the Lord's sake. It is no easy thing to live a life—a long, varied, tempted life. Though Peter's life was not long as measured by time, yet he was the first, the oldest of the disciples, and he fell! " Let him that thinketh," &c.

II. *He uttered the most emphatic declarations of constancy.* " Though all men forsake thee," &c., " I am ready to go with thee to prison," &c. There is a wide difference between strong conviction and strong language, they are perfectly compatible, yet where the language is always extreme it is probable that great inconsistencies will mar the life. In the deepest sense actions should speak louder than words, otherwise there will almost of necessity come a great halt in the Christian experience.

There is, however, one danger to be avoided; while there is a possibility of saying too much, there is also a temptation to say too little. Men may say, " Because Peter made a great profession and fell, therefore it is better not to make any profession at all."

III. *He was surprised into this denial of his Master.* We are to be prepared not only for formal and elaborate defence, but for sudden assault. " *Watch.*" " Pray without ceasing."

IV. *He was deeply penitential,*—" he went out and wept bitterly." There is hope of amendment where there is this sorrow for sin. Penitence is one of the first conditions of new life. What does penitence imply?—1. Consciousness of guilt; 2. Consciousness of responsibility; 3. Self-reproach and self-renunciation.

Where the whole story is intensely practical, it is difficult to assign superiority of claim to any portion. We may, however, look:—1. At the rapidity of descent in Peter's case, —he *denied,* he denied with *an oath,* then began he to *curse and to swear.* 2. We may look to the sudden quickenings of memory which mark the spiritual life,—" then remembered he the word of Jesus." By one flash the whole life is lighted up.

Though man fails, the truth proceeds to assert its claims

and establish its ground. The servant yields, but the Son is "obedient unto death." Peter is an example of what the strongest man would be apart from the Master. "Without me ye can do nothing."

## CHAPTER XXVII.

1. When the morning was come, all the chief priests and elders of the people took counsel against Jesus to put him to death :
2. And when they had bound him, they led him away, and delivered him to Pontius Pilate the governor.

TRAPP says: "They had broken their sleep the night before, and yet were up and at it early the next morning, so soon as the day peeped. So sedulous are the devil's servants. Esau began to wrestle with Jacob even in the very womb, that no time might be lost." The point to be noted carefully is, that the *religion* of the day was the destroyer of Christ. They were not pagans but Jews who bound the Lord's anointed with cords, and drove the iron through His flesh. Did ever "morning" lighten on such a scene? They carried everything their own way. Not a sign of resistance was offered by Jesus Christ. Is there no meaning in this continued and immoveable placidity? If the conception of it as a feature in fabled history be not the result of the most cunning knavery, the placidity must be traced to causes no less than Divine. It was foretold in prophecy; it was consistent with the whole tenor of Jesus Christ's spirit; and was in beautiful consistency with the object which He proposed to accomplish. The Jews resorted to the lowest expedient,—their answer to Jesus Christ's challenge was *death!* Can death permanently interrupt the progress of truth? History has told no fact more repeatedly than that truth cannot be destroyed; the Speaker may be killed, but the speech is immortal. These two verses, humanly viewed, present a dark aspect of Christianity,—but is not the *night* God's as well as the *day?* 1. Judge nothing in *parts;* 2. Human *extremities* are Divine opportunities; 3. The *very elect* may appear to be given over to the devouring enemy.

3. Then Judas, which had betrayed him, when he saw that he was condemned, repented himself, and brought again the thirty pieces of silver to the chief priests and elders,
4. Saying, I have sinned in that I have betrayed the innocent blood. And they said, What is that to us? see thou to that.
5. And he cast down the pieces of silver in the temple, and departed, and went and hanged himself.

1. Look at *the reaction of the moral nature.* Conscience resumes its function, and not a tittle of trespass is forgotten. 2. In this reaction see an illustration of *the retributive force of outraged right.* God does not destroy sinners, they destroy themselves,—every sinner is on the road to self-destruction. Emphatically, "the wages of sin is *death.*" When the Holy Ghost is quenched, man's existence is intolerable. This confession of Judas is valuable:—1. As a testimony to the life which Jesus Christ lived amongst his disciples; 2. As illustrative of the relative strength of conscience and selfishness; and, 3. As showing the uselessness of money as a compensation for moral loss. But for Christ's expression (John xvii. 12) concerning Judas, it might have been inferred that this repentance (though the word is simply μεταμεληθείς, hardly implying more than temporary sorrow) was all that was possible under the circumstances. Even in the expression referred to, as Dr. ADAM CLARKE points out, it is acknowledged that Judas was "given" to Christ. The theory that Judas took his part merely to hasten the development of Christ's kingly purposes is untenable in view of the facts:—1. That Judas was called a thief and a devil before the betrayal; and, 2. That his work was

distinctly ascribed by Christ Himself to the action of the devil upon the mind. The case of Judas shows these awful possibilities:—1. Of being *nominally* a disciple; 2. Of being an *unworthy officer* in Christ's kingdom; and, 3. Of repenting *too late.*

6. And the chief priests took the silver pieces, and said, It is not lawful for to put them into the treasury, because it is the price of blood.
7. And they took counsel, and bought with them the potter's field, to bury strangers in.
8. Wherefore that field was called, The field of blood, unto this day.
9. Then was fulfilled that which was spoken by Jeremy the prophet, saying, And they took the thirty pieces of silver, the price of him that was valued, whom they of the children of Israel did value;
10. And gave them for the potter's field, as the Lord appointed me.

The language of the chief priests shows how well they knew the meaning of their work. 1. "It is the price of blood,"—but of what is that blood itself the price? "Ye are bought with a price." "Ye are not redeemed with corruptible things," &c. 2. They bought a *burial place* with the money,—but what a scene of *resurrection* was about to be witnessed? All that men can do for their dead is to find them a burial place,—but Jesus Christ can recover and immortalise their life. 3. The ancient prophecy was fulfilled,—but how much brighter a prophecy opened its vision! On the human side of this transaction there is nothing but *death,*—look at the expressions, "hanged himself," "price of blood," "to bury strangers in," "the field of blood." On the Divine side there is redemption, resurrection, and immortality.

TRAPP's observations on the 8th verse are striking: "'The field of blood,' not the burial place for strangers, as they would have had it called (thinking thereby to have gotten themselves an eternal commendation, for their love and liberality to strangers), but 'the field of blood' (so the vulgar would needs call it, much against their masters' minds), for a lasting monument of their detestable villany, which they thought to have carried so cleverly that the world would have been none the wiser; and therefore they would not kill Christ themselves, as they did Stephen; but to decline the envy, delivered Him up to Pilate to be put to death. It is hard if hypocrites be not, by one means or another, detected; how else would their names rot?"

11. And Jesus stood before the governor : and the governor asked him, saying, Art thou the King of the Jews? And Jesus said unto him, Thou sayest.

12. And when he was accused of the chief priests and elders, he answered nothing.

13. Then said Pilate unto him, Hearest thou not how many things they witness against thee?

14. And he answered him to never a word; insomuch that the governor marvelled greatly.

There was no doubt much in the conduct of Jesus Christ to perplex observers, and it is of the highest consequence that all the perplexing circumstances should be referred to some general principle rather than connected with variations of mere temper. That Jesus Christ should have given answers so curt, or been silent under circumstances which even challenged self-vindication, is most singular, if His life and purpose be judged by ordinary rules. Most men would have hailed with gladness the opportunity of full explanations which Pilate afforded; when Peter and John were arraigned before the council they boldly defended the action which had been made matter of accusation; and when Paul was put upon his defence, he said, "I think myself happy, king Agrippa;" yet when Jesus Christ was called upon to speak for Himself He spoke the fewest possible words, or preserved the most embarrassing silence. Does this not hint the possibility of something being about to transpire which no speech could explain and no defence avert? Jesus Christ's part in these final proceedings clearly shows that the case was far removed from common ground, and suggests that if the man be all that he claims, the explanation will come afterwards. Whether that explanation did come must be answered by those who believe not only in the crucifixion but in the resurrection.

The 13th verse is remarkable: "Hearest thou not how many things they witness against thee?" Had it been a merely personal matter, Jesus Christ was bound, for the sake of the men whom He had drawn around Him, to explain and defend His course; His silence must be held to signify that there were events to be developed which alone could throw light upon present difficulty, and that knowing this, no good could come of intermediate and superficial references. We all know that cases arise in common experience in which explanation must be a question of time. Explanation cannot always be instantaneous and complete; the deeper the mystery the greater the time required for its solution. Regarded from this point of view, the conduct of Christ in the closing scene suggests:—1. That personal interests may require occasional subordination to public purposes; 2. That temporary silence is not to be ascribed to inability or self-accusation; 3. That after such silence there may come a command to preach the Gospel to every creature; 4. That complete judgments cannot be formed upon incomplete evidence.

15. Now at that feast the governor was wont to release unto the people a prisoner, whom they would.

16. And they had then a notable prisoner, called Barabbas.

17. Therefore when they were gathered together, Pilate said unto them, Whom will ye that I release unto you? Barabbas, or Jesus which is called Christ?

18. For he knew that for envy they had delivered him.

19. When he was set down on the judgment seat, his wife sent unto him, saying, Have thou nothing to do with that just man: for I have suffered many things this day in a dream because of him.

20. But the chief priests and elders persuaded the multitude that they should ask Barabbas, and destroy Jesus.

The preference of Barabbas to Jesus Christ shows:—1. That the care of the Jews was not to put down mere *crime*, for Barabbas was a robber; 2. That religion may degenerate into irreligion; 3. That envy is of the nature of murder.

The message which Pilate's wife sent shows:—1. The connection between the mind and the unseen state; 2. God's independence of human instrumentality in revealing the character of His Son; 3. God's power of troubling the conscience in defence of Jesus Christ; 4. God's method of employing one human being to warn another. Why not have troubled Pilate's own mind? Men are stimulated and strengthened by outside help; human life should be a mutual ministry. Have we not felt that if another voice than our own would but speak to us in certain crises of life, we should be encouraged to give effect to good impulses and convictions?

The influence of the chief priests and elders upon the multitude shows:—1. How power may be abused; 2. How leading men may make a convenience of the multitude; 3. That an action is not necessarily right simply because it is supported by the leading men of the day; 4. That men judge superficially who imagine that by destroying a teacher they have also destroyed his doctrine.

21. The governor answered and said unto them, Whether of the twain will ye that I release unto you? They said, Barabbas.
22. Pilate saith unto them, What shall I do then with Jesus which is called Christ? They all say unto him, Let him be crucified.
23. And the governor said, Why, what evil hath he done? But they cried out the more, saying, Let him be crucified.
24. When Pilate saw that he could prevail nothing, but that rather a tumult was made, he took water, and washed his hands before the multitude, saying, I am innocent of the blood of this just person: see ye to it.

These verses may be taken as showing the relation of Pilate to the whole transaction:—1. *The mind of Pilate was favourably disposed towards Jesus.* This was, had they known it, a severe reflection upon the Jews. Jesus was better received by strangers than by "his own." (John i. 11.) 2. *Pilate was embarrassed by the legal question on which the Jews laid so much stress.* They said that if Pilate let Jesus go he was not Cæsar's friend; they said further, "We have a law, and by that law he ought to die." 3. *Pilate openly expressed his conviction of the justness of Jesus Christ,*—"I am innocent of the blood of this just person." This was an independent and impartial testimony, showing the moral worthlessness of the charges which had been urged against Jesus Christ, as they were viewed by a man who was free of traditional prejudice. It does not appear just to condemn, as many have done, the spirit and conduct of Pilate. Speaking of Jesus Christ not having done any evil, TRAPP says: "If He hath done no evil, wherefore doth not Pilate pronounce Him innocent, *contra gentes,* and quit Him by proclamation? which, because he did not, but the contrary, was he not therefore by a just judgment of God upon him, kicked off the bench by the Emperor Tiberius?" The note of CHRYSOSTOM is in the same vein : "If he was just why didst thou not set him free, as the tribune did save Paul afterwards? Wherefore Pilate with the priests and people falleth into the same sin. The wicked priests instigate the people, the people have not the power to deny the priests, and the most weak and cowardly-minded judge had not the power to deny the people." The opinion of JEROME would seem not only more sensible but more accurate : "The judge who is compelled to give sentence against the Lord doth not condemn Him being offered, but reproveth those that bring Him, pronouncing Him to be just who was crucified. 'See ye unto it.' I am a minister of the law, it is your voice that sheddeth blood. In that he scourged Him before the crucifying, it is to be understood that Pilate served the Roman laws, whereby it was enacted that every man who was to be crucified should first be scourged."

25. Then answered all the people, and said, His blood be on us, and on our children.

This is the cry of murderers, yet by a change of spirit it may be made the prayer of a penitent world! The text may be used to show that in one of two senses the blood of Jesus Christ must be upon all people and their children; either—1. In the sense of destruction,—for every impenitent sinner crucifies the Son of God; or, 2. In the sense of salvation,—for without the shedding of blood there is no remission, and the blood of Jesus Christ cleanseth from all sin. No man who has heard the Gospel can escape relation to Jesus Christ's blood.

26. Then released he Barabbas unto them : and when he had scourged Jesus, he delivered him to be crucified.

27. Then the soldiers of the governor took Jesus into the common hall, and gathered unto him the whole band of soldiers.

28. And they stripped him, and put on him a scarlet robe.

29. And when they had platted a crown of thorns, they put it upon his head, and a reed in his right hand : and they bowed the knee before him, and mocked him, saying, Hail, king of the Jews!

30. And they spit upon him, and took the reed, and smote him on the head.

31. And after that they had mocked him, they took the robe off from him, and put his own raiment on him, and led him away to crucify him.

32. And as they came out, they found a man of Cyrene, Simon by name : him they compelled to bear his cross.

33. And when they were come unto a place called Golgotha, that is to say, a place of a skull,

34. They gave him vinegar to drink mingled with gall : and when he had tasted thereof, he would not drink.

35. And they crucified him, and parted his garments, casting lots : that it might be fulfilled which was spoken by the prophet, They parted my garments among them, and upon my vesture did they cast lots.

36. And sitting down they watched him there :

37. And set up over his head his accusation written, THIS IS JESUS THE KING OF THE JEWS.

38. Then were there two thieves crucified with him, one on the right hand, and another on the left.

39. And they that passed by reviled him, wagging their heads,

40. And saying, Thou that destroyest the temple, and buildest it in three days, save thyself. If thou be the Son of God, come down from the cross.

41. Likewise also the chief priests mocking him, with the scribes and elders, said,

42. He saved others; himself he cannot save. If he be the King of Israel, let him now come down from the cross, and we will believe him.

43. He trusted in God; let him deliver him now, if he will have him: for he said, I am the Son of God.

44. The thieves also, which were crucified with him, cast the same in his teeth.

45. Now from the sixth hour there was darkness over all the land unto the ninth hour.

46. And about the ninth hour Jesus cried with a loud voice, saying, Eli, Eli, lama sabachthani? that is to say, My God, my God, why hast thou forsaken me?

47. Some of them that stood there, when they heard that, said, This man calleth for Elias.

48. And straightway one of them ran, and took a spunge, and filled it with vinegar, and put it on a reed, and gave him to drink.

49. The rest said, Let be, let us see whether Elias will come to save him.

50. Jesus, when he had cried again with a loud voice, yielded up the ghost.

51. And, behold, the veil of the temple was rent in twain from the top to the bottom; and the earth did quake, and the rocks rent;

52. And the graves were opened; and many bodies of the saints which slept arose,

53. And came out of the graves after his resurrection, and went into the holy city, and appeared unto many.

The non-resistance of Jesus Christ, considering all that has been seen of His power over men and nature, is quite inexplicable, except on the principle that some object was to be wrought out which required the utter subordination of the individual will. Would He, who had been so careful over other people's lives, be wantonly careless of His own? Judged upon common principles Jesus Christ's conduct was not merely imprudent, it was immoral; so to speak, He was an accomplice in the work of His own destruction; without a struggle, without even a protest, He yielded Himself to the will of His tormentors. Did He prefer death to such a humble and exhausting life as He had been living? Did He choose the less of the two evils ? If so, He was no Saviour; He yielded because the pressure was too much for Him, —and therein He proved Himself to be but a common man.

If we accept this theory it must be at the expense of the testimony of the whole life. Jesus Christ never held human life lightly; He was never a silent party to any deed of mischief or oppression; where force was forbidden, He at least availed Himself of the right of protest; hence the whole bearing of His course must be consulted as the best interpretation of the final tragedy. The difficulty has been explained in a manner which not merely saves, but exalts and glorifies the consistency of the whole life:—" He was led as a lamb to the slaughter, and as a sheep before her shearers is dumb so he opened not his mouth." The case was not one for argument. Words were of no use. What was begun in Eden must be finished on Calvary,—human nature must exhaust its utmost capacity of wickedness. Look, with some minuteness, into the account:—*They stripped him, and put on him a scarlet robe;* there was nothing royal in the appearance of His own raiment. This is an incidental illustration of the simplicity of Jesus Christ's life. There was nothing artificial in His manner. It might have been inferred from this that He was not a rival of the earthly ruler; His was a Kingdom of the spirit; but His tormentors knew of no kingdom that could exist without scarlet, and crown, and sceptre. This act was a development of the idea of artificial kingdoms. Does the scarlet make the king? We answer *no;* yet do not many men think they have sufficiently recognised Jesus Christ's royalty when they have given Him a scarlet robe,—given Him, that is, a nominal and official position ? To say that Jesus Christ is King, and yet never to bow the heart under His sceptre, is to give Him the scarlet robe, and to repeat, with delusive modification, the cruelty of "barbarous and brutish men, skilful to destroy." (Ezek. xxi. 31.)

*And when they had platted a crown of thorns, they put it upon his head, and a reed in his right hand, and they bowed the knee before him, and mocked him, saying, Hail, King of the Jews!* Did not the thorns come of the curse? "Cursed is the ground for thy sake. . . . . . thorns shall it bring forth." Did He not, in the fullest sense, bear the curse for us? They put a reed in His right hand,—do not all insincere professors do the same? Partial sovereignty, often merely nominal sovereignty, is given to Jesus Christ even by those who avow His religion. The soldiers knelt before their victim in an attitude of mock worship; this, even more than crucifixion, is the uttermost depth of depravity; crucifixion may be a legal act, but mockery is the refinement of cruelty.

*And they spit upon him, and took the reed, and smote him on the head.* Truly, it was the hour and power of darkness. The *spiritual* temptation having failed, the lower instrument of physical torture is employed without mercy. The soul was untouched,—why fear them that kill the body, and after that have no more that they can do? They smote Him on the head—" or into the head, εἰς κεφαλήν, drove the thorns into His head with bats and blows."—(TRAPP.)

*They compelled Simon of Cyrene to bear his cross.* The writer just quoted well says: "Not so much to ease Christ who fainted under the burden, as to hasten the execution and to keep him alive till He came to it." Truly the tender mercies of the wicked are cruel! "They gave Him vinegar— cold comfort to a dying man; but they did it in derision, *q.d.*, Thou art a King, and must have generous wines. Here's for Thee, therefore."

The place where this was done was called "Golgotha, that is to say, a place of a skull." The ancients had strange notions about this place. ORIGEN says: "There came unto me a certain tradition, that the body of *Adam*, the first man, was buried there, where Christ was crucified, that as in Adam all die, so in Christ all should be made alive, and in that place which is said to be the place of an head, the head of all mankind, Adam, might find the resurrection." JEROME'S remark is probably more reliable: " I have heard some interpreting this, and saying, that Adam was buried here, and by reason that his skull lay in this place it was thus called; a favourable interpretation, and pleasing to popular ears, but untrue. For out of the city without the gate, persons condemned were beheaded, and from this, doubtless, the place had the name; and Christ was here crucified, that where the place of execution for evil deeds had been, there should be the beginning of martyrdom; in Him cometh deliverance to those who have done evil."

*They set up over his head his accusation written, This is Jesus the King of the Jews.* The victory of derision is a transient triumph. Some shouts of victory come too soon. The truth may be told unintentionally; it *was* the King of the Jews,— the King of all men.

*Likewise also the chief priests mocked him with the scribes and elders.* To mock the weak is no sign of true strength. Only cowards are capable of mockery. Had those men been in pursuit of the ends of justice they would have been satisfied with the crucifixion as such; they could not have stooped to the infliction of needless pain. This collateral barbarism shows at once the wickedness of their spirit and the intensity of their fear.

*He saved others, himself he cannot save.* No saviour ever sought to save himself. When any man seeks to save himself he proves by that very act that he has not the spirit of redemption. Thus does the world, judging by vulgar standards, mistake the very highest strength for the most abject weakness.

These notes may serve to show the kind of opposition which Jesus Christ had to encounter. Looking at the whole section we find the following practical points:—

I. ALL THIS SUFFERING WAS ENDURED FOR OTHERS.

II. IT IS POSSIBLE TO ABHOR THE CRUELTY AND YET TO BE UNDER THE DOMINION OF THE SPIRIT WHICH INFLICTED IT.

III. A GREAT LIFE EXTORTS UNINTENTIONAL COMMENDATION FROM THE VERY MEN WHO SEEK TO DESTROY IT,— *He saved others!*

IV. THE SOPHISM WHICH ARGUES THAT PHYSICAL DELIVERANCE IS THE TEST OF DIVINE FAVOUR,—" He trusted in God, let him deliver him now," &c.

V. AN ILLUSTRATION OF THE SYMPATHETIC UNION OF THE WHOLE CREATION,—earthquake, rocks, graves, &c. "Creation is dependent on Christ's consciousness."—(LANGE.) Application: Men *must* be crucified (sin will torment all sinners); they may be crucified with *Christ,* and so escape the bitterness of death. The cross cannot be *escaped;* men must be crucified either with the thieves or with Jesus Christ.

54. Now when the centurion, and they that were with him, watching Jesus, saw the earthquake, and those things that were done, they feared greatly, saying, Truly this was the Son of God.

55. And many women were there beholding afar off, which followed Jesus from Galilee, ministering unto him:

56. Among which was Mary Magdalene, and Mary the mother of James and Joses, and the mother of Zebedee's children.

57. When the even was come, there came a rich man of Arimathæa, named Joseph, who also himself was Jesus' disciple:

58. He went to Pilate, and begged the body of Jesus. Then Pilate commanded the body to be delivered.

59. And when Joseph had taken the body, he wrapped it in a clean linen cloth,

60. And laid it in his own new tomb, which he had hewn out in the rock: and he rolled a great stone to the door of the sepulchre, and departed.

61. And there was Mary Magdalene, and the other Mary, sitting over against the sepulchre.

62. Now the next day, that followed the day of the preparation, the chief priests and Pharisees came together unto Pilate,

63. Saying, Sir, we remember that that deceiver said, while he was yet alive, After three days I will rise again.

64. Command therefore that the sepulchre be made sure until the third day, lest his disciples come by night, and steal him away, and say unto the people, He is risen from the dead : so the last error shall be worse than the first.

65. Pilate said unto them, Ye have a watch : go your way, make it as sure as ye can.

66. So they went, and made the sepulchre sure, sealing the stone, and setting a watch.

## CHAPTER XXVIII.

1. In the end of the sabbath, as it began to dawn toward the first day of the week, came Mary Magdalene and the other Mary to see the sepulchre.

2. And, behold, there was a great earthquake: for the angel of the Lord descended from heaven, and came and rolled back the stone from the door, and sat upon it.

3. His countenance was like lightning, and his raiment white as snow :

4. And for fear of him the keepers did shake, and became as dead men.

This section vividly represents:—1. THE CROSS AS THE OBJECT OF UNIVERSAL ATTENTION. "The centurion and they that were with him;" "many women were there;" "all his acquaintance, and the women that followed him from Galilee" (Luke xxiii. 49); and from the previous verses we learn that multitudes of approving observers were present at the crucifixion. This circumstance suggests an enquiry into the relation of the Cross to all classes of men: —1. *To the impenitent sinner it represents the most desperate attempt to destroy a spiritual tormentor.* Impenitence or rebellion cannot go farther: the resources of depravity are exhausted! "*There,*" says wickedness, "is my last stroke; if *that* fail, I cannot do more." 2. *To the speculative student it represents a great mystery in Divine government.* Why should this just and humane Teacher be delivered over to the will of an implacable enemy? Is this fate worthy of the Man who has said so many deep and pathetic things about God? 3. *To a sorrowing heart it represesents the sublimest method of suffering.* Not one evil word; no attempt at vengeance; a committal of the spirit into the hands of the Father. 4. *To an accusing conscience a solution of the problem of pardon.* How can God be just, and the justifier of the ungodly?

This section vividly represents:—1. THE TOMB AS THE CENTRE OF THE MOST CONFLICTING INTEREST. We find at the tomb, Joseph of Arimathæa, Mary Magdalene, and the other Mary; the chief priests and Pharisees; and the angel of the Lord whose "countenance was like lightning, and his raiment white as snow." Looking at all the interest which was manifested in Christ's tomb we draw several lessons:—

I. *The possibility of doing more for the dead body than for the living man.* It is not necessary to undervalue the reverence which Joseph displayed, in order to feel the force of this doctrine. The doctrine is illustrated every day: building the sepulchres of the prophets; allowing a man to live in poverty, and then building him a splendid monument, &c. A course of neglect cannot be repaired by a course of expensive and pompous mourning.

II. *The danger of tarrying at the tomb instead of following the example.* The women were sitting over against the sepulchre; the feeling was proper, still it points towards a danger. The tombs of the mighty dead should be as starting points for the earnest living. Plant a flower upon the borrowed grave, but never forget to follow the example of the holy life.

III. *The impotence of evil-minded men in reference to the resurrection.* They "made the sepulchre sure, sealing the stone, and setting a watch." We have seen the *power* of those men, now see their *weakness*. God is often marking very distinctly *the limitations of depravity*.

IV. *The magnificent announcement which will eventually be made at every Christian's grave*—" He is not here,—he is RISEN."

> 5. And the angel answered and said unto the women, Fear not ye: for I know that ye seek Jesus, which was crucified.
> 6. He is not here: for he is risen, as he said. Come, see the place where the Lord lay.
> 7. And go quickly, and tell his disciples that he is risen from the dead; and, behold, he goeth before you into Galilee; there shall ye see him: Lo, I have told you.
> 8. And they departed quickly from the sepulchre with fear and great joy; and did run to bring his disciples word.

The angels had no message of comfort to " the keepers," but to " the women " they said, " Fear not ye; " looking to the dismayed men on the one hand, and to the reassured women on the other, we may see the different results of moral relations. There is:—1. *Fear;* this fear will come upon the bad man (*a*) *suddenly;* (*b*) *irresistibly;* (*c*) from *unexpected sources;* (*d*) *publicly*, to his open shame and confusion. There is:—2. *Faith;* there are three noticeable things about the Christian's faith in Jesus Christ: (*a*) it points towards a *higher condition* of life; its look is not *downward*, but *upward;* (*b*) it is in direct opposition to all malevolence, whether satanic or human,—its tone is *benevolent;* (*c*) its development and realisation are assisted by the highest celestial powers, —" are they not all ministering spirits ? "

The women who carried the intelligence of the resurrection to the disciples were really the first preachers of the Gospel. The resurrection is the fundamental, the allnecessary fact of the Christian system,—" if Christ be not risen from the dead then is our preaching vain, and your faith is also vain."

Looking at the account of the resurrection, generally, we find the following points:—

I. It disproved the prognostications of Jesus Christ's enemies.

II. It gave great reality to His offers of *life*.

III. It illustrated His sovereignty over the laws of nature.

IV. It revealed the depth of His interest in human salvation.

Collecting into one view the trial, death, and resurrection of Christ, they present a picture of the course and issue of Christian truth:—

I. *It has been promoted to a fictitious royalty.* Jesus Christ was clothed in a purple robe; his tormentors put a sceptre in His hand, and bowed the knee, saying, Hail, King of the Jews. So with the truth; it is possible to clothe it with the purple robe of *mere profession*; to put in its hand the sceptre of *financial support,* and to render to it a *hypocritical homage.*

II. *It has been abandoned when allegiance became perilous.* "All the disciples forsook him and fled,"—so with truth in the trying hour.

III. *Every interruptive expedient has been adopted.* Stone; guard; seal. The adoption of such expedients shews (*a*) *man's latent belief in the great truths of Christianity;* and (*b*) *man's awful dread of awakening a slumbering conscience.* He rolls a great stone, sets a watch, &c.

IV. *Homage has been developed where least expected.* Nicodemus; Joseph. So in ancient times, the seven thousand of whom Elijah had not heard.

9. And as they went to tell his disciples, behold, Jesus met them, saying, All hail. And they came and held him by the feet, and worshipped him.

10. Then said Jesus unto them, Be not afraid: go tell my brethren that they go into Galilee, and there shall they see me.

1. The resurrection puts an end to all *fear*,—"be not afraid." 2. The resurrection is the completion of the Gospel,—"go tell," &c. 3. The resurrection renews and brightens

human relationships,—" go tell my *brethren*." (Rom. viii. 29; Ps. xxii. 22; Heb. ii. 11.)

11. Now when they were going, behold, some of the watch came into the city, and shewed unto the chief priests all the things that were done.
12. And when they were assembled with the elders, and had taken counsel, they gave large money unto the soldiers,
13. Saying, Say ye, His disciples came by night, and stole him away while we slept.
14. And if this come to the governor's ears, we will persuade him, and secure you.
15. So they took the money, and did as they were taught: and this saying is commonly reported among the Jews until this day.

1. A picture of the ultimate confusion of the enemies of truth; 2. The corrupt spirit of defeated bigotry; 3. The miserable subterfuges of uncandid opposition; 4, The degrading influence of bad associations,—" so they took the money and did as they were taught."

16. Then the eleven disciples went away into Galilee, into a mountain where Jesus had appointed them.
17. And when they saw him, they worshipped him: but some doubted.
18. And Jesus came and spake unto them, saying, All power is given unto me in heaven and in earth.
19. Go ye therefore, and teach all nations, baptizing them in the name of the Father, and of the Son, and of the Holy Ghost:
20. Teaching them to observe all things whatsoever I have commanded you: and, lo, I am with you alway, even unto the end of the world. Amen.

This section may be regarded as shewing *the spirit* in which Jesus Christ rose from the dead. 1. It might have been a spirit of *retribution;* 2. It might have been a spirit of *contemptuous defiance;* 3. Instead of this it was *a spirit of profound and universal benevolence,*—" go ye therefore and teach all nations."

Looking at the evangelical commission, simply as such, we are here taught :—1. That it is founded upon the *personal power* of Jesus Christ,—" all power is given unto me in heaven and on earth;" 2. That it includes *the widest earthly scope*,—"and teach all nations;" 3. That it is associated with the highest mystery of the moral universe,—"the name of the Father, and of the Son, and of the Holy Ghost;" 4. That its doctrine is exclusively and unchangeably Christian,—"teaching them to observe all things whatsoever I have commanded you;" 5. That its execution is ennobled and sanctified by the *personal presence* of Jesus Christ,—"lo, I am with you alway, even unto the end of the world."

The practical point is—*The spirit which was found in Jesus Christ after He rose from the dead will be found in every man who has undergone spiritual resurrection,*—whoever rises with Christ will desire to evangelise the nations.

# ON BEING RIGHT IN THE MAIN.

*(See page 224.)*

" Then Jesus beholding him loved him, and said unto him, One thing thou lackest: go thy way, sell whatsoever thou hast, and give to the poor, and thou shalt have treasure in heaven: and come, take up the cross, and follow me. And he was sad at that saying, and went away grieved; for he had great possessions."—MARK x. 21, 22.

THIS young man presented some of the best and some of the worst aspects of human nature,—he may be regarded, therefore, as a representative man. First: *He displayed a degree of moral earnestness,*—"There came one running, and kneeled to him." Running and kneeling,—speed and homage, what more could be required? Second: *He employed the language of veneration,*—" Good Master,"—character and authority, how high the eulogium! Third: *He was well-instructed in Biblical ethics,*—" All these have I observed from my youth." He knew the law, revered the law, exemplified the law, yet he said—" What lack I yet ?" Fourth: *He was inordinately attached to worldly possessions,*—" He was sad at that saying, and went away grieved;" he found that it was easier to " observe " than to " give."

Christ's conduct in the case shewed—First: *That He compels men to look at the logical consequences of their own admissions.* The young man said—" Good Master;" Christ answered, apparently but not really in correction, " Why callest thou me good? there is none good but one, that is God;"—as if He had said—Mark the consequence of calling me "good;" if I am "good" then am I God, and being God, what I declare must be Divine and final! Second: *That personal regard may be entertained where full moral approbation cannot be expressed.* " Loved him, and said unto him, One thing thou lackest." There was a charm in the countenance of the enquirer, hope gleamed in his eye, and wonder broke his tones into a tremulous modesty; the outward man was prepossessing, but in the heart there was one grand lack.

Looked at as a whole, the text shows :—

I. THE NECESSARY LIMITATIONS OF THE MOST CAREFUL RELIGIOUS TRAINING. The young man was no barbarian; the voices of the lawgivers and the prophets had resounded in his hearing, and he was familiar with the harp of the holy minstrels who had turned duty and sorrow, victory and defeat, into music. With practical theology as pronounced in statutes and commandments he was perfectly familiar, and even to practical religion in the life he declared himself no stranger,—"All these have I observed from my youth." There may be most careful training of the memory, and most jealous watchfulness over the conduct among men, and yet the heart may not be the temple of God. Is such training, then, without advantage? Certainly not. By so much as the mind is occupied with right considerations it is indisposed towards that which is evil. Hence there is a great moral value in many pursuits which are not directly either religious or ethical. A young man, for example, cultivates the art of painting; day by day he watches the changing lights which play upon the landscape; he knows no greater gladness than to succeed in catching the precise expression of light and colour, and giving it a permanence on the canvass;—so far, good; refinement of taste is a high attainment, studying nature is an inspiring exercise, life on the mountain is incomparably better than existence in the den of the bacchanal. The study of art, then, which is not in itself religious, is of good tendency; by it the mind may be so pre-occupied that the force of many temptations may be broken. The power of temptation is in proportion to the nature of the soul tempted. A thoughtless miner takes an uncovered light into the mine; where there is but little gas there is but a wavering and flickering of a transient flame,—hardly flame indeed; but where there is an accumulation of gas, the uncovered light occasions an explosion which shivers the rocks and brings swift destruction upon all who are in the mine. In both cases it was the same mine, the same light, the same miner, but the condition of the air was different. So is it with the fiery darts of the wicked one; they are shot into all human hearts, and just in proportion to the materials, so to speak, which are found there, will be the success or failure of the enemy.

A formal religious education, then, may, by simply pre-occupying the mind, break the force of temptation and save the soul from the more violent forms of depravity. Yet not necessarily so; and this shows the weakness of the most careful training. A case in point is before me now: a parent is determined to preserve his son from social contamination; that son was watched well-nigh day and night, was forbidden to speak to the servants lest he should be "corrupted," was expected to read good books, and to attend public worship regularly,—was not this well? Was not this a beautiful picture of domestic government? That son felt the restraint,—the recoil was tremendous,—soon as he escaped parental surveillance he plunged into excess, and eventually was hanged as a felon!

The text shows:—

II. THAT THE FINAL ATTAINMENT OF EDUCATION IS THE CONQUEST OF THE HEART.

The young man knew enough; he was not perishing for "lack of knowledge," light shone upon his intelligence, but his affections were self-enclosed and self-encoiled. There was one "cross" he could not lift,—one surrender he could not make! Only *one*, but that was ALL!

The conditions which Christ thus imposed show:—

1. *That Christ-following involves self-abnegation.* Men cannot have a little of Christ and a little of self,—in other words, true men cannot combine public profession and private self-gratification.

2. *That Christ-following must be the expression of the soul's supreme love.* Men are not permitted to make a mere *convenience* of Christ. The young man loved his "possessions" more than Christ's word. There are men who are prepared to "observe" any number of "commandments" provided they can also hoard wealth and indulge passion.

3. *That Christ-following means self-giving.* Christ was the GIVER, and men are like Him in proportion as they "give." Giving is not yet understood as a test of discipleship. Giving is understood as a patronage, but not as a self-sacrifice.

Giving means different things to different people. There are men who give a thousand guineas at once, yet is their gift without value. If certain rich merchants, whose purses are always accessible, would but utter two sentences distinctly in favour of Christ as their personal Saviour, such utterance, under given circumstances, would be a greater gift to the Christian cause than all the gold they ever lavished upon public institutions. Man must give *himself*, else he gives nothing. When a man gives a guinea where he should give a life, he mocks God to His face!

> "The Christ Himself had been no Lawgiver,
> Unless He had given the LIFE too with the Law."

The text shows:—

III. THAT LACK OF ONE THING MAY BE LACK OF EVERYTHING.

The garden is beautifully laid out: the straight lines and the curves are exact; the terraces are arranged with artistic taste; but no *seed* is sown,—and the summer says—"One thing thou lackest."

The machinery is perfect: cylinder, piston, valve, are in excellent order; no flaw is in the wheel, no obstruction in the flue; finer engine never stood on the iron way; everything is there but *steam*,—and the intending traveller says—"One thing thou lackest."

The watch has a golden case, the dial is exquisitely traced and figured, the hands are delicate and well-fixed; everything is there but the *mainspring*; and he who inquires the time says—"One thing thou lackest."

Conduct may be regulated in two ways:—1. By the hand; 2. By the heart: as with a watch so with the life. The face of the watch may be made to represent the truth by simply altering the hands, or it may be corrected by touching the interior works. Here is a young man who says—What shall I do to make my watch tell the hour accurately? He is answered:—Thou knowest the great clocks by which time is kept in the city. He replies:—"All these have I observed." He is then told to open his watch and correct the regulator. So is it with human life: many seek to correct it by the outside; they search for models, they inquire for foot-prints; but they neglect the life-spring within, and consequently never get beyond the affectation of artificialism, or the stiffness of Pharisaic conceit.

Observation is continually noticing instances in which "one thing" seems to be everything; it is so in common life, it is so in all life. Here is a man listening to the most exquisite music; peal of trumpet, clash of cymbals, roll of drum, sweetness of the lute, sharpness of the clarionet, crash of a hundred brass instruments;—to him it is simply a tumult, he sees no idea in the tempest, he does not rise and fall with the swelling rhythm of the wave and billow. Why? What is wanting? "One thing thou lackest,"—that one thing is an ear for music! Of what account is it that jewellery sparkles on his fingers, or that perfume is shed by every waive of his hand, or that the finest cloth covers his shoulders? The man is harmonically *dead*, and the music which rushes like a storm through the appreciative soul is to him "sound and fury signifying nothing."

Two men walk by the same path: the gold of the same sunset is lavished on their way; they look at the same objects, and move towards the same goal. One of them reaches home enriched with many mental pictures; the landscape is impressed upon his memory; the clouds are massed and coloured in his soul; he is not a tenant but a proprietor: his hand may be poor, but his spirit revels in affluence. The other traveller saw nothing, heard nothing, felt nothing; his eye was on the road, merely the servant of his feet, not the servant of his soul. "One thing thou lackest," —an eye for the beautiful! It is only *one* thing, yet everything turns upon it, and without it garden and wilderness are equal in charm.

These reflections may serve to show the tremendous danger of the fallacy that *if a man is right in the main he will be admitted into heaven*. The man who had no ear for music was right in the main; he was well-educated, well-connected, rich and generous, yet all this did not interpret one passage of the music to his dormant soul. The man who saw nothing in the landscape was right in the main; he was honest, persevering, modest and gentle, yet his eye was blind to beauty, and he cared not for hill or dale, or stream or luxuriant wood. So is it with regard to the higher life; we may have much and yet have nothing. A man may walk well without being able to swim at all, yet all his strength as a pedestrian will not save him in the sea! The lack of "one thing" may involve ruin. A merchant may have a musical voice, but if he have no money he cannot maintain his credit; an orator may have great muscular strength, but if his *voice* should fail, what then!

Place yourself at the railway terminus: a traveller is there who has no ticket; is *that* of any consequence? It is only "*one* thing;" a very insignificant thing; why should the man be detained for want of it? He has an address card; he has a wedding card; he has a visiting card; will *they* not do? No! "One thing thou lackest." That "one thing" represents law, order, equivalent, authority, and in the absence of that *one particular thing* a thousand other things go for nothing!

Are we not thus all through life continually reminded that the absence of "one thing" is the ruin of all?

The text shows:—

IV. THAT THE SINCERITY OF MEN MUST BE TESTED ACCORDING TO THEIR PECULIAR CIRCUMSTANCES.

This young man had "great possessions," consequently the test had relation to the worldliness of his spirit. What is a test to one man may be no test to another: hence the difficulty of one man appreciating the "cross" of another, and expressing intelligent sympathy. No other test would have met the peculiarity of this young man's case; he might have fasted long and prayed much, or even given liberally to the poor, but to "sell *all*" that he had was a test which shook his soul. Here, then, is the rule of right self-crucifixion. A man must be prepared to surrender what he *values most*, or he must subdue, mortify, and annihilate the passion which rules his spirit. 1. Covetous man; 2.

Haughty disposition; 3. Self-indulgent nature; 4. Censorious tone; 5. Vanity of heart; 6. Love of approbation. The personal cross must be determined by the personal constitution. To one man it is no cross whatever to address a thousand hearers, yet to that very man it may be a heavy cross to speak a word for Christ to *one* individual. He is not, then, taking up a cross in addressing the multitude; his cross lies in another direction, and Christ points him to it.

The young, in particular, are apt to be impatient with this requirement of self-denial as the condition of entrance into the kingdom of heaven. Is their impatience reasonable? Is Christ demanding a condition which is out of harmony with the general process of life? Not for a moment. What Christ requires in the particular matter of Christianity, is required as a condition of entrance into all foreign kingdoms. Has the *student* not to deny himself? Has the *explorer* not to deny himself? Has the *apprentice* not to deny himself? Has the *soldier* not to deny himself? Trace practical life through all its variations, and it will be found that all promotion, progress, and extension of influence, demand self-denial as a fundamental condition; yes, and even the man who goes down to hell "denies himself" in a sense more appalling than can be expressed. There is no escape from self-denial; choose ye whether it shall be self-denial towards heaven, or self-denial towards hell!

www.ingramcontent.com/pod-product-compliance
Lightning Source LLC
Chambersburg PA
CBHW031849220426
43663CB00006B/549